The
AGE
of the
CLOISTER

THE STORY OF MONASTIC LIFE
IN THE MIDDLE AGES

Christopher Brooke

HiddenSpring

Photographic Credits
Permission to use photographs is gratefully acknowledged to Fran Barbara
Hesse for Plate 3, top (*see* p. 8 of 1974 ed.); to Peter Meyer and Adrian
House for Plate 8, bottom; and for all other photographs to the Research
Library, The Getty Research Institute, Los Angeles, Wim Swaan Photograph
Collection (96.P21.).

Cover design by Amy King

The front cover shows Le Thoronet Abbey, Provence, France.

Text design by Jennifer Daddio

Copyright © Verlag Herder Freiburg im Breisgau 2001, original title: Die
Klöster

This edition published by arrangement with Verlag Herder Freiburg im
Breisgau, Germany.

Library of Congress Cataloging-in-Publication Data
    Brooke, Christopher Nugent Lawrence.
      The age of the cloister : the story of monastic life in the Middle
Ages / Christopher Lawrence.
        p. cm.
    Includes bibliographical references (p.   ) and index.
    ISBN 1-58768-018-1
      1. Monasticism and religious orders—History—Middle Ages,
600–1500. I. Title.
    BX2470 .B75 2003
    271′.009′02—dc21

                                 2002153784

Published in 2003 by
HiddenSpring
an imprint of Paulist Press
997 Macarthur Boulevard
Mahwah, New Jersey 07430

www.hiddenspringbooks.com

Printed and bound in the United States of America

Contents

Note on the Plans of Monastic Buildings   x

Preface   1

Introduction   5

    1974–2002: Old and New Problems   5

    Cîteaux and Grandmont   8

    Women   17

PART ONE:
THE MONASTIC TRADITION

1. PRELUDE   25

    Origins   25

    St. Basil   34

    St. Augustine   35

    John Cassian   38

2. THE RULE OF ST. BENEDICT   44

117675

3. THE FORMATION OF THE MONASTIC TRADITION ... 52

From St. Benedict of Nursia to St. Benedict of Aniane ... 52

The Tenth Century ... 62

Cluny and Gorze in the Tenth and Eleventh Centuries ... 64

4. LIFE, WORK AND PRAYER ... 70

The Daily Round ... 70

The Officials and the Monastic Economy ... 77

Cluny, the New Monasticism and the Twelfth-Century
Renaissance ... 82

5. THE HERMITS ... 86

The Influence of Italy in the Eleventh Century ... 86

St. Romuald and St. Peter Damian:
Camaldoli and Vallombrosa ... 87

The Carthusians ... 90

The Contrast of Community and Hermitage ... 95

6. THE CLOISTER AND THE WORLD ... 100

900–1050: Monasteries as the Property of Kings
and Princes ... 100

Recruitment in the Eleventh and Twelfth Centuries ... 106

Social Change, 1050–1150 ... 107

Lay Offerings ... 117

Abbey and City: San Zeno, Verona ... 121

7. THE MONASTIC CONTRIBUTION
   TO THE TWELFTH-CENTURY RENAISSANCE   126

   Architecture and the Crafts   127

   Monks and Romanesque Art   132

   Monastic Involvement   134

   Theophilus   137

   Work and Books   139

   Books and the Apostolic Life   140

   Biography and History   142

   St. Anselm, Theology and Humanism   143

PART TWO:
NEW ORDERS

8. THE AUGUSTINIAN CANONS   153

   The Apostolic Life   153

   The Rule of St. Augustine   155

   The Movement in Italy, France and Spain   157

   Germany, Austria and the British Isles   158

   Distinguishing between Monks and Canons:
       The Canon of Liège   162

   Chaucer   164

9. THE CISTERCIANS   166

   Cîteaux, Clairvaux and St. Bernard   166

   The Cistercian Program:
       Choir Monks and Lay Brothers   169

   Seclusion, Self-Sufficiency and Manual Work   173

Puritanism and Efficiency   178

Uniformity, Architecture and the Cistercian Constitution   181

Rievaulx and St. Ailred   186

The Adventure and Its Victims   191

10. THE KNIGHTS   195

11. ON ABBESSES AND PRIORESSES   201

To the Eleventh Century   201

The Twelfth and Thirteenth Centuries   206

Lacock   214

12. ST. NORBERT AND ST. FRANCIS—
THE PREMONSTRATENSIANS AND THE FRIARS   217

Norbert of Xanten   217

The Apostolic Life in the Twelfth
and Thirteenth Centuries   219

Francis of Assisi   223

Franciscan and Dominican Friars   225

PART THREE:
GATHERING THE THREADS

13. THREE VISITS   235

I. Fountains   235

II. Mont Saint-Michel   245

III. Sant'Ambrogio, Milan   252

14. 1300: THE MONASTIC MAP OF EUROPE   261

15. EPILOGUE: 1300 TO THE PRESENT 278

    1300–1500 279

    Since 1500 283

Glossary 293

Notes 296

Bibliographcal Notes 318

Index 340

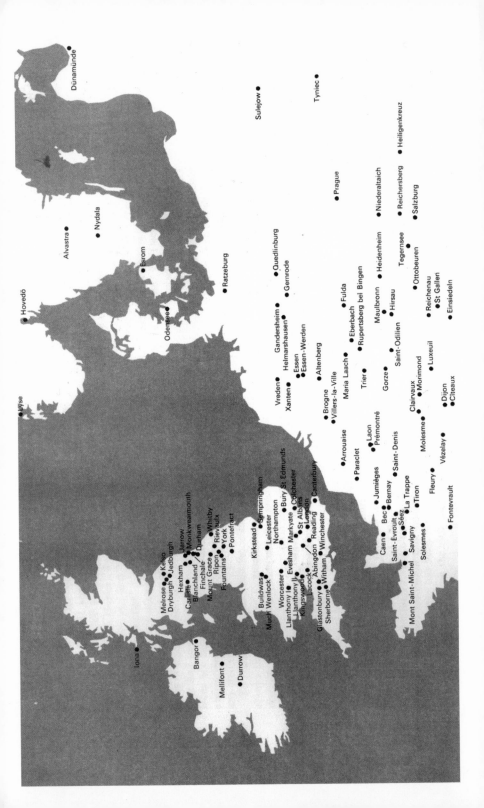

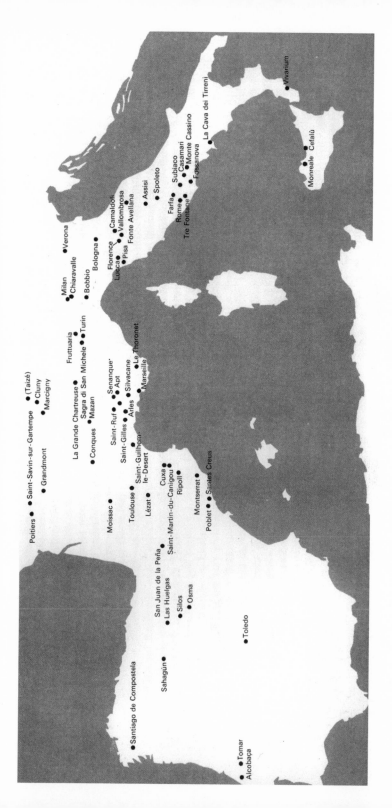

Map of Europe showing the monastic sites
used as examples in the text and plans.

Note on the Plans of Monastic Buildings

For twenty monastic houses discussed in this book plans are provided. To make these as intelligible as possible abbreviated names for the various parts of the building complex have been given in standard form; this saves us from an elaborate numerical code, though numbers are used in a few cases to explain special features of a plan. No attempt is made to identify every part of the buildings—indeed, the identifications that appear on some modern plans are sometimes very conjectural—but to clarify the normal and fundamental elements in the monastic plan.

A typical arrangement in a monastery of the mid or late Middle Ages comprised a large church, cruciform in shape, with a cloister garth nestling against its nave and south transept—a square courtyard, that is, with the main domestic buildings beside the remaining walks: chapter house and parlor(s), with dormitory above, on the east walk, kitchen and refectory on the south, offices and storehouses on the west— or, in a Cistercian house, the quarters of the lay brothers. Outside this central group lay the guest-house, commonly to the west, and the abbot's lodging and infirmary, sometimes around a subsidiary cloister farther east. This plan was subject to numerous modifications; even the most uniform order, the Cistercian, adapted their plans to the sites in a certain degree. In particular, they were comparatively indifferent whether the cloister lay south or north of the church: No doubt they shared the general preference for a sunny cloister, but essentially they looked for a site where they could lay a church on solid ground and the domestic buildings toward a river, for water supply and drainage.

The following abbreviations are used in the plans:

Abb = *Abbatia*, abbot's lodging

Arm = *Armarium*, book cupboard or room

Atr = *Atrium*, narthex, courtyard to west of church

Cal = *Calefactorium*, calefactory, warming room, monks' parlor

Cap = *Capitulum*, chapter house

Cla = *Claustum*, cloister (at Sant'Ambrogio, Milan, *Mon monachorum*, and *Can canonicorum*, monks' and canons' cloisters: see p. 255)

Conv = *Conversi*, lay brothers (quarters of)

Coq = *Coquina*, kitchen

Dor = *Dormitorium*, dormitory

Eccl = *Ecclesia*, church

Gal = *Galilaea*, galilee, paradise, western porch

Hosp = *Hospitium*, guesthouse

Inf = *Infirmaria*, infirmary

Lat = *Latrina*, latrine(s)

Lav = *Lavatorium*, lavabo, ceremonial wash-place
in cloister, near refectory

Nov = *Noviciorum cella,* novices' room

Pr = *Prioratus*, prior's lodging (and *Priorissatus,* prioress's)

Ref = *Refectorium*, refectory

A few minor features are only noted occasionally: Thus the
night stair from dormitory to church, normal in Cistercian
houses and not uncommon, for example, in Augustinian, is
marked on the plan of Maulbronn and noted on that of
Buildwas (see pp. 177 and 176, respectively).

Preface

"I embarked on this book in the conviction that the dialogue between the literature and the buildings of medieval monastic communities was a theme too little developed by historians." Thus I wrote in 1974, when the first edition of this book, entitled *The Monastic World*, was published by Paul Elek in London. I was inspired to write it by my admiration of the work of the architect-photographer, the late Wim Swaan, and the prospect of collaborating with him. Today, in revising the book I have tried to relive the experience of revealing how the visible remains of medieval monasteries reflect the history, culture, way of life and religious sentiment of the period from 1000 to 1300.

I have left it essentially as it was, correcting errors, revising details, bringing the bibliography into the twenty-first century with a light hand—and above all, in a new introduction giving my own view of what has happened to the subject in the last thirty years. Our knowledge has been greatly extended and much deepened, but the sources I used and the eyes with which I looked at documents and buildings remain essentially the same. I see many problems quite differently now, but the book still carries the inspiration I felt when writing it—witness especially chapters 9 and 13. I hope the introduction will make clear how I think it could be written now by a scholar thirty years younger than me of like convictions and interests.

The epilogue discusses ever so briefly the monastic life since 1300. I am well aware that it carries the hopeless burden of giving in epitome the history of an immense variety of religious orders over centuries of fundamental change. In the period of this book the dominant cultures of western Europe accepted monasticism as perhaps the most perfect way of life open to men and women. For very many in the twenty-first century a life dedicated to celibacy and worship seems perverse and wrongheaded. But human beings are infinitely various— however much historians, sociologists and journalists try to drive us into too-simple molds. The plain fact is that a life very close indeed to that led in a twelfth-century monastery may still be followed in a monastery today. To make this intelligible, what, above all, is needed is a sequel in which the monastic world of recent centuries is unfolded by an expert in the documents and the buildings of these centuries. Such a book will soon appear when Professor Derek Beales publishes his Birkbeck Lectures as *Prosperity and Plunder: European Catholic Monasteries in the Age of Revolution, 1650–1815* (Cambridge, 2003).

In 1974 I listed the many friends and colleagues who had helped me in the search of monastic sites and photographs, in preparing and publishing the book: To them all I repeat my thanks. I owed a most particular debt to Donald Bullough, Robert Markus and my wife, Rosalind Brooke; to Paul Elek and his colleagues, especially Moira Johnston; and, for guidance in monastic art and architecture, to Neil Stratford and George Zarnecki. The greatest of my debts was to my former teacher,

Professor Dom David Knowles, and to Wim Swaan—and to their memory I dedicate this new edition.

In preparing the new edition I have had kind help from Christopher Holdsworth, Robert Markus, Falko Neininger, Edna Pilmer and Rosalind Brooke—and to my new editor Jan-Erik Guerth and his colleagues. To Jan-Erik Guerth I owe the opportunity to explore the themes of this book once again, and I am indeed grateful.

Christopher Brooke
2002

Introduction

1974—2002: Old and New Problems

It may at first sight seem a paradox that we know less than we did thirty years ago on some of the major issues discussed in this book. Yet so it is. On innumerable details—of documents, archaeological remains, liturgy, religious life, mysticism, economy and so forth—we know far more. But the new knowledge has served to make some of the central problems more insistent and more, not less, puzzling, and some accepted solutions have been swept away.

The Rule of St. Benedict is a good example. Down to 1937 it had been taken for granted that the parallel passages in the *Regula Magistri,* the *Rule of the Master,* were due to copying by the Master from St. Benedict. In 1937 the first shots were fired in a long battle, and (as reported in 1974) the outcome was a general consensus that the Master came first. On this assumption were based some passages in chapter 2.[1] It always seemed contrary to common sense to make Benedict the derivative and the much inferior Master the source; but weighty arguments from their language, use of sources and other technical matters seemed to many to counter the simpler, traditional view. Then in 1990 Dr. Marilyn Dunne opened a new campaign

with a cogently argued paper in the *English Historical Review,*
aimed to undermine the consensus and restore priority to St.
Benedict. Her paper was very soon answered by Père de
Vogüé—and he in turn by Dr. Dunne. The debate continues;
meanwhile, the consensus has been shaken: What the outcome will be, it is too early to say, but it seemed wise to leave
my text as it was, with the proviso that my ingenious explanation of Benedict's use of the Master may one day go away
on the wind.[2]

If the Rule of St. Benedict was the foundation of the monks'
way of life, the cloister was the physical center of their world;
and even while the first edition of this book was in the press, a
major contribution to the history of the cloister was published
in 1973 in *Gesta,*[3] enshrining the Cloister symposium of 1972.
This helped me to reflect on one of the crucial meeting points
of documentary and architectural evidence—central to many
passages and plans in the book, but inadequately explored in
it—the amazing uniformity in the shape, design and function of
the cloister in a medieval monastery.[4] The dominance of the
cloister in monastic planning is a fact so obvious it is easily over-
looked. Nor was it always so obvious: Early monastic complexes
in the west, such as we know—like Wearmouth and Jarrow,
elucidated with patient care by Rosemary Cramp[5]—do not at
all suggest anything in the shape of a cloister, in the sense of a
four-square covered walk as the center of a complex; and my
limited experience of nineteenth- and twentieth-century
monasteries suggests that the medieval plan lost its dominance
long ago. An early example has been reconstructed in the
rebuilding of a Roman *villa rustica* at Lorsch in Germany in the
eighth century, and a cloister, and the earliest certain use of
claustrum in this sense, appear pictorially for the first time in the

famous St. Gall plan.[6] We may take it as reasonably certain that this plan was composed at Reichenau, and probable that it was sent as a kind of Christmas card by Haito, bishop-abbot of Reichenau, to his pupil the abbot of St. Gall, in or about the early 820s, and at St. Gall (Sankt Gallen), it has remained ever since. We know nothing else for certain of its context, or whether it was unique—or one of a large number of such drawings.

St. Benedict had used the word *claustra* for the enclosure, the whole area in which the monk was enclosed; and this sense of *claustrum* will survive as long as the Rule of St. Benedict is known and studied and followed.[7] The narrower sense of *claustrum* is commonly very difficult to distinguish from the broader in medieval texts: Meyvaert has found a possible use in the eighth century, but admits it is not certain; nor is any known before the St. Gall plan.[8]

The dominance of the cloister in monastic planning is a puzzle. Covered porticoes, with arches open to the weather, have been very common throughout historical times in southern Europe, where they seem wholly appropriate as shelters from the sun open to the fresh air. But the monastic cloister flourished fully as much in northern Europe as in the south; for Lorsch and Reichenau and St. Gall were among the main creative monastic centers of northern Europe in the ninth and tenth centuries. Such indications as we have suggest that it was in these regions—or at least in the monastic world of the tenth and eleventh centuries, with its centers in Cluny and Gorze and Glastonbury—that the cloister won its spurs. If we read the customaries of Cluny or of Archbishop Lanfranc of the eleventh century, we meet a life devoted to ritual—in worship, eating, reading, sleeping, bathing and shaving; and for this the four-square, ample cloister, ideally suited for ritual and procession from church to refectory, from refectory to dormitory, and so on, may seem well suited to its purpose.[9] But that still leaves many puzzles. Such was its grip on the imagination of religious planners that the monks of Mont Saint-Michel, who lacked the ample space a cloister needed, would nonetheless build a whole cloister in the early thirteenth century over their new domestic buildings as a kind of roof-garden (see p. 249–50), and the friars, who lived in many ways a different kind of life, contrived to fit their living spaces into monastic complexes with cloisters at their heart. Equally mysterious is why the cloister was (in the main) rejected by those who designed colleges in Oxford and Cambridge in the fourteenth century and later usually reckoned an open courtyard more appropriate than a cloister—even though their colleges were surrounded (and partly inspired) by the houses of the friars. Yet William of Wykeham, who built uncloistered courts for his scholars at Winchester and New College, Oxford, added cloisters for processions, burials and scholarly contemplation outside the main court or quadrangle.[10] The rejection of the cloister is as strange as the fashion which created it.

Cîteaux and Grandmont

In 1974 I commented at length on the special case of Cistercian planning: the pursuit of an ascetic uniformity, and the special design of the western range and the furnishings of the church to ensure that a large army of lay brothers could serve and service the monastery without having to mingle with the choir monks.[11] Through all the vicissitudes which the Cistercians have suffered or enjoyed at the hands of recent historians, the search for simplicity and uniformity remains unscathed. Beyond that, in 1940 David Knowles could still tell a very simple story based on the earliest Cistercian narratives and the *Carta Caritatis*—the charter of divine love—of Abbot Stephen Harding.[12] But in the years that followed, evidence began to accumulate that later in the twelfth century the story had in some measure been rewritten, and the *Carta Caritatis* extensively revised, in at least two or three different versions. Heroic attempts have been made to date the various recensions and plot the history of the Cistercian constitution by their progress. These attempts have foundered, for two reasons: because no consensus as to the dates of the various versions has emerged among the experts, and because the very attempt presupposes that constitutional theory and practice marched hand in hand, a doubtful belief in any age. Father Chrysogonus Waddell has indeed shown good reason to believe that Cistercian liturgical regulations passed through two phases: an early attempt to return quite literally (in liturgy as in all else) to the letter of the Rule, and a much later attempt, which he would date in or about 1147, to clear away some of the difficulties these attempts had created and take advantage of what was best in the music and worship of the age.[13] Less helpful has been the widely canvassed view that regulations for the making of new foundations must precede the decision in 1152 to forbid any new foundations at all. But monastic foundations took time to mature—and especially Cistercian foundations, which were normally not consummated until there were buildings to enter and a community to live in them; and it would be absurd to suppose that all the foundations under way in 1152 could have stopped in their tracks; regulations for new houses were still required. In truth it was a fertile year, in which the order scored at least six new houses. The plain fact is that the decree of 1152 had only limited effect.[14] There had been sixteen foundations in 1151; in 1162, when those of the later 1150s were coming to full fruition, there were fourteen. If we plot the progress of the order by the dates of final foundation, we get the following pattern:

1098–1115: 5
1116–33: 68
1134–May 1152: 260
June 1152–1170: 65

Clearly the very rapid expansion of the order was checked in the 1150s, but it continued to grow. It would be superficial to attribute the sharp fall in the 1150s solely to the decree. Some effect it may well have had. But 1153 and 1154 saw the death of St. Bernard, of the Cistercian pope, Eugenius III, of David king of the Scots and Stephen king of the English, two of the order's notable benefactors. The impetus of the years before had resulted in a plethora of specialized ascetic foundations. Some effect we may attribute to the decree; more to the anxieties that had inspired it. But the reasons—for example—why fashion in England and Scotland switched quite suddenly from Cistercian to Premonstratensian foundations in the early and mid-1150s are very far from clear.[15]

It was not in the nature of medieval legislation to provide a blueprint for future practice: It could lay down aims and ideals, as did the *Carta Caritatis* in its various recensions. If it forbade practices such as the possession of churches and tithes, we can only deduce that the Cistercians were being offered them—and we know in fact that these rules were breached from quite an early date.[16] An important rider to this is that items in the later recensions of the *Carta* may in fact represent early practice not enshrined in legislation till a later date. Thus it has been argued that the annual general chapter and the annual visitations by motherhouses were not primitive features of the order because the clauses defining them do not appear in the earliest versions. The history of the visitations is full of problems: We know that St. Bernard seems never to have visited his numerous progeny in England, and we know that there were complex disputes in later times as to who was truly the parent of whom.[17] But that there was a closely articulated system of communication among houses of the order is the inescapable inference from the plans and designs and character of the Cistercian complexes, as I argued in 1974 (see pp. 179–86).

The early constitutional documents suggest that the order was governed, not by a parliament of abbots, but by the paternal authority of the abbot of Cîteaux.[18] But there are very strong grounds of quite another character for believing that the parliament of abbots—the general chapter—was a primitive feature of the order.

One very significant document, or series of documents, has escaped the notice of the constitutional historians of the Cistercian Order—or, rather, has been taken for granted without a close scrutiny or the preparation of a modern edition. The great catalogue of the houses of the order published by Father Janauschek in 1877 was largely based on earlier catalogues, which he was able to trace back to late twelfth- and early-thirteenth-century manuscripts.[19] The earliest surviving versions were, quite evidently, attempts to tidy up the precise dates of foundation of all Cistercian houses so as to determine precedence at general chapter. It is clear that the catalogue had not been adequately kept up to date and that this led to differences of opinion among the reverend fathers gathered at Cîteaux. It is equally clear that a long history lay behind the earliest surviving versions. It is a very striking fact that the

Cistercian Order was the only one in the central Middle Ages whose members could tell to the day when their houses were founded.[20] As we have seen, these precise dates represented a human event: Sometimes in early days the departure of the monks to a new house, more often (and, one presumes, more correctly) the date of their entry into the new monastery. The catalogues have not been well preserved, or perhaps one should say, not well edited; and there are some lacunas. But from the foundation of Clairvaux and Morimond on, from the fourth and fifth foundations on June 25, 1115, all have a precise date. It is curious, and intriguing, that Clairvaux and Morimond were founded on the same day. But Arnold of Morimond was a humbler man in some respects than St. Bernard, and he does not seem to have challenged the priority of Clairvaux. In any case, the precision of the catalogues—however many uncertainties and false beginnings and compromises it may disguise[21]—seems to be decisive evidence that the general chapter was a formal meeting place in which it mattered very much where one sat, from 1115 at the latest.

From 1115 on, furthermore, the abbots who gathered for the chapter included Bernard himself, a superlative rhetorician, a man who was to prove himself prepared to dictate to bishops, kings and popes. One can scarcely conceive that the kindly, art-loving Stephen Harding could exercise tyrannical authority— or any kind of arbitrary rule—over the fiery, ascetic, puritanical Bernard. Whatever the constitutional documents might say or not say, from 1115 on the general chapter was first a committee then (as it grew in size) a parliament of abbots.

The Cistercians had a full share of space in this book's edition of 1974. In contrast, the modest Order of Grandmont received only a bare mention. Their founder, St. Stephen of

Grandmont, would have rejoiced in this obscurity; but his order of hermit-monks—which came to number 150 houses, mostly in France—was significant far beyond its numbers, and it had already been studied in the editions and articles of Dom Becquet, and has since been deployed before a wider audience in Carole Hutchison's pioneering book.[22] The early history of the order is indeed obscure: St. Stephen had a love of poverty and simplicity which made him a forerunner of St. Francis 100 years later; and in one respect at least he went further than Francis, for he seems to have cared little for the written word, so that we depend on later sources, based mainly on oral tradition, for our knowledge of him and the nature of his inspiration. Unlike the Franciscans, the Grandimontines lived a wholly enclosed life and never recruited women. But in his attitude to the lay brothers Stephen seems to have anticipated Francis to a remarkable degree. The functions of their lay brothers indeed were different: Stephen's were the managers and the drudges of the order; Francis's were the spearhead and the rank and file— the men whose poverty and simplicity made them natural companions to the poorest of the communities he wished to serve. But (anyway at times) he thought their prayers more efficacious than those of the learned clerical brothers. In both cases the class distinction established by the Cistercians was (in principle) wholly absent. In the late twelfth century the lay brothers of Grandmont asserted their managerial role in a world grown used to a very different relationship between the clerical and lay elements in an order. The Cistercian choir monks lorded it over the lay brothers, and this reflected the more fashionable view of the proper relations of clerical and lay religious. Not unnaturally, the managerial attitudes of the Grandimontine lay brothers led to friction; the clergy claimed a higher authority —and the lay brothers rebelled; so also did groups of Cistercian, Gilbertine and other lay brothers.[23] In the end, clerical principle and clerical fashion prevailed in these orders: the lay brothers were put in their place. Similarly, in the Franciscan Order, less than twenty years after the founder's (St. Gilbert's) death, the recruitment of lay brothers was forbidden.[24]

This is a striking example of the way in which the infinite variety of the religious impulses of the eleventh and twelfth centuries was subjected to the synthesising influence of fashion and canon law. The variety often led to paradox: the most gregarious of the religious leaders, for instance, were often those most addicted to the hermit life. The hermits indeed pose many paradoxes, and I was reasonably taken to task for portraying the hermit life in chapter 5 as something too radically distinct from the monasticism of the community. This was partly due to the limitations of the 1974 edition; partly because I wanted to deploy—though it was not sufficiently emphasised—precisely this paradox. In many respects the hermit life was utterly divorced from life in the community; but they were inextricably linked, sometimes in the lives of the same religious leaders. A careful reader of the edition of 1974 could observe the hermits in the hills above Cluny, the many communities which grew out of groups of hermits, the forest of Craon from whose hermitages were to spring three religious orders of a more conventional stamp, the manner in which Francis alternated life in the urban throng and in a remote hermitage.[25]

No one who has contemplated the hermitage of San Romerio a thousand meters above the valley of Poschiavo in southeastern Switzerland, or the vertiginous hermitages of the west coast of Ireland, or the cell of St. Francis in the Carceri high in the hills above Assisi, looking down a thirty-meter cliff, can doubt that these modest western versions of the pillar of St. Simon Stylites reflect a very different way of life from the ceaseless communal ritual of the cloister.[26] Yet the two ways were intimately combined in the religious impulses of the central Middle Ages, and the paradox that they were utterly different and yet equally part of the aspirations of many religious of the age is central to our understanding of this monastic world.

This fundamental mingling of contradictory impulses has been most fully and authoritatively expounded in Giles Constable's *The Reformation of the Twelfth Century*.[27] Constable has no special love of paradox, and most of the book comprises a comprehensive mustering of themes—the variety of reformers, the types of reform, their rhetoric and polemic, the way "reform" (as the word was used at the time—for he avoids the meaningless repetition modern historians give to the word) affected the inner life of monks and canons and their outward relations with the world about them, above all the spiritual aspirations of monastic founders and reformers—and the relation of this "reformation" to other movements of the day. But he lays some emphasis at the outset on "three contradictory tendencies, almost paradoxes," which I myself have no hesitation in calling paradoxes, for of such are human affairs compounded:

> The first was the tension between the reformers' emphasis on withdrawal from the world and their desire, fired by their own religious personalities, to take an active role in secular society....The second contradictory tendency was the conflict between the desire of the reformers to break out of the established forms of religious life and to find new ones suited to their spiritual

needs and their continued adherence to and confidence in existing institutions. The new and relatively formless communities felt a pressure to institutionalise both from their own need to survive and from the ecclesiastical and secular authorities, who wanted to fit them into a recognised and controllable framework....The third tension, more seeming than real, was between the backward-looking ideals based on models from the past, in accord with which the reformers tried to reshape existing institutions, and the forward-looking vision that opened the way to real innovations and to changes that now seem more significant than the type of issues that predominate in the polemical writings.[28]

With great learning and insight, Constable expounds a movement which included much, very much, variety—and yet also a remarkable degree of common aspiration and culture too. Something of the same perception had inspired chapters 6 and 7 below; but Constable has illuminated almost every corner of the subject from his unique knowledge of the early literature. On monastic architecture (though equally learned) he is much more reticent; and yet it illustrates these themes most clearly. The triumph of the monastic cloister and the exceptional—yet also conservative—uniformity of the Cistercian plan both show a striking mixture of the forward and the backward view. But the most fundamental consequence of Constable's ecumenical view of monastic reform does quite deeply affect the pattern of some chapters below:

The old view that monastic reform originated and spread from a single center of influence, such as Cluny in the tenth century, Vallombrosa and Camaldoli in the eleventh, or Cîteaux in the twelfth, is thus replaced by a view of these monasteries as the most prominent examples of tendencies that appeared in many houses, which differed (like modern universities and colleges) in specific ways but shared the same basic concerns. The changes in old black houses in the twelfth century, like those in older universities today, are easier to understand as responses to a broad pattern of development than as the result of influences or attacks.[29]

Easier to understand—but the messages of the different orders remain very significant. Thus the Cistercians spread because they encountered everywhere men and women of similar impulses. But their ideas and their identity remained: The influence of St. Bernard and of the chapter house at Cîteaux was as great as we have ever supposed.

Women

"More perhaps than at any other time in Christian history (not excluding the present), male religious leaders in the eleventh and twelfth centuries were responsive to the needs of women and welcomed their presence and influence in religious institutions." Thus Giles Constable, introducing his remarkable—though all too brief—account of women religious.[30] This is perhaps the greatest of all his paradoxes, for the attitudes to women among the religious leaders of the eleventh, twelfth and thirteenth centuries were exceedingly varied, and the final impression must be ambivalent. It is also the field that has been most extensively surveyed, and most deeply ploughed, since 1974. At first sight, Constable's examples seem widely spread, from Christina of Markyate, via Heloise, to Hildegard of

Bingen; and Robert of Arbrissel alone would place France, for a time, in the forefront of the movement (see pp. 203ff.). But ever and anon he returns to Germany: "[I]t has been estimated that the number of houses for, or including, women in Germany alone rose from about 70 in 900 to 150 in 1100 and to 500, containing a total of between 25,000 and 30,000 nuns, in 1250."[31] Furthermore, there were many houses of monks that gave shelter to nuns as well: Constable lists seven major houses in Germany that had nuns attached to them in the eleventh century; "…and in the twelfth century the presence of women was almost a mark of neo-Cluniac monasticism in Germany."[32] It is perhaps no coincidence that the Abbess Hildegard, one of the most learned and cultured, most imaginative and original of the great characters of the twelfth-century renaissance, flourished in mid-twelfth century Germany.[33] It is also significant that among the Cistercians—who tended in early days to keep the women at bay and even at times to deny that there were female Cistercians—it was in what we call Belgium that the first major patrons of Cistercian nuns appeared, and in the Low Countries and Germany that the female Cistercians had their greatest success, so that by 1300 there were more houses for Cistercian women than for Cistercian men in Germany (see pp. 213–14, 275).

It is instructive to compare Germany with England. There the statistics are at all points less impressive. There had been only thirteen houses of nuns in 1066, and the grand total never rose much above a hundred, even in the thirteenth century. The number of religious women in these houses has been estimated to have risen from about 250 to about 2500—less than a tenth of those in Germany, though all the estimates of numbers of nuns are very approximate.[34] The work of Sarah Foot and Sally

Thompson has shown that, as in Germany, there were small groups of nuns attached to male houses—sometimes living close to the male community, sometimes at a moderate distance; in a number of cases groups of nuns were removed from the male precinct to a convent some miles away. Most striking was the case of St. Albans, where there were women living close to the monastery at or soon after the Norman Conquest and where tradition had it that this was an ancient practice— and that Abbot Paul (1077–93) made them lead a more regular life, in the almonry of the abbey.[35] Even more striking was the readiness of the abbots of St. Albans, especially Geoffrey de Gorron (1119–46), to lend support to two small communities of nuns that had grown up in the entourage of local hermits at Sopwell and Markyate. This was a characteristic situation: It seems to have been common for would-be women religious to gather either in the peripheries of houses of monks or in the circle of a single holy man. If the *Life of Christina of Markyate* is to be believed, the hermit she first attached herself to died and was succeeded by one less holy than herself, and her success in the long run was largely due to her dominant personality, of which Abbot Geoffrey went much in awe.[36] Most striking of all was the case of St. Gilbert of Sempringham, who gathered a small community of pious women about him and his church at Sempringham—and in the end formed a new order to provide for their needs. In all these cases the needs of women were considered, but the dominant culture in England at this time meant that they were relatively soon segregated from the men, even in the double houses of the Gilbertine Order.[37] Two winds were blowing, two tides flowing over the sands: Woman was made to be man's helper, colleague, partner; but woman was also (in many men's minds) the successor of Eve, the temptress.[38] To many religious it was axiomatic that monks and nuns, or nuns and canons, must be kept firmly and effectively apart.

This ambivalence meets us everywhere in the twelfth century; and it confronts us most piquantly in the relations of Francis and Clare in the early thirteenth.[39] Francis inspired Clare to join him, and in early days they worked together as friars. But before long the dominant culture of clerical Italy led Francis to lock her in a convent and cease to visit her: In later years he was alleged to have claimed that he only knew two women by sight—so far had he traveled from his call to Clare to be a colleague in earlier years.

The question remains: Why were nuns so much more numerous in Germany and the Low Countries than in the other countries of western Europe? Some attempts have been made to explain it, none very convincing: it remains one of the most fundamental puzzles in the history of medieval religion and of medieval women. Three elements seem necessary to account for the great number of nuns and nunneries in these lands in the twelfth and thirteenth century: generous patronage, an ample supply of recruits, and a religious culture friendly to women and their aspirations to the religious life. Germany in particular had a long tradition of royal and princely patronage to nuns; and Ottonian princesses had lived out their lives at Essen and Gandersheim and elsewhere. In marked contrast to England, there were houses of nuns that recruited only from the aristocracy—and for whose support, therefore, the aristocracy were ready to pay. This does not, however, apply to the very numerous foundations for Cistercian women; and we must suppose a social convention that made it possible for women fully to participate in the aspirations of male religious to have been especially characteristic of Germany and the Low Countries. Some have argued that there was a surplus of women in this region or that, but the evidence is too sparse to have any confidence in it.[40] Attempts have been made to align the role of women religious with other cultural developments in the attitude toward women—the romances and the cult of so-called courtly love. Leaving aside the question whether secular and carnal love is the natural ally or rival or enemy of the love of the celibate spiritual life for women, there is no clear pattern or relationship that makes any sense. The most one can say is that an enhanced role for women is visible in the best of the German vernacular epics and romances of the turn of the twelfth and thirteenth centuries, especially in the epics of Wolfram von Eschenbach. He reveals a highly sophisticated respect for women far beyond what one finds in the French romances of the era. But in the *Tristan* of his contemporary Gottfried von Strassburg one meets perhaps the most devilish of all the notable heroines of the age, Isolde, a character certainly not calculated to improve the image of women among the admirers of the poem. Both great poets reveal a remarkable sophistication of ideas in this region—and also the wide range and variety of sentiment and attitude that one might expect in a cultural milieu which could produce opportunities for women so much above those in other Western lands. That is the most one can say.

Undoubtedly the causes were complex and interwoven; but by far the most tangible and promising was the spiritual movement that produced the mystics and Beguines in the same regions at much the same time. The Low Countries fostered a distinguished dynasty of female mystics from Hadewijch of Brabant on—overtaken by an equally distinguished mystical tradition in the mid– and late thirteenth century in Germany in Mechtild of Magdeburg and her circle. They were also the first and most notable home of the Beguines, women who lived the religious life both in their homes and in communities, and formed very influential groups in many parts of western Europe—for it was an exceptionally cosmopolitan age. But their most notable center was in Liège in Flanders, where they were fostered and recorded by Bishop Jacques de Vitry—later cardinal and one of the central figures in giving support and countenance to the aspirations of women—whose *Life of Mary of Oignies* is the chief document of the movement in its early phases.[41] These movements help us to understand the geography of the religious foundations of the twelfth and thirteenth centuries. But they do not fully explain it: the concentration of women religious in the Low Countries and Germany is one of the most fascinating of the problems we have explored. Many scholars have surveyed the paths and bypaths of medieval religious history; yet there is much still to explore, and to elucidate.

Part One

THE
MONASTIC
TRADITION

1.

Prelude

Origins

From the very beginnings of Christianity the question has been asked: Can the good life, the Christian life, be led in the world; is it compatible with earthly joys and pleasures?—or must it, in its highest and truest forms, involve renunciation, stern discipline, an ascetic life, and celibacy? There is a single chapter in Matthew's Gospel[1] in which the claims of family life, and of children, are bewilderingly juxtaposed with the call to renounce both family and the resources to support it.

> And they twain shall be one flesh....What therefore God hath joined together, let not man put asunder....[To refrain from marriage] is something which not everyone can accept, but only those for whom God has appointed it. For while some are incapable of marriage because they were born so, or were made so by men, there are others who have themselves renounced marriage for the sake of the kingdom of Heaven. Let those accept it who can....

> Let the children come to me; do not try to stop them; for the kingdom of Heaven belongs to such as these....

If you wish to go the whole way, go, sell your possessions, and give to the poor, and then you will have
riches in heaven; and come, follow me.... It is easier for
a camel to pass through the eye of a needle than for a
rich man to enter the kingdom of God.

Then who can be saved?...For men this is impossible;
but everything is possible for God....Anyone who has
left brothers or sisters, father, mother or children [and in
a similar context St. Luke demands renunciation of
one's wife as well], land or houses for the sake of my
name will be repaid many times over, and gain eternal
life.

There is clear justification in this chapter for many varieties of
personal and religious experience; it is impossible to convert
the moral teaching of Jesus into a code. One can only cut out
the apparent inconsistencies by surgery so extreme as to be
fatal. The reason is clear enough: Jesus' teaching was addressed
to actual human situations; it was *ad personam*; if it was to have
any depth, subtlety, truth to human experience, it could not be
at the superficial level consistent. In a similar way the married
and the ascetic have over the centuries both derived some
comfort from Paul. "It is a good thing for a man to have nothing to do with women" is an unpromising start to his account
of marriage and its problems in 1 Corinthians, and he clearly
prefers his own state of celibacy and thinks women something
of an encumbrance on men and on the church. In the Epistle
to the Ephesians[2] the union of husband and wife in marriage is
likened to the relation of Christ and the church. It is clear that
Paul had to deal with a bemusing variety of views and practices, and that in 1 Corinthians he was trying to save marriage

from total disrepute, while not condemning celibacy, in the comparatively brief space before the world—as he believed—would come to an end. As it became clearer that the world would survive awhile, and the church had to come to such terms as it could with society, a clearer, and, one is bound to say loftier, doctrine of marriage was propounded. In the Pastoral Epistles, especially in 1 Timothy, there is a warm domesticity.

But coming to terms with society could not involve renunciation of the standards and ideals of Jesus and Paul. The austere ascetic life which the author of 1 Timothy had authorized for older widows remained a feature of many churches; beside chastity, a moderate poverty was from the first natural to many in a community largely made up of the poor. In a passage of the Acts quoted in almost every monastic Rule that has ever been written, Luke describes how "The whole body of believers was united in heart and soul. Not a man of them claimed any of his possessions as his own, but everything was held in common...."[3] And all the Synoptic Gospels described the poverty and simplicity in which the disciples had been sent to preach, taking nothing for the way.[4] Whenever we are allowed a real insight into early Christian communities, we find a variety of experience and approach, some rejoicing in family life and in the world as God's creation, others looking to the austerer words of the New Testament for their inspiration. But while variety seems to most modern readers of the New Testament to have been the practice and expectation from the first, there seem always too to have been voices raised that proclaimed a single element in the Christian tradition as the only true path. Many a monastic founder of early and medieval times read the Gospels and Acts and concluded that he alone was imitating the apostles; the *vita apostolica*—the apostolic way

of life—was a rallying cry for all manner of religious reformers.[5] Out of the early ascetic groups scattered all over the
Roman Empire developed the movement that has since been
specifically known as monastic.

In its original, etymological sense, a monk was one who
dwelt alone (μονος in Greek), and the first monks of the
Egyptian desert were hermits or anchorites. But from very
early days there came to be communities of monks living in
monasteries, *coenobia* (from the Greek κοινος, or common) and
most of the monks who are the subject of this book have
lived in communities and hence were called coenobites. The
monastic ideal, however, is commonly reckoned to owe its formation to St. Antony (c. 251–356), and he was the first great
anchorite and leader in the Egyptian desert at the turn of the
third and fourth centuries; it is beyond doubt that it was in the
deserts of Egypt in the early fourth century that monasticism,
as a large-scale movement, was born. Three men conspired to
create the tradition of orthodox monasticism: Athanasius the
bishop and theologian, Antony the hermit, and Pachomius the
coenobite.[6] They hardly knew one another; but they seem to
have known that on their cooperation the survival and success
of much of what each stood for depended. Antony and
Pachomius were the founders; Athanasius, bishop of
Alexandria, helped to give their work fame and respectability.
He is generally reckoned the author of the first *Life of Antony*,
and so the man primarily responsible for recording and dis-
seminating knowledge of his life and ideals. Beside Antony, in
early tradition was set a colleague and rival called Paul; but
Paul is a shadowy figure and it is evident that Antony, if not
precisely the first hermit in time, was the true founder of the
movement. We cannot be sure of all the reasons for the primacy

of Egypt, but two are particularly clear. First, though many early monks were very simple men and Antony himself no theologian, monasticism was partly inspired by a powerful intellectual stimulus. The Christian Platonists of Alexandria—perhaps the most remarkable group of theologians of the day—had brought together, in a unique world of learning and devotion, the known deposits of Greek philosophy and religious practice with the traditions of early Christianity. The greatest of them, Origen, made himself a eunuch for the kingdom's sake and preached an extreme asceticism; celibacy was to him as holy as martyrdom. Yet for the rank and file of the Egyptian church, martyrdom was the highest aspiration of the Christian, and as Christianity ceased to be the religion of a few devout souls and became a popular religion, the contrast between heroic Christians ready to face martyrdom and fair-weather Christians who came and went with the crowd became increasingly evident. It seems that it was in Egypt that large masses of people first joined the church and, by a paradox, Antony and his colleagues and followers fled into the desert to escape both popular religion and persecution. In the late third century the crowd must have seemed the greater menace; in the opening years of the fourth century came persecution by the colleagues of Diocletian; then peace for the church: first tolerance, then favor, then—at the end of the fourth century—the era in which Christianity was the official religion. All others were frowned on and suppressed.

"After the death of the apostles," wrote John Cassian in the brief summary of monastic history contained in his *Collations* (c. 400) "crowds of strangers and men of different races flowed into the Church....And as day by day the number of converts at home and abroad grew, and the primitive Christians lost

their fervour...the Christians who were still fervent...and
remembered the original and perfect way of life, left their cities
and the company of those who thought that they could live
negligently and comfortably in God's Church," and formed
communities apart from the world.[7] A long stretch of history is
here considerably foreshortened. Yet it is evidently true that it
was when Christianity, for long the sect of a minority, officially
proscribed and sometimes persecuted, became a popular religion, that the need for a separate way of life for the more fervent, vigorous and ascetic was first seriously felt.

Cassian held that all the early fervent, ascetic Christians
were "coenobites," and so he could say: the "coenobites...
were...a stem from which grew many flowers and fruit—the
hermits. Everyone knows the founders of this way..., Paul and
Antony. Their motive for choosing the solitary life was not
cowardice nor intolerance of community living, but a wish to
advance further in the contemplation of God, though Paul is
said to have been driven into the desert to escape arrest during
the persecution." The followers of this way "are called
anchorites....They have not remained satisfied with defeating
the attack which the devils secretly plan in human society, but
have been ready to meet them in open war." In the first
instance, and in some cases, the flight to the desert may have
been an escape from worldly entanglements and even temporal embarrassment and persecution, but the monks of the desert
rapidly found that psychological warfare became more and not
less acute in the desert. It was there (as they characteristically
put it) that the devil's onslaught was most fierce. We have
stressed that the monastic movement was in its origin—as all
the great ascetic movements of Christian history have in some
measure been—reaction by men of fervor to the laxer standards

of the church in the world. But it was much else besides; and so it rapidly became a popular movement, and a widely recognized way of life of much variety, with causes and inspiration too rich and complex for brief analysis. Crucial for the direction it was to take was the personal influence of a small group of early ascetics who showed that the life was possible and who inspired men of varied talent to imitate them; among these the central figure was Antony himself. Equally important was the deep influence of the Christian Platonists of Alexandria, and in interpreting their ascetic teaching and the segments of Greek philosophical tradition congenial to ascetics, the central figure was Evagrius of Pontus (c. 346–99). He developed the familiar Greek theme of *telos*, the aim toward which the human soul tended or strove; he first analyzed the "eight principal temptations" that stand between the soul and purity of heart: greed, lust, avarice, anger, melancholy, accidie (see p. 36), vanity and pride. Their conquest, their stripping, leads to freedom from passion, *apatheia*—a word often misunderstood to mean a negative, passive state—in which charity is born; and hence the soul may advance to *gnosis*, knowledge of God.[8]

The combination of powerful personal influences and teaching with the reaction against worldly prosperity takes us a fair way to understanding the success of early monasticism. But there is much still to ponder and to puzzle us; for we shall presently witness a similar movement in the Celtic west, in a country which had never felt either the Roman peace or Greco-Roman wealth (see pp. 55–56).

How can one begin to characterize a movement of the human spirit so distant and so strange? There are indeed many monks today. Nonetheless, to most of us the rigor and asceticism of the desert seem utterly alien. It grew from a conviction

that the world and man's body, though created by God, were
terribly corrupted by the fall and that even if redemption came
by God's free gift, intense human striving was needed if God's
will was to be in any adequate sense fulfilled; that a life of rigor
and renunciation was pleasing to God; that it was possible for
humans to strive, by intense mortification and ceaseless fight
against the devil, to something approaching "the perfect life."
In the fourth century the monastic call drew large numbers
into the desert; this, and the rich and varied intellectual milieu
from which many of them came, gave great variety as well as
intensity to the movement. Hence the ideal, not only of the
hermit Antony but of the coenobite Pachomius; hence too the
"Sarabaites," Cassian's third variety of monks,[9] those who have
abandoned discipline and obedience and live in wickedness.
For, as we should expect, as soon as there were monks there
were bad monks: It is in the nature of great human experi-
ments that they lead to failure as well as success, and no human
adventure can be kept within safe paths. This the founders of
monasticism themselves clearly understood. The lives of the
fathers of the desert, as recorded in their own and later generations, were full of the marvelous and extraordinary: Incredible
feats of endurance, marvelous battles with demons, encounters
with fantastic monsters. But the recorded sayings of the really
eminent directors of the desert are full of inspired common
sense, psychological wisdom and experience and, above all,
pleas for moderation. This remains an outstanding characteristic of early ascetic literature. However strange their way of life,
it is abundantly clear that their teaching was based on accumu-
lated insight and psychological subtlety that make the writings
of Cassian and others, who enshrine the teaching of the desert,
more sophisticated reading than anything of the kind that we

shall meet again before the twelfth century. The variety and the nature of this teaching will become clearer if we observe how monasticism spread through the Christian Roman Empire, north and west until it came to Gaul and Britain, and yet in how pure a form the basic ideals of the desert fathers were preserved in Cassian's *Collations*.

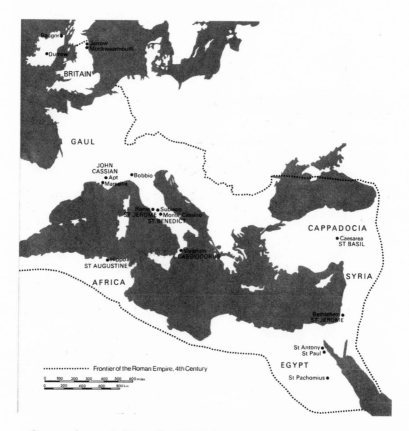

Centers of monastic life, c. 250–735. Only major centers mentioned in early chapters are named; the areas of work and influence of a few of the major leaders of the fourth and fifth centuries are also indicated.

St. Basil

In the mid–fourth century, as monastic communities and groups of hermits grew up in many parts of Egypt, similar communities, under a very similar inspiration, were formed in Palestine and Syria. In Cappadocia in eastern Asia Minor an essentially coenobitic way of life developed out of the old communities of pious Christians into specifically monastic institutes under the leadership of St. Basil (died 379). St. Basil's teaching, advice and instructions, enshrined in the Rule that passed under his name after his death, have played the part in Greek Orthodox monastic life that the Rule of St. Benedict has played in the west.[10] Yet it is not easy for Benedict's disciples, or students accustomed to the terse clarity of the best of western Rules, to appreciate the quality of Basil's Rule, even though they may recognize the common inspiration. St. Basil's Rule is a continuous flowing exposition by a great leader to assorted groups of monks; it is a series of brief sermons dealing with a host of different situations; it is descriptive rather than mandatory, though it lays emphasis enough on discipline and obedience. Above all, it contains a series of meditations by a man who set particular store on meditation based on the Scriptures. No disciple of Calvin ever attempted to set the Bible in the center of his life more fully than St. Basil.

Basil knew the Egyptian hermits and cared little for them; he was uncompromisingly coenobitic. His view is inward-looking, but not individualistic.

> The solitary life has one aim, the service of the needs of the individual. But this is plainly in conflict with the law of love....The Lord for the greatness of His love of men was not content with teaching the word only, but

that accurately and clearly he might give us a pattern of humility in the perfection of love He girded himself and washed the feet of the disciples in person. Whose feet then wilt thou wash? Whom wilt thou care for? In comparison with whom wilt thou be last if thou livest by thyself? How will that good and pleasant thing, the dwelling of brethren together,...be accomplished by dwelling solitary?[11]

Though western readers are not entirely wrong in thinking that Benedict had a clearer idea of legislation and of organization than Basil, even a hasty glance at Basil's Rule gives some understanding of the enormous influence he had throughout the Greek and Byzantine world, and the admiration Benedict himself felt for his eminent predecessor.

St. Augustine

Like Basil, the African father St. Augustine of Hippo (354–430) cared greatly for the monastic life and little for the desert. Augustine's later life as bishop of Hippo was spent, so far as he could arrange it, surrounded by a group of devout, intellectual and hard-working fellow ascetics. Their asceticism was not of heroic stature, but a natural expression of what he and they considered the best Christian tradition of good living. The essential purpose of such groups was practical: to provide for Augustine's need of human company and intelligent conversation, and for the need of his see to have hard-working, dedicated men to manage its spiritual life and temporal welfare. He naturally lent encouragement to other such groups, both of men and of women; and in a famous letter a community of women whose holiness had been called in question were told how such a life should be led. From this letter stemmed the later developments to which the name "The Rule of St. Augustine" came to be attached.[12] Whatever its true connection with the African father, it reflects his interest in monasticism. The description of the interior life of the monastery is spiritually inspiring, but practical; it is only the foundation for useful work in the world. Augustine was himself the most introspective of men, as he reveals in every page of his *Confessions*; but his view of the monastic life was outward-looking. The monastery was a center in which one could meditate, and converse with men of like mind and lead one's own spiritual life, then go out into the city and the diocese to do one's work. Some monks in a neighboring diocese quoted to their bishop the Gospel saying, "Behold the fowls of the air: for they sow not, neither do they reap, nor gather into barns; yet your heavenly Father feedeth them."[13] This, they argued, was an instruction to those leading the good life not to work. Augustine, called in by the bishop to help, was not amused, and wrote a treatise explaining the place of work in God's scheme, and how he wished he could set aside the endless chores of his bishopric, especially the lawsuits he had to settle, and work with his hands. The idea that work was essential to human dignity, or a divine gift, was entirely alien to the teaching of the early church and the fathers. St. Antony and his successors had taught that manual work was an essential of the monastic life, since it prevented idleness and the listlessness which could lead to depression and accidie, commonest of monastic vices—the sense of emptiness, uselessness and futility that naturally afflicts the lonely and the idle. Augustine went further, and although accepting that work was no part of the life of Adam and Eve before the fall of the blessed in heaven, taught that work was always an essential part of the good life on earth.[14]

Thus Augustine's view of monasticism had a strong outward-looking element and was essentially coenobitic; but he had a mind so capacious that hardly any element in the religious and philosophical tradition of the Greco-Roman world failed to find a corner somewhere in it, and he tells us in his *Confessions* that a talk about the Life of St. Antony played a crucial part in his conversion.[15] His monasticism was a macrocosm of his own mind and spirit: in its center lay intense introspection, meditation and contemplation.

The communities Augustine supervised included some for women, and these were important in the formation of the monastic tradition. Some of the very earliest ascetic communities had been those of widows described in 1 Timothy; and in the late fourth century Augustine's eccentric contemporary St. Jerome was inspiring small groups of wealthy women to lead a life of renunciation, celibacy and good works. A small coterie of holy ladies followed him from Rome to Bethlehem, adapting their lives to his harsh, unsympathetic counsels. He rewarded their heroic dedication to the ascetic life with a flood of pamphlets, widely read and imitated in the Middle Ages, in which he inveighed against the fickleness of women and the danger of female company. In his own extraordinary way, he inspired in the widow Paula and her family, and in countless successors who read his works, a sense of the possible dignity of the ascetic life for women. In combining this with passionate statements of the contribution of Eve and her descendants to the world's evils, he revealed attitudes and influences that make him a kind of parody of Paul. There was an absurd, perverse, theatrical element in Jerome; yet he greatly influenced the development of the religious life and helped to ensure that women played a distinguished role in it in the early centuries of the church's history (see pp. 201 ff.).

John Cassian

In the late fourth and early fifth centuries the monastic movement was spreading to many provinces of the Roman Empire, including those in Italy and Gaul. In the very early days, this monasticism was in touch with the eastern sources from which it sprang: the eccentric, ascetic, learned, cantankerous St. Jerome passed between Rome and Bethlehem, and John Cassian himself, one of the most acute observers of the monks of the desert and their most profound interpreter, was born near the Black Sea, brought up in Syria and Palestine, served his monastic apprenticeship in Egypt and settled in the south of Gaul just before the barbarian hordes broke across the Rhine and began the destruction of the western Empire. These invasions were to lead in due course to the separation of Greek and Latin, of eastern and western. Before Cassian there were already monks in France; most famous was St. Martin, first leader of a group of recluses near Poitiers, then bishop of Tours. Thus Cassian, when he arrived in Provence about 400, came to a land ready to receive the message of the desert, and he came just in time.

Cassian had sat at the feet of the leading abbots and spiritual directors of Syria and Egypt, and he ended his days head of a monastic community in Marseille. From his home in Provence he spread about the west a knowledge of the way of life he had studied in the east: first the framework of monastic, coenobitic discipline and spiritual life in his *Institutes*, written for a community recently formed at Apt about forty miles from

Marseille; then a deep and searching inquiry into the teaching on the personal life, contemplation and prayer of the great eastern fathers in the *Conferences*, the *Conlationes, Collations*.

The *Institutes* describe the framework of monastic life, and also the more elementary stages of the individual's progress on the ladder to knowledge of God. The novice is told that:

The fear of the Lord: leads to
compunction of heart: leads to
renunciation of all that is the soul's own: leads to
humility: leads to
mortification of the will: leads to
driving out of the vices: leads to
flowering of virtue: leads to
purity of heart: leads to
perfect charity.[16]

The earlier stages form the "active life"—active in pursuit of virtue—the later the contemplative. The active life witnesses the destruction of the eight sins, that is, the eight temptations of Evagrius translated into Latin—and later in western tradition reduced to seven by the amalgamation of pride and vanity. The *Institutes* were in due course replaced by the Rule of St. Benedict as the fundamental description of the coenobitic life in the west. The contemplative life is the theme of the *Collations*. They were the most elaborate and sophisticated statement of fourth-century teaching on the spiritual life, and one of the supreme masterpieces of early Christian literature, rarely surpassed for subtlety, depth and insight.[17] Thus it was right and natural that the book should become a classic very widely read; and every monastic library of any pretensions in the mid or late Middle Ages possessed at least one copy. It became the normal practice for a chapter of the *Collations* to be read before the service of Compline in the evening in many monasteries; when this became an hour of refreshment, the collation, from its original meaning as a monastic conference—the heart and center of the ascetic life—then became the term for a meal.

The *Collations* take the form of dialogues between Cassian and another young monk and the great leaders of the Egyptian monastic life of Cassian's youth. They bear much the same relation to the actual words of the hermits as did Plato's *Dialogues* to the teaching of Socrates. They reflect the immense respect Cassian had for his teachers, and the fact that he still felt the inspiration of the desert and the call to the solitary life of contemplation. But they are all interpreted according to his own mature thought and set in a literary form of his devising. The highest life, the life of perfection, is still that of the contemplative alone in his cell; yet for all a preparation in a community is now prescribed, and for most this is the true vocation. Thus he writes for coenobites; and he takes pains to emphasize the elements of moderation and common sense in the teaching of the fathers. He had no use for the exaggerated gymnastics of Symeon Stylites and the other saints who made their homes on pillars. And yet a hot wind from the Egyptian desert blows through his writings, and we are brought face to face with an ascetic ideal of great power and depth.

This is all the more striking because a modern reader, however remote he or she may feel Cassian's ideas and ideals to be, cannot fail to be struck by his psychological insight and understanding of human nature. His analysis of temptation avoids the contortions of an overanxious conscience, but cuts like a sharp knife through flourishing roots of self-deception. "It is no proof that our hearts are not plagued with ambition, if we abstain from worldly occupations in which we could not engage even if we wanted…but only if we eschew everything which ministers to our own power, even when it seems to be clothed in a garment of right." And in his study of the approach to purity of heart, he takes special note "why some people, who have given away worldly wealth in gold or silver or lands, are afterwards agitated about a knife, a pencil, a pin or a pen."[18]

Purity of heart is the immediate aim; the kingdom of heaven the ultimate goal. "It is for this end—to keep our hearts continually pure—that we do and endure everything, that we spurn parents and home and position and wealth and comfort and every earthly pleasure….To this end everything is to be done. Solitude, watches in the night, manual labor, nakedness, reading and the other disciplines—we know that their purpose is to free the heart from injury by bodily passions and to keep it free; they are to be the rungs of a ladder up which it may climb to perfect charity."[19] The *Collations* as a whole are a powerful exposition of the methods of climbing this ladder, culminating in the heights of perfection, and in contemplative prayer. In the Gospel story, Martha had been engaged in good works, and reasonably asked for help; but the Lord told her that Mary had chosen the good part: "The Lord, you see, placed the chief good in divine contemplation."[20] Here is an uncompromising statement that the monastic life is interior, first within the community, then within the individual soul; the outside world is mere distraction. Yet Cassian's ideal was neither so individualistic nor so egotistical as could easily be thought. The monastic life is led within, not apart from, the sacramental life of the church. He does not expect his monks to be priests, but he insists on frequent communion; he has no use for the desert

hermits who never communicated at all. Further, he follows a
New Testament scheme in dividing prayer into four elements
or states: first, supplication, that is a cry of penance; then an act
of dedication; next intercession; finally thanksgiving.[21] By
intercession he means prayer "in moments of fervour, for other
men and women—our family, the peace of the world. To use
Paul's words, we pray 'for all men, for kings, and all in authority....' From each of these four kinds rise other opportunities
of richer prayer." He goes on to explore the heights of mystical experience with a richness and clarity never equaled in the
Middle Ages, save perhaps in the mystical doctrine and experience of the twelfth and fourteenth centuries. Cassian never lost
sight of the fact that monks were limbs of Christ's body, members one of another and of the whole body of Christian
people, of the church on earth and in heaven. Though he
reckoned himself a teacher of moderation, there is often an
uncompromising note in his asceticism, and he declared war
on distraction of every kind. The Abba Isaac is made to recall
how he had heard St. Antony grumble at the sunrise: "Why do
you hinder me? The rising of your light draws my mind away
from the true light!"—a saying we shall remember when we
meet St. Bernard in the twelfth century driving every distraction out of his order's churches, especially the glitter of jeweled
shrines and painted glass.[22] Yet the attack on worldly distraction
in Cassian or Bernard's puritanism was not coupled with dis-
trust of all human emotions and values. In the most fundamental sense of the term, in their interest and belief in human capacity and human emotions, both were humanists. Cassian indeed
had indicated in one of his writings the possibility that the first
step on the path to perfection might be taken without God's
free gift of grace, and for this he was execrated as a heretic in

some quarters after his death. But it was in truth a small lapse, for he and Bernard both saw the whole process of man's perfectibility within the economy of divine grace; yet, granted this premise, Cassian laid before the monks who followed him a programme of heroic effort, an intensely strenuous yet feasible attempt to answer the appalling challenge: "Be ye...perfect."[23]

2.

The Rule of St. Benedict

The sixth century saw the final separation of Greek east from Latin west, the collapse in the west of all semblance of Roman Empire. But it also witnessed two notable additions to the literature of the cloister. The first of these was probably written somewhere to the southeast of Rome soon after 500, and is usually known as the Rule of the Master.[1] It is a long, rambling document, full of striking phrases and ascetic wisdom, lacking the form and refinement and clarity of Cassian's *Collations* and yet in its way more of a rule than Cassian's *Institutes*. The Master's monk was subjected to a discipline of personal poverty, and chastity, and total obedience; he was ruled by an abbot who had all the powers of a Roman paterfamilias—that is, a discretion virtually absolute, an authority dissolved only by his death: an abbot whose business it was to guide his monk and also, on occasion, to fuss over him, to see that he blew his "nose in a way likely to give least offence to the attendant angels."[2]

Soon after, perhaps about 530, and certainly in Italy south of Rome, at Monte Cassino, the second and more famous of these Rules was written by Benedict of Nursia. The opening chapters of St. Benedict's Rule consist of an abbreviated and adapted version of the opening of the Master's, and there are echoes and borrowings throughout. But the result is something much more than a second edition, for in numerous points of principle and practice the Master's teaching is modified; and the whole structure is tightened and clarified. In former generations it was assumed indeed that Benedict's was the earlier document, the Master's derivative, and the Master was generally undervalued. It came as a great shock to the monastic world when in 1937 the doctrine was first propounded that the Master was the earlier and Benedict the copyist. The result was a controversy. In the words of Dom David Knowles, "the heather had been set alight and fire-fighters and fire-raisers alike hastened to the spot."[3] Now a majority of the scholarly world, Benedictine and non-Benedictine alike, has agreed that the new doctrine is correct—but see p. 5–6. If Benedict was a modern author, publishing under modern laws of copyright, he would be convicted of plagiarism on a large scale. In his own world, he stands convicted of an act of extraordinary humility; it remains a curious and intriguing fact that his Rule should be so far superior to the document from which it was adapted.

"We must form a school of the Lord's service," said the Master in his prologue; "We must form a school of the Lord's service," said Benedict, "in which nothing too harsh, nothing too heavy, do we hope to see established....As we lead our life in the faith, when our heart has been enlarged, the path of God's commands is run in a sweetness of love beyond words."[4] Though for the most part much more succinct than the Master, and commonly content to use his words, Benedict takes pains to draw out essential points and everywhere to clarify the message. Moderation, common sense and a measure of organization are qualities much in evidence. He recognized that there were two kinds of monks: coenobites, "those living in a monastery under a rule and [or] an abbot"; and anchorites, "that is the kind of hermits who have learned, not in their first prentice fervour, but by long trial in a monastery, having studied many men's example, can fight against the devil and can go out from the ranks of the brothers fully instructed to the single combat of the hermitage." Here Benedict is not only following the Master: he shows himself, as so often, faithful to the tradition and teaching of Cassian.[5]

> We have laid out this Rule so that we may show that those who observe it in their monasteries have in a measure soundness of character or the beginnings of the good life. For anyone who hastens on to the perfect way of life, there are the teachings of the Holy Fathers, the keeping of which leads a man to the peak of perfection. For what page or what sentence of the divine authority of Old and New Testament but is a rule of human life of the most precise? Or what book of the holy catholic Fathers but echoes this word, that by a straight course we may come to our Creator? What else are the *Collations* and the *Institutes* of the Fathers and their *Lives,* and the Rule of our holy father Basil,[6] but instruments of the virtues of monks who lead the good life in obedience? But to us who are idle or live bad or negligent lives every page is shame and confusion.
>
> Whoever you are, therefore, who hastens to the heavenly country, fulfil completely with Christ's help this little rule written for beginners—and then at last, with God's protection, you may come to the greater heights of teaching and virtue which we have listed above. Amen.

The little rule for beginners describes a life of great earnestness and severity; to those of us who lead the life of ordinary mortals in the early twenty-first century, a life of dedication and monotony beyond our dreams. Yet the historical record shows that there is far more to it than that; and there are many thousands still obeying St. Benedict's precepts today. What is the secret of its astonishing success? To this there is no single or simple answer; the historian who asserts that he or she understands the problem and can give a crisp and clear answer has failed to take the measure of two of Benedict's most notable qualities—his humility and his practical good sense. Unless we have grappled personally with this problem, the excitement of exploring a medieval monastery or of monastic life will not begin to unfold.

In a curious way Benedict seems almost to anticipate his own achievement. "Whoever you are…" has a universal ring about it;[7] and so definite and precise and concrete are all his instructions that it is easy, when under the impress of his book, to feel that he knew it would have a large, long-lasting and universal impact. Nothing is less probable. He spoke from a comparatively narrow experience, and never strayed outside it; he legislated for the type of monastery he knew. But the doors of his mind, like the doors of his monastery, were not closed to strangers.

The "rule written for beginners" is homely, devout and practical; it shows shrewd and subtle insight into human nature; it combines unyielding demands for obedience and stability with moderation and humanity. It is no masterpiece of coherent legislation, yet it combines something of the genius of Roman Law and of the spiritual teaching of Cassian, legacies of an intellectual world more sophisticated than

Benedict's. Nor is its elementary nature to be taken to mean that it was easy. At its heart lie the precepts of complete obedience (a precept to be sternly maintained), personal poverty and chastity; the life it describes is frugal and severe and monotonous. Later generations of monks often found it impossible to maintain in every syllable, and it had to be reinterpreted to suit conditions other than those of the sixth century and harsher climates than that of Italy. It is a difficult rule to keep, but not impossible, and therein lies its genius. It was the fruit of a lifetime spent in trying to control an intractable body of monks often inspired with genuine devotion, rarely well equipped with native staying power. Externally, what was needed was a set of regulations sufficiently rigid and clear to command unquestioning acceptance from all members of a community. The monk in Benedict's Rule spends most of the day in silence: he is occupied either in the communal worship in church (eight services or offices and the mass are spread over various hours of the day) or in private meditation and spiritual reading, or in manual labor for the support of the community, or in eating and sleeping. The principal psychological dangers of such a life are neurotic extremes of depression and exaltation; and the answer to these, humanly speaking, is to maintain regularity and devotion. The regularity of the Rule is as inexorable as a doctor's prescription, and it has proved very effective.

Benedict was deeply influenced by Cassian, and most of the lineaments of his ideal can be found in the *Institutes* or the *Collations*. This is particularly evident in the mixture of sternness and mercy on which Benedict lays such emphasis. The abbot is owed complete obedience, and in the end the monk must obey him—after a pause for proper inquiry—even if he thinks the order wrong. Yet Benedict emphasizes at the outset that the abbot's business is to help the monks; and the spirit of the passages in which obedience and authority are discussed has far more to say of the abbot's responsibility, of help and cooperation, than of his ultimately dictatorial power. The idea of obedience comes from Cassian, and most of the chapter on the abbot from the Master—including the famous adjuration to remember the day of judgment and the abbot's responsibility for his flock in the judge's presence.[8] In Benedict's Rule, however, this is immediately followed by a chapter on taking counsel, which has only the vaguest counterpart in the Master's Rule. On crucial matters the abbot is to take counsel of the whole community, "for often the Lord reveals to a young man [or the young] what is best" (c. 3); on lesser matters he consults the seniors only, following the counsel of Ecclesiasticus: "Do nothing without advice."[9] After taking counsel, the abbot makes up his own mind, for this the Rule binds him in the end to do. He cannot evade his responsibility nor pass it to others: Much of the strength, and weakness, of the Rule lie in this vision of the abbot, who is assumed to be both a notable spiritual director and a master in handling human relations. Such men are rare.

Benedict followed Cassian in making the communal life a necessary foundation for all kinds of monks; whether he thought that the anchorite ideal was in the end higher than the coenobite is far from clear. His opening, in which he claims that the coenobites are the strongest or best of monks, seems to deny it; his epilogue—which is probably a later addition, representing his final view—seems to allow that the anchorite's may be a higher call for a minority, and commends the reading of Cassian in the strongest terms.

This reveals the ambiguity, the tension between the coenobite and the hermit ideal that was to remain a characteristic of
western monasticism. As for the other common tension in
monastic history, that between the inward and the outward
view, Benedict's monastery was clearly a little world, an oasis
of sanity in a barbarian kingdom. Yet the outer world was not
excluded. "All guests who arrive should be received as Christ
himself would be received…" (c. 53), and precise instructions
are given for their entertainment in a modest but becoming
fashion; a special duty of hospitality is laid upon the abbot. The
outer world is not to be entirely ignored or neglected; its presence is to be accepted in a practical way as well as in a spiritual sense, in the monks' prayers. Yet the monastery of the Rule
is presumed to be a place in which the essential aim is the
good life and the salvation of its own inmates. Social work,
pastoral work are not included; nor are they specifically mentioned in order to be rejected. From this silence many consequences have flowed.

It is also assumed that the buildings of the monastery are
much more modest than they later became in many communities in western Christendom. The church is called the oratory—it is simply a place of prayer, where the community can
gather for mass and offices or the individual can go to say his
prayers. It is the place where God's work is done, just as the
kitchen and outhouses are the place where the necessary tasks
of the monastery are conducted. The monks' life was passed in
God's work and their own, which was to include some of the
chores of the monastery and the monastic garden, though
Benedict evidently regarded agricultural labor as exceptional.
There emerges a vivid picture of a small and compact and
almost self-contained community in the heart of barbarian

Italy. But Benedict's vision is more than that; it is a link between the early Middle Ages and our own. For in many regions of the world today there are communities of monks calling themselves after his name, living by his Rule and constantly studying it and reciting it.

The Formation of the Monastic Tradition

From St. Benedict of Nursia
to St. Benedict of Aniane

Benedict prescribed spiritual reading for his monks, and he called their common worship "God's work"—*opus Dei*. But he assumes no great learning, nor a large library, and the liturgy lacked elaborate ritual or music. Learning never became a normal characteristic of any medieval religious order or of any large group of monasteries; nonetheless, the monastic library, along with the cathedral library, became the repository that ensured the survival of some part of the legacy of ancient literature. Thus when men of a scholarly turn of mind grew up in the cloister, they could thus sometimes find the food they needed to hand. In a similar way, the growth of liturgical elaboration was at first sporadic and occasional; but in the end it became a normal and inescapable feature of all monasteries of the ninth, tenth and eleventh centuries.

The intellectual tradition began with Cassiodorus (c. 485–c. 580), a retired civil servant who spent his declining years in a monastery called Vivarium, even further south in Italy than

Monte Cassino. He was the last of the great scholars of the ancient world seriously to engage in transmitting Greek thought and literature to the west. His library was the last really massive collection of books that the ancient world produced. Both monastery and library disappeared soon after his death, but a few books were carried to Rome, and it is probably to this that we owe the survival of more than one of the masterpieces of ancient literature. Even before his death his own *Institutes*, a treatise on the principles and techniques of the study of divine scripture, had reached the eternal city. The second part is a complete system of education in the chief Roman disciplines—grammar, rhetoric and the rest—which as a cultivated man he regarded as a necessary preliminary to the study of the Bible. The first part outlines the approach to the Bible itself. This remarkable enterprise was too much for all but a handful of the scholars of the centuries that followed, and it is a symptom of the failure of Cassiodorus's intention that the two parts circulated for several hundred years quite separately. In the eleventh and twelfth centuries, when learning revived for good and all, his scheme provided one of the chief foundations for the reintegration of learning, sacred and profane, of Roman literary science and Christian theological science based on the study of the Bible.

Cassiodorus was one of the most distinguished of a group of men who tried to gather in encyclopedic form the best of ancient learning before the failure of education and the barbarian onslaught destroyed it. One of the liveliest and ablest minds in this tradition was Pope Gregory the Great (590–604), not as cultivated as Cassiodorus nor as modest as Benedict, and more the man of affairs than either: There was scarcely a department of ecclesiastical life which his comprehensive genius and organizing ability did not stamp. His liturgical reforms were first implemented in the churches and monasteries of Rome, and so entered the monastic tradition alongside the books of Cassiodorus. He conceived an immense admiration for St. Benedict, whose praises he sang while chronicling his miracles in the Second Book of his *Dialogues*. He commends the Rule for its penetrating wisdom and clarity *(discretione praecipuam, sermone luculentam);*[1] it seems to have impinged curiously little on his own writings and teaching, but the phrase stuck and helped to make the Rule's fame. In particular, the Rule was taken to England in the course of the seventh century, and some of the monks of the second generation in England, notably St. Wilfrid of Ripon, York and Hexham, and St. Benedict Biscop, founder of Bede's monasteries at Monkwearmouth and Jarrow, paid it particular respect. The characteristic monastic rule book of these early centuries contains an anthology, sometimes up to half a dozen rules; even in the ninth century St. Benedict of Aniane, from whose work the unique place of the Rule in later monasticism sprang, was the author of just such an anthology. Undoubtedly there were monasteries in various parts of Europe much earlier than this dedicated to following his Rule and honoring the first Benedict's memory. The earliest surviving manuscript of the Rule, now in the Bodleian Library at Oxford, may possibly reflect the special devotion of St. Wilfrid to it.[2] Another center of the cult of Benedict was established in the seventh century at Fleury in France. After Benedict's death the Lombards had come and destroyed Monte Cassino; the remains of his community gathered up his bones and fled. After many wanderings and the passing of several generations, they came to rest in the late seventh century at Fleury on the Loire, where they have been honored to the present day and where the great abbey church of Saint Benoît-sur-Loire still stands, with massive westwork, aisles and ambulatory to provide space for the pilgrims to his tomb.

In the Britain of St. Wilfrid and St. Benedict Biscop there flourished another monastic tradition uninfluenced by Benedict of Nursia. Columcille (Columba) and Aidan were the most famous representatives in sixth- and seventh-century Scotland and England of the monastic movement that had captured the Irish church in the generations following the death of St. Patrick (probably late fifth century).[3] The heart of this movement lay in sixth-century Ireland in such places as Durrow and Bangor; and although it owed much to continental influence and inspiration, it was also a powerful native growth. Here we have an ascetic movement entirely different in its origin from that of fourth-century Egypt. It flourished in a barbarian society hardly or partly converted; it had from the first a strong missionary element within it. It also bred stern ascetics and the most ruthless denunciation of the human body recorded in western Catholic ascetic literature before the eleventh century; yet it could not in the nature of the case be a protest against lax standards in the church, for the Irish were poor (compared with the Egyptians) and recently converted. But in truth the Irish monastic experience was exceedingly varied, and in this it was not so different from the continental monastic scene of the sixth and seventh centuries. The Irish monks, like the Roman monks of Gregory the Great, became fervent missionaries. Their sternest leader was Columban, who went from Bangor to found Luxeuil in Gaul and Bobbio in Italy; his disciples spread Celtic monastic influence as far as St. Gallen in what is now Switzerland. Less fierce and more ready to compromise with native social customs were Columcille, founder of Durrow and Iona, and Iona's most celebrated son of the next generation, St. Aidan, a man of a gentler nature still than Columcille, the subject of one of the most attractive pen-portraits of the Venerable Bede.[4] Columban despised the body; yet among Irish hermits and monks an exceptional devotion to the beauty of nature can be discerned. A similar variety appears in the Irish monks' treatment of native society, from those who rejected it root and branch to those (especially of the seventh and eighth centuries) who melted into their Celtic background so as to become indistinguishable from it. To accommodate Irish society and the Christian faith had been in the first instance a notable achievement. But in course of time it seems that whole families became monastic in name; while some members might lead a fervent religious life, others married and gave in marriage and ruled the monastery as if it were a secular community. A similar process of assimilation can be detected in England in the age of Bede, and the disappearance of specifically monastic features from communities of monks has been common in many ages. The attempt to check such decadence and to establish a clear framework of monastic discipline was to bring the Rule of St. Benedict to a new peak of fame in the ninth and tenth centuries. Meanwhile this movement was most obviously prepared for in the intervening centuries in the Northumbria of Bede (died 735) and the German monasteries founded by the missionaries of the early and mid–eighth century, many of whom were also English. Most influential of these was St. Boniface, who started in Friesland in 716, transferred to Germany soon after and was consecrated bishop for Germany by the pope in person in 722; before his martyrdom in 754 he laid the foundations of the German church, in

organization and spiritual life, and inaugurated the reform of
the church in West Francia (France and the Rhineland) too.
For an English monk it was natural to make a group of monasteries the center of his work and life, and to set them in close
relation with the pope and under a discipline owing much to
St. Benedict. Some of his colleagues studied the monastic life
in Monte Cassino, recently revived, and elsewhere in Italy.
From Spain or southern Gaul came St. Pirmin, founder of
what soon became the chief center of monastic life in southern Europe, the Reichenau, securely placed on its small island
just to the west of Constance. Reichenau performed in the
south of Germany the role of Boniface's abbeys farther north.
The chief of these was Fulda, which remained a center of
monastic observance and of pilgrimage after Boniface had
been buried there.

It was natural too for an English monk to look for female
helpers in his work. Of the many great English abbesses of the
previous generation the best known is St. Hilda of Whitby, of
whom Bede spoke at length and with admiration, and who
dominated a large community of both nuns and monks. One
such double monastery appeared in Germany in the time of
Boniface, at Heidenheim in Thuringia, first under the rule of
Boniface's cousin Wynnebald, then of Wynnebald's sister
Walpurgis or Waldburg. Other Anglo-Saxon ladies, notably
Leoba and Thecla, founded abbeys for nuns in Franconia; they
established a tradition of female involvement in the monastic
life that was to survive and flourish in Germany more abundantly than in England (see pp. 202–3).

In the remains of Bede's monasteries in Northumbria we
may still gain something of the impression of the tiny monastic oratories characteristic of the eighth century. Fleury is of

the eleventh; and it reflects the new fashions of the Romanesque period (see p. 126 ff.). There is a dramatic contrast in scale, and this reflects two movements: the liturgical movement, which began in the Roman basilicas about 600 and became a general feature of western monastic life in the ninth and tenth centuries; and the popular religious movement, which brought throngs of pilgrims to churches like Saint-Benoît from the early eleventh century on. Behind these movements lay the work of Benedict of Aniane in the ninth century and the monastic revival of the tenth.

It has been implicit in what we have said of the influence of Cassian and Benedict and Cassiodorus that the survival and spread of the ancient books of Christian devotion and theology and classical learning were due to their long life, waking or sleeping, in monastic libraries, and to the reawakening of intellectual interest in old books at various epochs of the Middle Ages. Thus it is natural to look for a major development in the study of Benedict's Rule in the Carolingian renaissance.

The coronation of Charlemagne as emperor in Rome on Christmas Day 800 marked the alliance of Roman tradition and Frankish monarchy, the assurance that the Roman Empire was still thought to be alive in the west. But it was in his new Rome north of the Alps, in Aachen, that Charlemagne organized the center of an empire rooted in divinely ordained kingship, military power and central administration—such as it was in the ninth century. It was in this milieu that religious and monastic reform and intellectual revival had their nucleus. The emperor himself provided the force and power of the movement; in middle life, he felt himself thoroughly involved in everything that went forward, and sat on his lofty throne in the palatine chapel during mass directing the service. But the intellectual climate was made by men like Alcuin, by a group of scholars with a modest but definite reverence for the antique and a clear idea of how the treasures of ancient literature and the needs of contemporary schools were to be matched. Their central idea was to find and copy pure and exact texts of the Bible, the fathers, the classics and the liturgies and rules of the church. To this process the modern world owes the survival of a number of ancient works of literature and learning, and the purity of text of still more. It is characteristic of the achievement of Alcuin and his colleagues that, although the oldest text of the Rule of St. Benedict now surviving comes from seventh-century England, the best derives from the court of Charlemagne. This is the famous manuscript preserved for many centuries at St. Gall, Sankt Gallen, the Codex Sangallensis.[5] It was once supposed to be a direct copy of the original manuscript, preserved in Rome after Benedict's death and the dispersal of his community. Its story is now thought less simple and satisfactory; yet it remains a faithful copy, made by Carolingian scholars, from a model very close to Benedict's own text, still close enough to mirror the degenerate spelling and syntax of sixth-century Latin much more faithfully than the copies to which we are used today.

Charlemagne's successor, Louis the Pious, decided that if the monastic life was to flourish in his empire as he wished, a major effort of reorganization must be set on foot. To this end he appointed the second St. Benedict, Benedict of Aniane, archabbot of all the monasteries of Francia—or at least of those within reach, or of those capable of reform. The dissemination of the Rule of St. Benedict and the appointment of Benedict of Aniane were grand gestures whose practical result at the time was extremely limited. But they sowed the seeds from which the traditional monasticism of the tenth and eleventh centuries, with all its branches, was to grow. Of ancient Aniane itself, Benedict's first home, nothing remains; but its near neighbor, Saint-Guilhem-le-Desert, is a remarkable monument to his generation of monks. For here in a wild cleft in the hills above Montpellier, a great noble of Charlemagne's day, William of Toulouse ("Guillaume d'Orange"), sought refuge. His hermitage became the center of a fine monastery, which grew and flourished when William the saint drew pilgrims to his shrine and William the hero was inspiring epic songs, culminating in Wolfram von Eschenbach's *Willehalm*.[6]

If we ask when was the Benedictine Order formed, then the first, simple, strict answer is: never, or not yet. The history of Benedictine communities has been the story of a long struggle to preserve the independence that was traditionally regarded as an essential mark of Benedictine monachism. The abbey of the Rule is a world on its own, and Benedict's monks have commonly been inclined to prefer it that way. In the eleventh century groups of monasteries under a common head began to be formed, sometimes very large groups indeed, but still following the Rule of St. Benedict; in the twelfth century articulated orders grew up with a constitution and a central organization, some of them following the Rule. In the thirteenth century a powerful pope and a great council (the Fourth Lateran of 1215) put it on paper that the independent houses of Benedictine obedience should form themselves into provincial or national congregations, and on paper for the most part the doctrine stayed. In thirteenth-century England the first congregation was formed; but it was not until many centuries later that every Benedictine community had been dragged into some net or other, and not until the days of Pope Leo XIII in the late nineteenth century that a single abbot primate, a single head to the whole "order," was set up; but the Benedictines are still not governed by the primate or gathered into a single, authoritative order; his primacy is one of honor, not of power.

A former generation of Benedictine historians viewed the early efforts at centralization with a marked coolness, and this accounts for the comparatively bad press that Benedict of Aniane received, together with some of his most distinguished successors, including sometimes even Cluny itself. Yet even the great liturgical scholar Edmund Bishop, a devout upholder of the traditional Benedictine life, admitted that: "After the great founder himself, Benedict of Nursia, no man has more widely affected Western monachism than did the second Benedict, he of Aniane."⁷ Stern and puritanical by temperament, authoritarian in intention, Benedict of Aniane found that the world in which he lived and the responsibility laid on his shoulders increasingly mitigated both his puritanism and his austerity. In 816 or 817 at a council at Aachen he was the central figure in the promulgation of a series of monastic customs that, joined to the Rule, was to form the basis for the traditional monasticism. Its most essential features were liturgical. God's work, the *opus Dei* of the Rule, ceased to be merely a part of a divided routine and became the raison d'être of the monastic life, and a liturgy of ever increasing elaboration grew up to match its new vocation—new, or partly new, because in a measure this was the consummation of accretions to the Benedictine life begun in the Roman basilicas shortly after the death of Benedict of Nursia. But even more important than the growing liturgy was the consecration of the book itself. St. Benedict's Rule ceased to be, what it had been for Bede, a revered model, one of many, and became the basic norm—to be studied and learned by heart as no other Rule or model was studied.

The Tenth Century

When Benedict of Aniane died in 821 his schemes collapsed, and the ninth century marked perhaps the lowest point in the history of monastic observance since the sixth. There are exceptions. Here and there about Europe great abbeys flourished; and this was the first golden age of Reichenau, secure on its tiny island in the Bodensee (Lake of Constance), and St. Gall (Sankt Gallen). From both these monasteries venerable confraternity books survive, revealing that already in the ninth century each had an alliance in prayer with a group of abbeys in southwestern Germany and Switzerland.[8] These alliances were not institutional, like those of the later orders, yet they created unions in some ways very much like congregations of more recent times, and helped the knowledge of Carolingian monasticism to survive through the collapse of the Carolingian empire. The buildings of Reichenau remain perhaps the most striking monument today of this epoch in monastic history: The Mittelzell, the main abbey church, has a nucleus of the ninth century, and was greatly enlarged at the turn of the tenth and eleventh. What we admire today is a great Romanesque basilica in its heyday. In the ninth and tenth centuries it was a center of life and learning, able to furnish even St. Gall with skilled painters. But in the ninth century centers such as these were exceptional.

It was between 910 and 940 that the foundations for the true monastic revival were laid, and laid over a wide area. From Cluny in Burgundy (910), northeast to Brogne (c. 920) and Gorze in Lorraine (c. 933), then west via Fleury, where St. Benedict's relics rose again to preside over the temporal and spiritual revival of his

flock, to Glastonbury in England (*c.* 940): In this ample space
the Rule of the first Benedict and the customs of the second
found practical expression. The monastic life revived and flourished in several hundred monasteries in France, Germany,
England, Italy and Spain. The scale and the variety of the
modes of monastic life became far greater in the twelfth century, when monastic houses came to be counted in thousands.

Map to illustrate the monastic movements of the tenth and eleventh centuries.
Any attempt to plot the shifting pattern of influences, often very widely spread,
must be impressionistic. Yet such a map is genuinely revealing, so long as the
boundaries and arrows are not taken too literally, and so long as we make no
attempt to put frontiers to the influence of Cluny, save where the sphere of
influence of Gorze was felt (see pp. 67–69)

From the tenth to the late twelfth century the foundation and endowment and support of monasteries of every kind are the characteristic forms which the endeavor of the pious, lay or clerical, was to take. Numerous men of moderate wealth and conventional piety—and many supposed less than pious by their fellows—invested large sums, a substantial part of their wealth, in founding or enlarging monasteries where monks or nuns could pray for their souls till the day of judgment. Here are facts of deep and lasting interest for the social, cultural and economic history of western Europe—also for the understanding of its politics, as we shall see—as well as facts of religious history.

Cluny and Gorze in the Tenth and Eleventh Centuries

The houses that flourished in the eleventh century had mostly been founded or refounded in the tenth; all accepted the Rule of St. Benedict of Nursia and the legislation of St. Benedict of Aniane as the basis for their life; all accepted a much larger liturgy and much less manual work than the earlier Benedict had expected. Two main streams of influence flowed down from the tenth century into the eleventh and twelfth. First is Cluny, whose prestige grew steadily as more houses accepted her customs and as she continued to flourish under a succession of abbots of exceptional ability and saintliness, and also of exceptionally long life, for St. Odilo (994–1049) and St. Hugh (1049–1109) spanned the whole eleventh century between them. Numerous abbeys were reformed under the inspiration of Cluny. Commonly the patrons asked Odilo or Hugh for monks, books and advice; sometimes the monks themselves took the initiative in applying to Cluny; frequently the abbey remained for a time under the jurisdiction of one of

Cluny's leading men or of the abbot himself. In the end, down to the mid–eleventh century, they became independent houses once again. But though these abbeys, reformed under Cluny's aegis, later owed no allegiance to the motherhouse, they continued to bear her stamp upon them. A visitor would find in the customs, liturgy, music, sometimes in the architecture and ornaments, signs that monks from Cluny had been there. From the mid–eleventh century on, Cluny began to collect houses large and small that remained dependent on her, so that by the late twelfth century, spread over most of western Europe except Germany, there was a community of many hundreds of houses in the Cluniac allegiance. This meant that the abbot of Cluny was himself the patriarchal head of all these communities; the monks professed obedience personally to him. The kind of constitutional or parliamentary structure established by other orders in the twelfth and thirteenth centuries was foreign to the simple hierarchy of Cluny.

Much of Cluny's influence was indirect, through disciples of her abbots and houses reformed by her that had preserved or recovered their independence. This can be seen most characteristically in Italy and Spain. In both lands Cluny had daughter houses. But in Italy its most powerful influence came through St. William of Volpiano, abbot of Fruttuaria, who led a movement deeply influenced by Cluny, which spread her customs and the communal ideal of the traditional monasticism in Lombardy, especially at Sant'Ambrogio at Milan, south to Farfa, and from Farfa to Rome itself; and also in Dijon, where William was already abbot of the house of Saint-Bénigne; and from Dijon to Normandy, where he inspired and led the remarkable renaissance of monastic life with its centers in Fécamp and Jumièges, which also influenced monasteries already under way, such as Mont Saint-Michel (see p. 246). In Italy, the abbots of Cluny had already established their customs in a number of houses, including San Paolo fuori le Mura at Rome, when St. William started his work; he greatly enlarged and extended the area over which Cluny's influence spread. Later in the eleventh century a number of Italian houses were refounded or revived under the direct sway of the abbot of Cluny, but the most widespread movements of Cluniac reform were technically independent of her authority. Monte Cassino itself, St. Benedict's home, became a major center of observance, monastic influence and craftsmanship under Abbot Desiderius, who was for a brief time at the end of his life Pope Victor III (1086–87). After the formation of the Norman dominion in southern Italy and Sicily in the mid– and late eleventh century, a new monastic center was established at La Cava dei Tirreni, not far from Salerno—under Cluny's inspiration but never dependent on her. In the early twelfth century it came to number in its obedience about seventy-five houses, including some that had replaced the Greek communities of southern Italy and others, like San Paolo at Rome, which had formerly been in the ambience of Fruttuaria.

In the Christian kingdoms of northern Spain and on the frontiers of Spain and France, in the tenth and eleventh centuries, there was a similar juxtaposition of influence direct and indirect from Cluny and other major centers of monastic observance farther north. In the late tenth century, for example, the abbeys of Lézat and Cuxa (now in the south of France), in different ways already influenced by Cluny, became the center of an independent congregation, and in the early eleventh century Cuxa joined Ripoll to form the headquarters of a small monastic empire ruled by Oliba, abbot of both houses, under whose inspiration both Saint-Martin-du-Canigou and Montserrat were founded. Soon after, the king of Navarre appointed an abbot trained at Cluny to San Juan de la Peña. Later in the eleventh century, Cluny and her southern-French daughter Moissac, one of the greatest of Cluniac houses, had a measure of direct influence in Spain; but the real successor to Oliba's congregation was that which was formed in the 1070s and 1080s under Bernard de Rodez, abbot of Saint-Victor at Marseille, and his brother, Richard, who succeeded him as abbot and became a cardinal. Both were admirers of Cluny, though not subjects of St. Hugh. But Richard overreached himself as an empire builder, and some of his Spanish dependencies regained their freedom; more remained for a while under Saint-Victor, especially the great house of Ripoll, subject until the late twelfth century. In Spain, as in Italy, we see the direct and indirect influence of Cluny at work, helping to form a series of local centers and congregations sustaining the type of observance that had won Cluny her reputation.

Thus "Cluniac" is a label with two distinct meanings: It is correctly applied to the houses that remained under Cluny's allegiance, and it is no less correctly applied to those which retained or resumed independence but nonetheless were infused with Cluny's customs.

The other chief source of influence flowed from Lorraine, especially from the great house of Gorze, near Metz, then in Germany. The houses reformed by Gorze and her children numbered over 160 by the early twelfth century. But the ripples spread further than the direct influence, and in the monastic revival in England in the mid– and late tenth century the customs and influences of Cluny and Gorze met. There, in the work of St. Dunstan and St. Ethelwold and St. Oswald, they mingled with local traditions and customs, but the monasticism of Glastonbury, Abingdon, Winchester and Worcester was visibly of the same pattern as that of Cluny and Gorze.

England apart, it is broadly speaking true that down to about 1050 the frontier of France and Germany, as it then ran, divided the sphere in which Cluny reigned from that of Gorze. The essential reason for this seems to have been political. The patrons of almost all these abbeys were kings and princes; it was not till the late eleventh and twelfth centuries that it became common for lesser men—barons, knights and burghers—to found and play the patron to monasteries. In the tenth century the German kings, alias emperors, had kept a tight grip on their abbeys, whereas those outside their frontiers, especially those like Cluny, which were remote from any center of kingly or princely power in France, had developed a tradition of independence. Cluny herself had from the start a considerable measure of secular freedom, and in due course became wholly independent of every power save that of the pope; to put it another way, she was founded in direct dependence on the pope, and was able in due course to draw out the logical consequence of her status. Successive kings of Germany had close personal relations with St. Odilo and St. Hugh, but the pattern of Cluniac independence was alien to them. Thus for their own monasteries they looked to Lorraine, then a part of their kingdom, and Gorze and its kin developed a system of external relations much more dependent on the king and the princes than Cluny's.

One of the central figures in German monasticism at the turn of the tenth and eleventh centuries was St. Godehard, who ruled over Niederaltaich and Tegernsee abbeys, and by the purity of his observance influenced many more. Late in life he settled in Niederaltaich, his biographer tells us, intending to end his days there. One night, after spending many hours in prayer and worship, he retired to his chamber just as dawn was breaking and laid down on his bench for a short rest. His sleep was disturbed by a dream, in which he saw a great olive tree in the midst of the cloister garth, and under it he was sitting and reading. Presently there came messengers from the king-emperor, Henry II (1002–24), saying that their master had sent them to dig up the tree and carry it off for his use. Although they encountered roots of exceptional depth and other difficulties, the abbot awoke feeling sure that he would himself be presently uprooted. Sure enough, Henry insisted that he become bishop of Hildesheim, and as bishop he served both the monastic movement of his day and the king. In combining these two roles, Godehard showed himself a true disciple of Gorze and the German monastic ethos of his day, and relations between the king and the monastic reformers were especially close under Henry II.

In the mid– and late eleventh century the borders of France and Germany ceased to be a frontier between Cluny and Gorze; and one of the most powerful movements of the century had its center in Hirsau in south Germany, and its founder in a disciple of St. Hugh of Cluny. Yet the influence of William of Hirsau did not necessarily involve the waning of the older traditions that had flowed from Gorze, for in many parts of Germany allegiance to the king still meant adherence to the type of monasticism that had inspired St. Godehard. Thus when a loyal count founded Maria Laach in 1093, he looked to St. Maximin at Trier, a house firmly set in the Gorze mold, for the monks and the monastic customs on which the house was to be founded.

The differences between Cluny and Gorze were mainly external. Their internal life represented still the customs of the ninth and tenth centuries, based on the Rule of St. Benedict.

4.

Life, Work and Prayer

The Daily Round

What did monks do? How was their life spent? First of all, they dedicated a great share of their time to communal worship in the monastic church; in some communities, at some epochs, almost all the time that was left over from eating and sleeping. In all communities paying any kind of allegiance to St. Benedict and his Rule the day was punctuated by services. From soon after midnight till late in the evening the bell rang every hour or two to summon the monks to the office, to the recitation of psalms, hymns, prayers and readings from the Bible: in the middle of the night to Matins,[1] in the small hours to Lauds, at dawn to Prime, about two hours later to Terce (the "third hour"), about noon to Sext (the "sixth"), early in the afternoon to None (the "ninth"), early in the evening to Vespers, a little later to Compline. The times have been stated with deliberate vagueness. It is indeed possible to state the hours of the day when these events were supposed to have happened according to the Rule; but what these hours really meant, in the centuries before the clock (as we know it) was invented, is impossible to say; and a natural vagueness covers most medieval customaries. They had sundials and they had hourglasses. To what extent they used them is an insoluble mystery. In practice, for most monks most of the time, the hour was announced by the bell, and we should be wrong to think in any terms more precise than the fairly regular toll of the bell punctuating a very regular day.

In winter, the monastic day may be roughly defined as running from 2 A.M. to 6:30 P.M.[2] By any standard, this meant an early start and a long day; though not unduly long. It meant an early start, but ended not long after dusk, at least in Mediterranean lands. The southern influence is still clearer in the summer timetable, for from Easter until mid-September the Rule allowed for a siesta in the early afternoon, and so a longer evening. Perhaps the strangest feature is the arrangement for meals. In winter and Lent only one was allowed: at about two in the afternoon in winter, in the evening (half-past five or six) in Lent. In the summer there were two, about noon and in the evening. Eggs, fish and cheese, beans, milk and honey provided the basic fare, with many variations in different times and places. Meat was forbidden by St. Benedict, but it was widely held that he had not intended to include birds in his prohibition, and a number of special relaxations had already begun to creep in by the eleventh century. It was assumed that the very young monks and those who had serious difficulty in fasting would have breakfast or at least a drink between Terce and Sext; occasional extra dishes, "pittances," were added in most monasteries on Sundays and feast days and on a number of occasions that tended steadily to increase as the centuries passed. At the abbot's table, and in the infirmary—that is, where distinguished guests and the sick had to be fed—meat was commonly allowed.

In the refectory, then as now, an uplifting book was read from a pulpit or lectern. The monks were not allowed to talk—

and silence was the rule throughout the day, save at certain times
in special places, and apart from the public utterance of prayers
and praises and instructions in church, chapter house, refectory
and cloister. Thus a whole language of signs had to be devised to
enable the brothers to communicate without breaking silence. A
common sign for bread was a circle described by the thumbs and
two fingers of both hands, for bread (we are told) was usually
round; and for cherries a finger placed under one eye.

Apart from the brief time allotted for meals, the monk's day
was divided between prayer, public and private, and work.
"Idleness is the soul's enemy," wrote Benedict, "and so at certain times the brothers ought to be engaged in manual work,
and again at certain times in spiritual reading" (c. 48). It is clear
that he presupposed a routine in which communal worship,
private prayer and reading, and manual work were roughly balanced; on the interpretation of this simple sentence innumerable passages in monastic history turn.

Let us consider first of all three possible approaches to
work.[3] We may view it simply as the job to be done, like washing up or cooking: something essential for the life of any
household, but not necessarily anything more. We may view it
as a way of passing time, for the prevention of boredom or idleness. Or we may view it as a sacred thing, as the dedication of
hand and brain to a lofty purpose. Now it is clear that if we
start with the third view as our premise, then St. Benedict's
words must assume an enormous importance. But it is equally
clear that it had never occurred to Benedict himself to interpret work in any such way. The passage itself describes work as
the avoidance of idleness, and is evidently intended to provide
some variety in the day to prevent the intense monotony that
can follow from too homogeneous or monolithic a routine.

But Benedict also goes on to define work as what is necessary, what has to be done, and it seems that he is essentially thinking of the chores of a community. He had no idea that the monks should be entirely self-supporting, should till the fields or grow the wool or spin the yarn or weave the cloth from which their habits were made. He was concerned to see that the jobs that had to be done were accomplished, and in the process a useful element of variety enter the monastic day.

When one turns from the small and poor communities for which Benedict wrote to the large, elaborate and wealthy abbeys of the eleventh century, one can readily see why this chapter was interpreted in a manner very different from Benedict's intention. Granted a large team of monastic servants and a fairly large number of officials and specialists to do the various administrative and routine tasks of the community, there came to be little necessary work for the rank and file to perform. At the same time the development of more elaborate liturgy and of church music meant a much greater part of the day was spent in church.

Of how this worked the traditional monasticism of the eleventh century has left us many accounts, though none is perfect and all leave gaps; but far and away the best are the descriptions of the customs of Cluny. About 1075 a monk of Cluny called Ulrich visited the abbey of Hirsau in south Germany and was eagerly crossquestioned by the abbot, William, on the customs of Cluny. On his return, Ulrich wrote the fullest surviving account of Cluny's customs. These writings have for us a double interest, since they not only open windows on every aspect of monastic life in the abbey, but also show very clearly how one monastery influenced another, how the customs of the traditional monasticism were passed down.

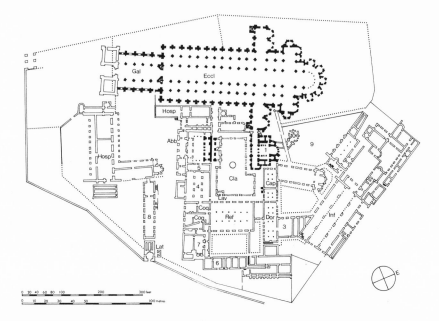

Plan of Cluny in the twelfth century (after professor K.J. Conant), showing the third church, Cluny III (begun 1088), and the remnant of Cluny II (tenth and eleventh centuries). 1. Choir of Cluny II. 2. Galilee of Cluny II. 3. Dormitory extension (?). 4. Storehouse. 5. Almonry. 6. Workshops. 7. Bakery. 8. Stables etc. 9. Cemetery. 10. Cemetery chapel.

A great part of Ulrich's book is taken up with a description of the rituals and liturgy of Cluny. First he goes through the regular hours, from the moment the bell rang in the middle of the night for Matins, when the monks rose, dressed and went down through the cloister to the church; he treats of how the office was sung, of how one of the brothers went round with a lantern to check that none was asleep in his stall; of the progress through the later hours and the arrangements for mass, that is for the two masses attended by the whole community and the private masses said by each of the monks who was a priest. Then he turns to the church's year and observes the varieties of the feasts and fasts, from Holy Week round to Lent again. The ritual splendor is like a pendulum, swinging to the extreme of magnificence at the great festivals, to the extreme of simplicity in Lent. In Lent the ornaments, crucifixes, candelabra and reliquaries were hidden behind veils, and in place of the splendid golden frontal, the high altar had a cloth of white linen. On Easter Eve tapestries and carpets were hung round the church and all the finery restored to its place of honor; at Easter and Christmas nearly 500 candles were lit, and the altar was surrounded with candles and ornaments.

Ulrich freely admits that the services in the abbey church took up a great part of the day and night. The offices or hours consisted essentially of groups of psalms, with antiphons, hymns, prayers and readings or lessons interspersed. When a monk died during the winter, the whole psalter was recited the following night; if he died in summer, they were content to commemorate him with 100 psalms. Even allowing that their chanting was probably fairly crisp—medieval injunctions more often rebuke monastic choirs for going too fast than too slow —this was a marathon exercise. So were some of the readings: Ulrich tells us that he heard the whole of Isaiah read in six nights during one Advent. Thus there remained little time for manual work, and not even a great portion for private prayer and spiritual reading.

It is clear that the frontier connecting the *opus Dei,* God's work, public worship, and man's work, be it reading or laboring with the hands, had been redrawn; and the reasons for this throw a flood of light on the nature of medieval monastic life. The community at Cluny in the mid–eleventh century was perhaps a hundred strong; when St. Hugh died in 1109 the number had risen to three hundred. All books were handwritten on parchment at this period, and thus extremely expensive and, by our standards, extremely scarce. A thousand books made a large library in the Middle Ages, and if a hundred or two hundred monks wanted to read the same book, it could only be accomplished by public reading. Public reading was a much more essential part of their life than we can readily grasp; this helps to make sense of the long lessons at Matins and the solemn readings at mealtimes in the refectory. We have indeed a list of the books issued to sixty-four monks during Lent for private reading in the 1040s, and the list is a fascinating cross section of the contents of the library and the interests of the monks. The Bible, St. Augustine, Cassian and Gregory the Great reflect the basic literature of medieval monasticism; other fathers of the church and the classics of the early Christian centuries, such as St. Isidore of Seville, are well represented; the list also contains the lives of saints, a few works of history, including ecclesiastical history from Josephus to Bede, and one of purely secular history, Livy's *History of Rome,* rather rare in monastic libraries.[4]

Thus we can see that there was a practical element in the arrangements at Cluny and that the Advent readings enabled the whole community to "read" Isaiah simultaneously, which could not otherwise have been accomplished. But this only slightly lessens the ritual nature of the Cluniac routine. Ritual entered every aspect of the monastic life, and its effects are very visible in the buildings of the eleventh and twelfth centuries. Privacy was no part of the life of the period, whether for rich or poor. A peasant lived huddled with his family in a small cottage or hovel with a single room; a rich burgher or a knight spread himself a little more amply, but in two rooms at the most; even a great castle might essentially consist of two main rooms and a chapel, without private apartments of any kind.

Only a palace enjoyed a multiplicity of rooms of various sizes, and this was not because kings were more private than their subjects—this was hardly so still in the days of Louis XIV and Versailles—but because of the multiplicity of tasks that had to be performed. At first sight, a monastic complex seems more like a palace than any other kind of building of the age. But this was essentially because of the variety of folk and functions it had to provide for. In the church, God, the saints, the monks and their lay visitors had each to have their compartments, linked in a unified whole, but yet separate and distinct. The center of the domestic buildings was the cloister, in which much of the monastic work was accomplished. It was definitely a work room, but it was also the center for much ritual. On great festivals the community processed right round the cloister. Every day they processed from church to the chapter house, their business center. In the chapter house they listened every day to a chapter of the Rule—hence the name of the room; they solemnly considered their own and their colleagues' faults; they conducted business of a formal kind; on occasion they held discussions or listened to a discourse from the abbot or a senior monk on the spiritual life. At meal times they gathered at the wash-place, often a splendid and ornate affair, for ceremonial hand washing, followed by a very elaborate grace in the refectory, and a meal as much punctuated by ceremony as by food. Liturgy and work had lapped over into each other's space, and the portion of the day allotted to necessary tasks had been severely curtailed.

The Officials and the Monastic Economy

It became increasingly the practice to allot many tasks to specialists, and to release a number of monks from the full liturgical round to minister to other needs and wants. St. Benedict had assumed a small body of officials under the abbot's close direction: a provost or prior to be the abbot's second-in-command; deans (literally, men set over ten monks each) to supervise groups of monks; a cellarer to attend to all their bodily wants; and door-keepers to guard the gates and the enclosure. By Ulrich's time these officials had grown more numerous and independent at Cluny. The abbot had often to be away visiting daughter houses, performing some mission for the pope or attending to the abbey's affairs. In his absence two or more priors had to be ready to act: one as general administrator of the whole family of houses, a second "claustral" prior to look after the domestic affairs of Cluny herself and later (in all probability) a whole hierarchy of priors to whom the abbot could delegate his task. The deans at Cluny were external officials, administering groups of manors, seeing to the flow of food and money to the abbey's central funds and also to the welfare, bodily and spiritual, of the abbey's tenants. Under the claustral prior there was a team of *circatores,* wandering spies as we are tempted to call them, whose business it was to tour the monastery and see that every monk was at his allotted task. The master who taught the young monks had one of the most crucial tasks in the cloister. The liturgy in the church was organized by the precentor, and in his charge came all the books, not only for the chant, but in the library—the book cupboard as it was called, reminding us how modest a space a monastic library of this age filled, even in a great abbey like Cluny. The chamberlain and his assistants attended to the clothing, washing and shaving of the monks. The cloth was bought already woven and dyed,[5] and it was tailored in the chamberlain's department; he also supervised the occasional washing of the monks' habits.

The razors for shaving were kept by one of the monks under the chamberlain's jurisdiction, locked in a box in the cloister near the door to the dormitory. At the appointed time he organized a group of monks in two rows in the cloister, one row to shave, the other to be shaven, and the task was performed to the accompaniment of a psalm. Normally the monks shaved weekly. "As to our baths," says Ulrich candidly, "there is not much that we can say, for we only bath twice a year, before Christmas and before Easter."[6]

The central figure in the administration of the abbey and its temporal welfare was evidently the cellarer, who had the largest team of assistants: a general assistant or subcellarer; a granarer, who saw to the delivery of food supplies and to their storage, and organized the baking of the bread; a keeper of wine, who supervised the carting of wine from the abbey's extensive vineyards, its storage and use within the abbey; the gardener and the keeper of the fishponds; the refectorer, who organized the kitchen and the meals; and other officials who managed the guesthouse and the stable. The work of two other major officials is described by Ulrich: the almoner and the infirmarer. The almoner organized poor-relief in the neighborhood of the abbey; and since a large part of its revenues consisted in tithes from the parishes under its jurisdiction and tithes were intended for the relief of the poor as much as for the support of the clergy, in principle at least the almoner should have handled very substantial quantities of money, food and clothing.[7] How substantial they actually were is impossible now to say; in times of dearth and in later centuries they tended for various reasons to be whittled down. In this too a ritual element entered in, and in most monastic customaries we hear as much of the almoner's duty to collect poor men for the

liturgical feet-washing and serving by the monks on Maundy
Thursday as we do of practical relief. But Ulrich has much to
say of practical matters, and we may be sure that the almoner's
office was onerous and important, that in such a society many
men depended on charity, and that charity was abundant at
Cluny in the days of St. Hugh. In the infirmary lived sick
monks and some others who for various reasons were excused
the full routine. Once a month or so all the monks had a
blood-letting and a holiday, when they could enjoy the less
arduous, more relaxed routine of the infirmary, where meat
might be eaten and a briefer round of services attended.

Substantial as the bureaucracy appears when compared with
the officials described in the Rule of St. Benedict, the catalogue
given by Ulrich is incomplete. He says little of the sacrist,
who was in charge of the church, its fabric and ornaments—
suggesting that they were more modest than those later obtain-
ing in large Benedictine and Cluniac communities. And it is
clear that the officials at Cluny in Ulrich's day were not independent landlords, as many later became.

There is, too, a certain simplicity about the economic life
of Cluny at this date that is interesting to observe. Its basic
needs were corn, especially wheat, beans, milk, butter, cheese
and honey; wax for candles; cloth for habits; sheepskins and
pigskins for parchment; timber and stone for buildings and furniture. In vine-growing country, such as the heart of the
Mâconnais or, for Hirsau in the Black Forest, there were vineyards and grapes. From the large estates near the abbey came
corn and wine in the enormous quantities needed to support
a large community; from farther afield the produce came transformed already into money, with which the other needs could
be purchased. Beans and vegetables such as were used in the

eleventh century—onions and leeks, for instance, but not later discoveries such as cabbages or potatoes—were grown in the monastic garden and the home farms; milk in modest quantities was presumably to be had from the cows and goats of the neighborhood, and also butter and cheese. Students of Cluny's estates have been struck by the absence of sheep, or large flocks of any kind.[8] This seems to be partly due to the absence of meat from the diet, and the practice, in Benedictine and Cluniac communities in the eleventh and twelfth centuries, of buying cloth ready-made; and this meant too that for the most part the animals whose skin provided the parchment had to be purchased, no doubt at considerable cost. Candles for the monastic church were probably made from pure beeswax in the Middle Ages, and honey was extensively used to sweeten the diet before the import of sugar began in the fifteenth century. Thus bees and beehives were an important part of a monastic economy. In every large community the fishponds were vital, providing some relief from the salt fish that seems to have played a heavy role in the monastic diet—though it is probable that the fishponds would have been rapidly depleted if salt fish from more distant waters had not been available: for, needless to say, fresh fish could only be transported very short distances.

The sacrist had the largest burden of all: the fabric of the church and the maintenance of its treasures and its equipment. He also had the chief charge of one of the largest sources of income, offerings given to the church by visitors, pilgrims, friends and patrons. If we contemplate his work and imagine the army of assistants he must have needed when the great church was being rebuilt, and the complexity of the relations between the sacrist and the many other leading monks and the master masons and the multitudes who cut and carried timber and stone and the other materials needed, fashioned and set it in the new building, we are almost tempted to think that the material structure had become so heavy as to obscure, for many monks, the worship and the prayer for which it all existed.

Cluny, the New Monasticism and the Twelfth-Century Renaissance

This would be a superficial view of the case, however, for the sense of devotion, the impact and the image of Cluny was something deeply felt by numerous visitors in the eleventh and twelfth centuries. No doubt the enormous increase in population in Hugh's later years made it difficult to sustain such standards. Furthermore, Hugh's death in 1109 was followed shortly by a crisis in the abbey, since his successor, Abbot Pons, proved a failure. The disasters of Pons's abbacy coincided with a growing challenge from the new monastic movements of the early twelfth century, and his successor, Peter the Venerable (1122–56), was faced with war on two fronts—against disruption and decay within, and fierce criticism without. Criticism came above all from the new orders, and St. Bernard of Clairvaux poured out his wrath against rich monasteries, including Cluny, in his youthful, intemperate *Apologia*.[9] Bernard accuses them of being too rich, of living too delicately, of adorning their churches with preposterous ornaments and of not testing the vocation of their novices or giving them sufficient instruction before admitting them. This is no doubt a brief and unsophisticated statement of a large dispute, but it reflects at once certain essential features of Cluny as it had been under Hugh and remained under Peter. It was a traditional way of life, not greatly different in standard of living from the harsh, uncomfortable world of the eleventh century. As living standards rose in the twelfth century, the difference between the ascetic Cistercians and the more luxurious secular aristocracy became much sharper, and the Cluniacs were tempted in some measure to follow the latter. The Cluniac life was a traditional mode, based on the Rule of St. Benedict, no doubt, but based even more on custom, a tremendous ritual, which left little time over for most of its members for much adventure in the life of prayer or intellect.

But if we ask which had the better of the argument, Bernard or Peter?—the answer must be: both. Peter instituted a number of reforms intended to meet Bernard's scorching criticisms where they could not be rebutted; Bernard was conquered by the abundant charity and diplomatic skill of Peter the Venerable, so that they became close, even intimate friends.

We should perhaps expect to find, in the early twelfth century, the variety and number of recruits coming to Cluny drying up. It was no longer avant-garde, no longer in the van of monastic movements; it represented the old world. Or so it seems to us. Yet the opposite is true. In the eleventh century Cluny had been famous for its splendor and devotion; under St. Hugh it had grown in a spectacular fashion. Yet it had not, before the end of the century, been conspicuous as a center of literature or art. Both these things it became for a time in Hugh's later years and under Peter the Venerable. Perhaps it should be remembered more as a patron than a center of art, but the little that survives of Cluny herself and the riches of Vézelay, the most sumptuous of Cluniac abbeys, brilliantly illustrate one aspect of the twelfth-century renaissance (see p. 136). Cluny in the 1070s was no great intellectual center; it was the home of a way of life of immense prestige, and the books that came out of it were practical treatises on that life, like

Ulrich's. In 1140–41 it became the last home of Peter Abelard. Although Abelard's theology had little to do with Cluny or the monastic life, it is significant both of Peter the Venerable's wide range of interests and of his charity that Abelard found there a safe haven after the disaster of his final condemnation. Indeed, in the eyes of intelligent contemporaries, Cluny stood at the height of its reputation in the late eleventh and twelfth centuries.[10]

Peter the Venerable was a theologian of considerable accomplishment. How he found time, in a busy life, between the endless routine at Cluny and his long journeys round the Cluniac world, in France, Italy and Spain especially, to write at all, seems to have puzzled him as much as it puzzles us. His was not an original mind, but wide-ranging. He was a theologian who took pains to study Islam—he commissioned the first translation of the Qur'an into Latin—and contemporary heresy. His aim was to refute Muslims and heretics; but what is remarkable in that age is that he troubled to study them first and that he showed something of the same charity toward them that won the friendship of both St. Bernard and Peter Abelard.

The splendor of Peter's human insight comes out above all in his letters. They are verbose and over-rich, reminiscent of St. Bernard's picture of the black monk's diet, and so defy translation. But through the endless periods one can discern a mind of extraordinary sympathy and understanding. One of the most remarkable is a long letter, almost a treatise, addressed to Brother Gilbert, who was a hermit living in close association with Cluny or one of its daughter houses. Peter reveals at every point a sense both of the differences and of the common ground between the hermit life and the life of a large community. Essentially, he sees them both as expressions of the spiritual life set between earth and heaven. He outlines four elements in the life of the recluse—prayer, meditation, spiritual reading and work. The recluse cannot plant trees, water his plants or engage in any rural pursuit because he is enclosed in his cell; so he engages in the more useful task *(quod est utilius)* of copying books, cultivated the fruits of the spirit and the heavenly bread of the soul.[11]

The hermits who lived in association with Cluny lent variety to its life and added, for some, a dimension to its character and appeal. For others the sharp difference between life in a hermitage and in a community represented a challenge, which inspired them to look for novel modes of the religious life. Where the hermit inspiration was deep and widespread, the first shoots of the new monasticism grew.

5.

The Hermits

*The Influence of Italy
in the Eleventh Century*

Life at Cluny was a continuous round of activity, both ritual and communal: regular and dignified, yet without privacy and without leaving a large space for individual spirituality or private endeavor. In practice the variety of men who felt its inspiration was reflected in a greater variety of life than the customs suggest; in the surrounding hills there were hermitages for those who felt the call to live in solitude.

No monastic community that took any note of the ancient literature of the religious life could fail to know that it had first sprung up in the desert and that Cassian and Benedict had allowed a place in their schemes of life for a few to look for a more lonely and heroic approach to the divine presence. The anchorite ideal was never entirely forgotten; groups of hermits can be found in almost every part of western Europe where the monastic life flourished in the early Middle Ages—in Ireland, England, France, Germany, Switzerland; above all, in Italy.

The wastes of Egypt or North Africa were not accessible to them; but the word *desert* literally means any remote, uninhabited place, and they looked for, and found, the desert on the hilltops, in the valleys, on small islands and in other secluded places in western Europe.

The Italian contribution to the monastic movements of the central Middle Ages can easily be undervalued. Most of the houses that gave their names to religious orders were in France or (as the boundary then ran) western Germany. Assisi and St. Francis have overshadowed all earlier Italian founders since St. Benedict. Yet the traditional monasticism owed much of its influence to Italian monks in the eleventh century, notably to St. William of Volpiano and the creators of La Cava, and it was from Italy that the anchorite revival stemmed.

St. Romuald and St. Peter Damian: Camaldoli and Vallombrosa

In the later Middle Ages there were recluses in every country, in every corner of western Christendom, in innumerable secluded valleys and in many places not at all secluded, for man must live and even a hermit needed to be sufficiently under the public eye to attract alms and food. But the farther one goes north, the weaker becomes the influence of the desert. The prehistory of the movement was in the tenth century, in the persons of a Greek and a Bohemian, Nilus and Vojtech, or Adalbert.[1] They came to Rome in the third quarter of the tenth century and began the revival of its monasteries and the formation of new ones in the neighborhood. Adalbert died as bishop of Prague and martyr-apostle to the Prussians in 997; Nilus, still a monk of comparative obscurity, near Rome in 1005. Their work was taken up by a more dramatic figure, the restless, heroic St. Romuald, who began as a Cluniac monk and ended by founding Camaldoli. Camaldoli represented an attempt to interpret the final chapter of St. Benedict's Rule quite literally. In a secluded valley near Arezzo in Tuscany he founded a Benedictine monastery for beginners, and on the mountaintop above, a group of hermitages to which those long and carefully trained in the communal life could go to recreate the life of the desert. The monastic life in general was seen by its finest proponents as a constant striving, "you cannot stand still...: you go up, you go down; if you try to stay, you are ruined," as St. Bernard was to say.[2] A similar inspiration can be seen in Romuald's younger contemporary, St. John Gualbert, who chose an even more dramatic site near Florence and founded a remote, contemplative house among the leaves of Vallombrosa, strictly coenobitic, yet deeply influenced by the desert. Both became centers of small groups or orders of similar monasteries, and both survived, small but persistent, into the modern world. Their monastic offspring included French houses and orders, above all Grandmont and the Chartreuse, which were strongly influenced by the disciples of Romuald and the call of the Italian desert; but to gain first the flavor of the movement, let us stay in Italy a little longer and consider the most remarkable offshoot of the movement, St. Peter Damian.

Peter Damian was a hermit and an intellectual. He had enjoyed the best education that the Italian schools of the day could offer; and in Italy, for all their vicissitudes, there were never lacking from the tenth century schools in which a fairly cultivated Latin and quite a wide knowledge of the deposit of ancient learning could be acquired. We see in Peter Damian himself the beginnings of something more than this—he wrote a Latin of a quality, and showed an understanding of ancient books of an intensity, to make him one of the first notable figures of the twelfth-century renaissance, although his life lay wholly within the eleventh (c. 1007–72). His inspiration came partly from Romuald; equally, perhaps more, from a deep study of Cassian, of the lives of the fathers, and of the ascetic literature of the patristic age. In his hatred of secular entanglements, and especially of marriage, in his great learning and eccentricity of temperament, and above all in his admiration for the monks of the east, he was almost a replica of St. Jerome. Like Jerome's, his writings can be at once inspiring and absurd. On the whole, he disliked his fellow men, hated and despised their foibles and temptations, but just sufficiently remembered that they were God's creatures and that Jesus had died to save them, to wish them all monks. He settled at a hermitage at Fonte Avellana, similar to Camaldoli and also inspired by Romuald; and there he lived the life of his ambition—a recluse, secluded in prayer, occasionally emerging with a fiery tract or sermon, for the most part hidden from the world.

But he was not permitted to stay in seclusion. When the new spirit of ecclesiastical reform captured Rome in the person of the German Pope Leo IX, Damian was one of the small group of great personalities—inspired, contradictory, quarrelsome monks for the most part—who changed the face of Christendom in the mid-eleventh century. Damian found himself in due course cardinal bishop of Ostia and a frequent visitor to places near and far from Rome as papal legate or ambassador. On one occasion he went to Milan with his "holy Satan," the future Pope Gregory VII (see p. 114), and Damian, by force of character, polished eloquence and total indifference to what men might do to him, quelled a dangerous riot. Presently he returned to his hermitage, but not before he had helped to lay the foundations of one of the most remarkable movements within the papal reform, the attempt to make all clergy monks or quasi-monks, from which the orders of canons regular were to spring (see pp. 154–56).

Meanwhile, the stature of Damian's writings and the opportunities his office gave him to travel and to preach made him what his predecessors had not been, an effective propagandist of the life of the hermitage.

> The solitary life is the school of heavenly doctrine, the training ground of heavenly skills. There everything that is taught is God. He is the path one treads, by which one comes to the knowledge of the highest truth. For a hermitage is a garden of heavenly delights; just as one might in a garden find the scents of different kinds of herbs, or the fragrance of luscious flowers, so in a hermitage the scent of virtues fills the air with fragrance. There the roses of charity burn rose-red, there the lilies of chastity shine in their snowy vesture; there too the violas of humility enjoy their lowly stature, and can be blown by no stormy winds. There the perfect myrrh of mortification abounds, there the incense of constant prayer ceaselessly rises....[3]

And he likens the hermit's cell to a shop in which transient goods are exchanged for eternal; to a soldier's tent in God's camp; to the Holy Sepulcher, where sin died and the dead rose again.

The Carthusians

Peter Damian's writings were one of the means by which the knowledge of the hermit ideal, and of monastic ideals in general, spread through Italy and over the Alps into France and the Low Countries. Local movements partly inspired by Damian and other Italian leaders grew up in various parts of northern Europe. In the forest of Colan in eastern France Robert of Molesme presided over a group of monks and hermits in the late 1070s and early 1080s; their ideas and ideals were later to inspire him to found Cîteaux. About 1080 a learned teacher from Rheims called Bruno came to join him. In 1084 Bruno and two companions passed on to found their own hermitage in a spot yet wilder and more remote; with the aid of the bishop of Grenoble, they settled in a high wooded valley and established the first hermitage on the site later known as La Grande Chartreuse. Bruno presently moved on to Rome, where he worked for the pope, and he died in 1101 in the south of Italy, in the act of founding another group of hermits. But his hermitage at Chartreuse survived and prospered sufficiently to become the center of a small but stable order. The founder of the Carthusian Order as an organized, regular pattern of life was Guigo I, who ruled the Chartreuse from 1110 to 1136 as prior: The order had no abbots. He wrote down the customs and laid firm the foundations of the institute, which have never since been fundamentally altered. In particular, they allowed for a much reduced liturgy, which gave ample time for private prayer, meditation, spiritual reading and work. The characteristic work of the early Carthusian was copying books, which helped to provide their priories with fine libraries. Meanwhile, from the start, though they lived in groups and communities and had certain communal buildings such as a chapel and a chapter house, most of their days were spent in their own individual cells; they formed groups of hermits, that is, living in permanent stone cells grouped round a

large cloister. But it is not till the second half of the twelfth
century that we are really well informed about their life.

One day in the middle of the twelfth century, about 1163,
a young canon regular from the diocese of Grenoble, of noble
origin and austere life, called Hugh of Avalon, came on a visit
to La Grande Chartreuse. Hugh felt there an urgent call, an
intense desire to join the community set "almost in the
clouds…far removed from the turmoil of the world." He
approached one of the older monks, "with groans and tears,"
asking for counsel.[4]

> My son, how can you dare even to consider this? The
> men whom you see inhabiting these rocks are harder
> than the stones themselves, and have compassion nei-
> ther on themselves nor on those who dwell with them.
> The very aspect of the place is frightening, but our way
> of life is even harder. The roughness of the hair shirt
> which you would wear would cut through skin and
> flesh to your very bones. The sensitiveness which I per-
> ceive in you would cause you to break down com-
> pletely under the austerities of our way of life.

This discouragement, says his biographer, simply made Hugh
hungrier for the banquet—for like St. Lawrence viewing the
instruments of torture with which he was martyred, he found
the old man's horrid vision of Carthusian life draw him to it the
more. It was indeed no easy course. His own superior, the prior
of his house, put every kind of pressure on him not to go. The
move from a less strict to a stricter religious community was a
frequent event in that age, and must have caused many human
difficulties and separations of this kind; but Hugh was shortly
installed among the brothers at the Chartreuse, and stayed there

in quiet contemplation and prayer and study of the scriptures
and of the large library that the community had built up.

> During this period Peter, the most venerable arch-
> bishop of Tarentaise, a Cistercian, used often to come to
> Chartreuse, and there alone in a cell among those of
> that holy community, dwelt for several months like an
> industrious bee making honey in his hive.[5] He might
> also be compared to the mild and gentle dove living in
> security and tranquillity with Noah in the ark, and flee-
> ing from the tumult of the world as from the onrush of
> the waters of the flood sent to overwhelm almost the
> whole face of the earth. Passing his time in meditation
> and in converse on spiritual matters with these holy
> men, he believed that like Paul he had found himself in
> Paradise, and was often on the wings of contemplation
> borne up to the third heaven.

> The duty of waiting upon him was allotted to Hugh.
> Who was more fitted to be the companion of such a
> man?...To see the old man and the young one together
> you would imagine that Peter and John had once more
> returned and been reunited....

> There still exists on the side of the mountain, on the
> way from the cells of the monks to the lodgings of the
> lay brothers, a seat made as a resting place for the holy
> [arch]bishop, who became tired and hot through often
> passing up and down. [He] would seldom ride when
> there because the prior was forbidden to do so. The seat
> was of this type. There were two large firs growing side
> by side with a space between them. Horizontal cuts

were made in these into which a squared pole of yew
wood of no great thickness was inserted. This was the
only seat provided for the [arch]bishop.

In later years, after he had become bishop of Lincoln
(1186–1200), Hugh was able once at least to visit Chartreuse,
and so his biographer had accompanied him there:

> We sometimes saw Hugh sitting on that seat, telling us
> affectionately this and certain other anecdotes about
> this former archbishop, now reigning in heaven, and
> wiping the perspiration from his venerable counte-
> nance, for the ascent was no small labour to him [Hugh
> was short and stout]. It was a pleasure also to us, who
> heard these stories from him, to sit on that lofty throne.
> It amazed us that as the trees grew the timber plank
> became so firmly fixed that the mark left by the inci-
> sion could scarcely be detected. It also seemed wonder-
> ful that, although the trees had been growing vigorously
> upwards for fourteen years or more, the seat was never
> any higher, but remained near enough the ground for a
> small man to sit on it in comfort. It always seemed as
> fresh as if its original sap had not yet dried.

The most remarkable character at the Chartreuse in Hugh's
time (to judge from Hugh's Life) was William, ex-count of
Nevers, who had abandoned the world, but not his native wit
or bluntness of speech.[6] When asked whether he thought King
Solomon was in heaven, he asserted firmly that he was—for
Jesus called David his father, and David would undoubtedly
have seen to it that his other son was properly treated. On
another occasion he called on Louis VII of France (1137–80),

a pious man and by no means a coward, but in great awe of Brother William. The chessboard with which the king had been relaxing was hastily removed when William was announced, but not hastily enough; William coolly observed that all his time should be spent trying to make amends for his failures as a king, "not on these idle allurements."[7]

William reveals one remarkable consequence of the monastic life. Its comparative rigidity and uniformity have often been supposed to breed conformism, to diminish individual traits and eccentricities. This is not wholly untrue: Communities can carry a single stamp, and the communal life has undoubtedly bred certain common characteristics. Yet the outsider who visits a lively community today is commonly struck by the opposite impression: that the common life has sharpened and strengthened the individuality of many of its adherents. This can be in even greater measure true of the more secluded breeds of monk; and brother William and, in a different way, Hugh himself, reveal this very clearly.

The Contrast of Community and Hermitage

The hermit ideal revived in a world in which its opposite, the communal mode of life, flourished as never before. The significance of this contrast is vividly revealed in such buildings as the dormitories at Eberbach in Germany or Sénanque in Provence. They are austere and simple and Cistercian, but they will serve as representatives of dormitories in any monasteries of moderate size. They are open, bare and unfurnished today, but all that we need to add to each in imagination is two lines of palliases filled with straw, and some rough bedding. In later times such dormitories were fitted out with paneling and

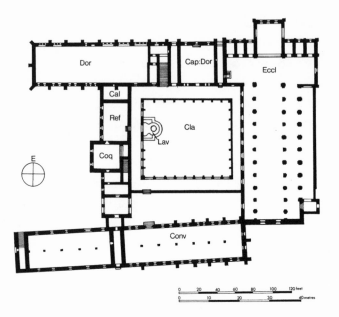

Plan of Eberbach as it was in the late Middle Ages. A very characteristic plan, see p. 175, save for the small refectory, which was, however, larger at the end of the Middle Ages. Most orders perferred to have their cloisters to the south of the church; here, as often, the shape of the site forced the Cistercians to put it on the north side.

cubicles, and the monks of some houses abandoned them altogether for more domestic quarters; eventually the practice
spread of providing monks with private cubicles in which to
sleep. But privacy, or the use of small rooms, was the practice
neither in the monastic life nor in the secular world in the
eleventh and twelfth centuries.[8] A modern observer, accustomed to privacy, needs no further persuasion of the attraction
of the hermit life than a picture of a common cloister, refectory and dormitory. A brief visit to the most celebrated of
medieval hermitages—to the Chartreuse, to Camaldoli, the
Carceri above Assisi, each set in a position of great natural

beauty and quiet, surrounded by woods and streams and moun-
taintops—reveals some of the positive attractions of the hermit
life. Not all the hermits lived in such places; surprisingly
enough, the monks of the Chartreuse and Camaldoli set up
houses in the middle of towns such as Pisa and Bologna, but
their natural habitat, and the country which inspired their
founders, lay in the hills and woods. It was the solitude and
peace that first attracted the hermits to these places. If they had
thought of natural beauty as an alluring or distracting thing, no
doubt they would have rejected it. In this guise it presumably
appeared to Milton, when he counted the leaves of Vallombrosa:

> Thick as autumnal leaves that strow the brooks
> In Vallombrosa, where th'Etrurian shades
> High overarch't imbowr—

and likened them to an army of devils. Yet if the founders of
the Chartreuse, Camaldoli and Vallombrosa rejected the idea
that the natural beauty of their new homes could be a temptation, they were in each case positively attracted by a dramatic
piece of scenery nonetheless. The Italian sites are on hilltops, by
an elementary symbolism felt to be—not nearer to heaven, a
concept cruder than any they entertained—but above the
habitations of men, as it were on Mount Sinai or Mount
Horeb. More important, they were inspired by the feats of the
fathers of the desert, whose manner of life in sober fact, not
without some embellishment in the *Lives,* was often a heroic
struggle against natural forces unnaturally made as tough as
man could devise.

The Carthusian life has always been a vocation for the very
few. From the first, there were some who felt a superficial call,
tasted the rigors and fled. From approximately 1180 to 1186

St. Hugh was prior of the first English Carthusian house, at Witham in Somerset, and his biographer records how one of his monks, called Alexander, fled from Witham after a bitter complaint.

> Wretch, you have deluded us...and have brought us to this wild and lonely place, taking us away from our pleasant dwellings and a civilised way of life. You have forced us to lurk amongst beasts and thorns, as if there were not places of monastic retirement in the world. The whole land is full of communities of monks, and the mutual support provided by the communal life provides us with a sufficiently good example of religious perfection. Here, alone and without companionship, we become torpid and dull through boredom, seeing no one for days at a time whose example can inspire us, and having only the walls which shut us in to look at. Your apparently unanswerable arguments shall not convince us, since what you have to say is always in opposition to our sound and excellent judgement. The yoke of this new law which you tell us must be borne, as if all Christians everywhere would be damned except the Carthusians [a doctrine of which Hugh was conspicuously innocent] and the way of salvation open to very few, is almost unendurable in this world. Since we know better, we must not and cannot endure this unprofitable and narrow way of life any longer. We are going to seek something saner, and absolutely refuse to stay for a further period."[9]

Alexander became a Cluniac monk, and later in life begged to be allowed to return; but Hugh refused.

Most of the traffic described in the *Life* was in the other
direction, though Witham, like the Carthusian Order itself, was
always of modest size, reflecting its call for the few. What is
noticeable is that it flourished when other orders were lan-
guishing; in England especially it enjoyed an Indian summer in
the fourteenth and fifteenth centuries, when its most famous
house, the London Charterhouse, brought silence to the very
edge of the city, and the priory of Mount Grace in Yorkshire,
the one English house whose remains can still be inspected,
was also founded.[10]

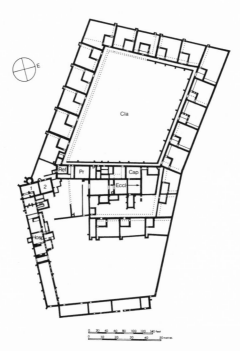

Plan of Mount Grace, a Carthusian priory in Yorkshire founded in 1398, with
the outline of its buildings of c. 1400 still clearly visible. Characteristically, the
cloister is very large, with the monk's cells, each with its garden grouped
round it; the conventual buildings in comparison were modest. 1. Brewery.
2. Bakehouse.

The Cloister and the World

900–1050: Monasteries as the Property of Kings and Princes

From 900 to 1050 the movements, Benedictine in character, which had begun in Cluny, Gorze and Glastonbury spread and flourished; this is the period in which monastic influence rose to its peak in the political and social life of western Europe. Yet the number of monasteries and monks was comparatively modest; in population and variety the century following 1050 is the age of growth. Between 1050 and 1150 the numerical strength of the monastic world increased out of all recognition, but the place of the monks in the life of the church and the world did not grow in proportion. Western Christendom was a richer, more varied, more complex world, and the monks had to take their place as one among a number of active, influential social groups. Between 1150 and 1300 the numbers of houses and religious continued to grow, and the orders of friars appeared to lend a new dimension to religious activity. But if we leave the friars out of account, monastic influence in society and culture sharply declined. The difference between the two graphs—between that of monastic population, always on the increase, at least till the early thirteenth century, and monastic influence, first rising steeply, then taking an erratic course before falling quite dramatically in the late twelfth and thirteenth centuries—must be studied against the background, first of the European economy and social life, then of the cultural life of the twelfth-century renaissance.

Looking back from many centuries later, it is easy to underestimate the effect of the change. Society was still dominated by emperors, kings and warriors; an aristocracy bred to war ruled in many parts of Europe much as it had done in 1000, or even in 900. A struggling peasantry under seignorial domination still fought off poverty—even sometimes famine—by long hours of toil. In many respects medieval society was static, and of this the military nobilities and agricultural techniques bear witness; yet in certain respects the pattern and quality of life changed out of all recognition in these centuries, and the center of this change was the urban renaissance that made towns and cities flourish all over western Europe as they had not flourished since the fall of Rome.

The first era of monastic expansion is most closely tied to the traditional pattern of royal and aristocratic power. Traditional, and yet in certain ways novel too; for the lavish endowment and social prestige of the houses reformed under the aegis of Gorze and her children over much of the German kingdom reflected the growing power of the Saxon king-emperors of Germany, the Ottos and their successors. It also reflected the first awakening of the creative urges of the eleventh and twelfth centuries, the pursuit both of a peaceful life and of a cultivated life by a significant, if still small, proportion of the population. The first beginnings of most large historical movements are very obscure, and this is no exception. Any examination of its cause and inspiration must take equal account both of the patrons and the converts; for without patronage monks starved, and without vocations, or at least recruits, they failed to provide enough men for existing communities or a surplus to revive those in decay or bring new ones to birth.

The religious ideas of the late tenth and early eleventh centuries were predominantly monastic. It was still widely held in the late eleventh century that only monks had more than a reasonable hope of salvation,[1] and this induced many to seek refuge, at all periods of life, in the cloister, and motivated rich men and kings to the endowment of houses where fervent and continuous prayer could be offered for a safe passage to the gate of heaven. In Germany Otto the Great (936–73) and his successors, and especially Henry II (1002–24), later canonized, and in England King Edgar (959–75), were the central, royal figures in this patronage. At the level of lofty monarchical doctrine, the choirs of men who prayed for kings were an essential part of the jewels of their crowns. Among their social assumptions a central belief was that their business was to ensure peace on their own domains by carrying war into their neighbors' territory—or, at least, by ample provision for such a need. Monasteries and monastic estates provided havens of peace in lands otherwise dominated by aristocracies of warriors or thegns. At the same time their enormous estates could be much more closely controlled by royal authority than those of lay notables, and they could be used to provide support for troops, especially for the heavily armed cavalrymen or knights of Germany. More obscurely, we can see the traces of similar arrangements in England even before the Norman Conquest and settlement of Norman knights in the late eleventh century. Thus the German imperial armies were in great measure recruited from the tenants of bishops and abbots, and the great monastic estates formed an essential element in the structure of German political power as well as in the social pattern of the land. Nor were their only patrons the emperors, for the nobility were encouraged to add their gifts to their overlords'; but in Germany and England it was still normal for a great monastery to acknowledge the king as immediate overlord and patron, and thegnly or baronial monasteries only began to be at all numerous in the eleventh century.

In France and Italy the pattern was different, because royal authority in France was slight, in Italy distant and intermittent. In France, to all intents and purposes, the Capetian kings were great nobles ruling over one principality among the many in their kingdoms. This was not quite the whole truth, and over bishops and monasteries the royal hand spread considerably farther in the eleventh and twelfth centuries than over lay barons. In any event, lay princes were more often to be found among the founders and patrons of monasteries than were kings. At Cluny herself and among some of her disciples a new model of independence from local lay control had sprung up. The abbots of Cluny often had close personal relations with the surrounding princes—with emperors indeed—and with the bishops of Burgundy; but they lived in border territory, in the Mâconnais, where it was still doubtful if any allegiance was owed to the king of France. They had been founded on Burgundian soil by a duke of Aquitaine.[2] Thus it was natural for their founder to set them free from secular ties to a rival dynasty, and in due course they won from the papacy, their temporal and spiritual overlord, exemption both from temporal and spiritual control, save that of Rome herself. They were exempt, that is, in principle, from the rule of kings and of bishops. But in practice a close relationship with many princes and bishops was needed to preserve the large estates and the numerous churches that Cluny came to rule; over the houses reformed by her, or which in the eleventh and twelfth centuries became subordinate to her, a varying pattern of relationship with kings, princes and bishops came to be established. In Italy variety was in principle even greater, for the kings of Germany were kings of Italy too, but only rare visitors; local nobles and the reviving cities had in practice a larger part to play in their fortunes, even in the early eleventh century, than the king-emperors.

What was common to the monasteries of Germany and England, and in some measure to those of France and Italy too, was that the lay overlord regarded his monasteries in a very special sense as his own property. What was common to them all was the sharp social division and difference of function between the monks who prayed and the peasants who worked and supplied them with food and the material basis of life.

There was a sense in which a monastic complex could never be a piece of property. A king or prince was not a priest or bishop; the functions of priests and monks in choir and cloister were tasks he could not himself fulfill and could only imperfectly understand. In a real sense the monastic community was a spiritual power complementary to his, not subordinate to it. In a sense too the monastic estates, which supported peasantry, soldiers and the monks and their servants, were governed by a multitude of complex legal and social rules that divided the rights over them so that the whole social hierarchy was fed and protected and governed; and all were linked together as beneficiaries of the monks' prayers. And yet in another compartment of their minds kings and princes and lesser men regarded churches and abbeys and bishoprics as pieces of property just like the clothes they wore and the dogs they followed in the chase. If they were very secularly minded, like the Anglo-Norman William Rufus (1087–1100), they regarded them all as pieces of secular property, like manors; if they were spiritually minded, like Henry II of Germany, they were part of the whole system of kingly authority, over which the king ruled as Christ's vicar.[3] The phrase used in English formularies of Elizabeth I in the late sixteenth century, "supreme governor of this realm...as well in all spiritual or ecclesiastical things or causes as temporal," very appropriately describes the attitude of Edgar or the Ottos or Henry II of Germany, save only that it in no wise implied—as it did for Elizabeth—any denial of the spiritual supremacy of the papacy. Henry II reckoned he could found and suppress monasteries, appoint and remove abbots, organize and reorganize, at will. They were in a quite direct sense the jewels in his crown, for they were his property and the symbols of his divine authority.

It was a society in which freedom of choice was exceedingly limited. The sons of a baron or a knight were expected to learn the arts of war and the pleasures of the chase, the management of an estate and of a wife, but were not put to letters. The sons of the peasants were expected to work like their fathers and on their fathers' plots. But the estates of peasants and of lords could be extremely inflexible and insensitive to changes in population. In the eleventh and twelfth centuries growth in population was one of the main reasons for profound changes in society; already in this early period, it was becoming not uncommon for the well-to-do to place their younger sons in monasteries.

An essential element in the traditional monasticism was that it was for many a whole way of life in which they joined as children, and all, save the apostate or those who passed to a stricter or a higher role and became hermits or bishops, left by way of the cemetery. This is perhaps to us the most surprising feature of many monasteries of the early eleventh century: that a large number of their monks were not there of their own volition, at least in the first instance.

Recruitment in the Eleventh and Twelfth Centuries

There is in the British Library a manuscript written in Winchester in the time of King Cnut (1016–35) with a famous drawing of the king and queen presenting a splendid cross to the monks of the New Minster, the abbey which lay immediately beside the cathedral and was later moved to a more convenient site outside the city, called Hyde.[4] The manuscript contains a list of the community and of all its friends and benefactors, including not only kings and earls and citizens of Winchester, but the monks of the Old Minster, the cathedral community, and several other abbeys besides. We are here provided with a complete list of all the monks of the New Minster from its foundation in the 960s on—and it was kept up, not perhaps entirely faithfully, until the eve of the dissolution in the early sixteenth century. The most interesting part is that which reveals not only the names but something of the structure of the community in its first two centuries. It opens with the names of monks grown old or dead when the book was begun in 1031. These are mostly noted as having been priests or deacons. By the tenth century already, it seems, something approaching half a monastic community would be in priests' orders, though it was not until the twelfth or thirteenth that it became the normal practice for all monks to aspire to priesthood and all priests to celebrate mass every day.[5] Some are merely *monachi,* monks, which may have no significance or may mean that they never aspired to any orders. The forty-eighth recruit is the first called *puer,* boy—the first to be noted as dedicated to the community as a child. From the moment when the record is contemporary, and when we may be tolerably sure that the names are being entered as the monks arrived, the *pueri predominate.* From some point in the 1030s we have a run of boys, with scarcely a mature recruit among them: Between then and approximately 1072 there are forty-one names, thirty-five of them *pueri,* two unspecified, two deacons and a priest, and one noted as "convert and priest." The convert in this setting was a man of mature years who came of his own volition.[6] True, in strict law the *puer* could not take solemn vows till he was of man's estate; but by then, long since, his estate in life had been determined by his parents' choice. If he returned to the world there was no easy way to a livelihood open to him. The world accepted that a man's or a woman's vocation was neither more nor less than what their parents had determined. From 1072 on, the pattern begins to vary. Men who joined as lay and priestly converts alternate with the boys, and a class of "young men," *iuvenes,* a term of various connotation, also appears. By 1150 the *conversi* much outnumber the *pueri,* but the last group that bears these designations, from the early to mid-1180s, still included three boys to five converts. These facts are the outward and visible sign of a period of rapid social change.

Social Change, 1050–1150

In the late eleventh and early twelfth centuries the extreme pessimism of St. Peter Damian or St. Anselm as to the chances

of any but monks escaping the pains of hell gradually subsided.
"The married are not condemned, but the continent are more
easily saved" was the view expressed by Abelard in the early
1130s.[7] He was by then a eunuch and a monk, prescribing rules
for the conduct of nuns; the view is, even so, notably less harsh
than Anselm's. As heaven appeared more attainable, we might
expect the monastic life to lose some of its attraction; nonetheless, it is a striking fact that as the numbers of layfolk expected
to reach heaven increased, so the number of monasteries and
their population increased with equal rapidity.

By 1050, as far as we can judge, the general rise in the population of western Europe, which is so marked a characteristic
of its social and economic history between the late tenth and
thirteenth centuries, was well under way. In the twelfth and
thirteenth centuries the population rose steeply, to level off
about 1300 and fall sharply again when plague struck in the
1340s. We cannot hope to know the fundamental causes for
this rise. Even in much more recent times, the substantial
increase in the European population of the late eighteenth and
early nineteenth centuries is still a mysterious phenomenon on
which till recently the experts feuded;[8] small chance of
describing with any precision what lay behind the rise of the
central Middle Ages. It seems clear that most western countries
were somewhat more peaceful and that people were somewhat
more inventive in the late eleventh and twelfth centuries than
before. An increase in numbers by itself might only have led to
widespread shortages and hunger; no doubt in some places, at
some times, hunger was a very real threat, especially perhaps in
the thirteenth century when the expansion had here and there
outstripped the capacity of underdeveloped Europe to expand
the land under cultivation or to adapt its techniques. What is

striking, however, is that the growth of population coincided with a very marked increase in prosperity in many parts of Europe, and in a cultural and social movement that greatly added to the variety of art, literature, occupation, expectation and opportunity open to men, and even in a measure to women.

This was one of the notably creative periods in European history. The growth in population doubtless provided manpower for new occupations, and a challenge to those who grew food to grow substantially more; but it cannot in itself be called a cause of this prosperity—rather, it was a result, for the economic progress, however limited, was sufficient to feed far more mouths than hitherto. But in truth it is better quite simply to say, it was a part, and a crucial part, of the elements of change in a society that would still seem to us, if we viewed it with twenty-first-century eyes, exceedingly static.

Change was most evident in two institutions especially characteristic of this period of the Middle Ages: its monasteries and its cities.[9] In Italy, the towns had never declined to anything like the extent that the cities of the north decayed after the barbarian invasions. In the eleventh and twelfth centuries the Italian cities staged a spectacular revival: they became once again teeming and rich; as the grip of the emperors and the old aristocracy weakened in the late eleventh and twelfth centuries, the rich citizens argued with the bishops as to who should enter into their inheritance. In the late twelfth and thirteenth centuries innumerable cities were ruled by citizen oligarchies of local landowners and merchants—often the same people, or closely related. Even north of the Alps, where few cities achieved either the wealth or the independence of places like Pisa, Lucca, Florence and Siena, the urban renaissance fundamentally altered the pattern of life—altered it by reintroducing the town as an element in the social scene, with permanent markets where corn could be sold to town dwellers and others who no longer grew their own food; and in this way the foundations were laid which created a large world of commerce affecting the whole community. Money came to play a leading part in the affairs of peasants as well as their lords, of merchants and artisans, clerks and monks.

The rise in population by itself does not explain the growth in monastic population, for that far outstripped the general increase. It is very hard to give precise figures; but they have been worked out for the English monasteries with some degree of precision. Between 1066 and 1154 (the accession of Henry II of England) the number of monasteries for men rose from just under fifty to about five hundred; these are figures that can be documented with fair exactitude.[10] Less certain, but probably not far wrong, is the calculation that the population of the English monasteries, the number of monks and nuns, rose seven- or eightfold or perhaps even more over the same period of just under one hundred years.

England was relatively rich, and the Norman Conquest ushered in developments in some ways specially favorable to monastic endowment; yet we have no reason to suppose that conditions were greatly different elsewhere. In Spain the rapid extension of the area under Christian sway provided conditions as favorable as in England, though the monastic population was always much smaller in this period. Germany was relatively less prosperous in the twelfth century than before, and in the western parts earlier endowment had been lavish: Its expansion was probably less rapid than England's. In eastern Germany and those countries of central and eastern Europe that had become part of western Christendom, especially Poland, Hungary in fair measure, and Bohemia, the spread of monasticism was very slow indeed before the mid–twelfth century; then it proceeded apace (see pp. 267–69). But Italy and France were the twin centers of the church and of the cultural and spiritual movements of the eleventh and twelfth centuries, and there, and especially in France, we have no reason to suppose the growth of monastic population slower than in England. Yet it is impossible to believe that the general rise in population between 1050 and the late twelfth century was anywhere in the region of sevenfold; even a doubling in one century puts some strain on credulity.

Nor can the monastic rise have been won at the serious expense of any other sector of the community. It may be that even with the number of monks and clergy as it was in the 1150s the celibate element among the European peoples was not enough to check the growth of population in any significant degree. But in every walk of life—among the barons and knights, among the citizens and burgesses rich and poor, and among the peasants—the increase, with many local variations, and with all allowance for the large areas of our ignorance, went on steadily and, by the standards of a developing society, relatively fast.

In older monastic houses, so far as we can tell, the number of boy recruits remained fairly steady, or only slowly declined in the twelfth century, while the number of older recruits, of men who found their own vocations, rapidly increased. In the new religious orders of that period recruitment was mainly confined to adults. Thus, although we may reckon that some of the increase in monastic population was due to fathers at their wit's end to provide for surplus children in a world where growing population could mean growing competition, it is among the grown-up men and women of the age that we have mainly to look for the explanation.

No doubt it owed a great deal to social impulse and fashion; success multiplied success. In some parts of Europe the old fashion, represented by the German aristocratic ladies of the tenth and eleventh centuries (see pp. 202–3), for the highly born to monopolize some cloisters spread in this age and became a permanent feature of the landscape for centuries to come. This remained especially the case in Germany, though there are a few cases in France, Spain and Italy as well. To the general explanation of monastic recruitment, aristocratic interest contributes nothing, for although monks and nuns continued to be recruited in the main (so far as we know—and so far as our evidence suggests) from the well-to-do, it is precisely in the country where our evidence of growth is most secure, in England, that the aristocracy seem to have been most indifferent. Every age, even in England, saw a few men and women of the highest birth enter religion, such as Leofric (d. 1066), nephew of the earl of Mercia and abbot, perhaps, of half a dozen monasteries under the complacent regime of Edward the Confessor; or Henry of Blois, favorite nephew of Henry I, brother of King Stephen, who was abbot of Glastonbury and bishop of Winchester from the late 1120s on. Yet as a class, the English aristocracy conspicuously turned its back, almost throughout the later Middle Ages, on the clerical professions. They lavished money and land in the twelfth century and occasionally showed generous patronage later,[11] but their sons seldom became monks and their daughters almost equally seldom nuns.

If we cast our minds back to the age most nearly analogous in monastic history, the fourth century, we can recall that a similarly sensational and mysterious growth coincided with two features of the contemporary world—an intellectual and spiritual drive toward asceticism sponsored by men like Origen and his disciples in the generations immediately preceding the age of St. Antony, and rising living standards, general prosperity and worldliness among the Christian community itself, as it became first socially respectable, then officially permitted, then the religion of the Roman Empire. The analogies in the eleventh and twelfth centuries cannot be exact; but they are at least helpful. Cluny and her friends and rivals had played a leading part in the wider movements of popular religious revival in the tenth and early eleventh centuries. Then, in the mid-eleventh century, came reform at the heart of the church's hierarchy, led by monks or quasi-monks, in the papacy itself. At the same time a rapid growth in the wealth of at least a sector of the population caused a kind of revulsion that has been common in economic history; and the great sayings—"Blessed are the poor....Blessed are the peacemakers"—reverberate through all the religious movements of this age. The richer men became, the more they might fear, for themselves or their neighbors, the torments of Dives or the eye of a needle. Yet revulsion was not the only feeling Christian men felt, then or since, for material prosperity. Increased wealth added greatly to the resources available for monastic foundations, and it became increasingly easy in a society in which silver and even, in the far south, gold flowed more readily than it had done for many centuries, to add penny to penny for a building fund or finance a new monastery from a syndicate of men of moderate means. Patronage ceased to be a monopoly, first of kings, then of nobles; it came within the reach of everyone who had an earthly surplus with which to pile up treasure in heaven.

The reform of the papacy and the advance of Mammon—strange allies in the monastic upheaval of the eleventh and twelfth centuries—affect our story in numerous different ways. The great popes from Leo IX (1048/9–54) to Gregory VII (1073–85) fervently believed that the clergy should lead ascetic lives, that as many as possible of them should be monks or at least live according to a rule. The separation of the clergy from the allurements of the secular world, from women and money above all, lay at the heart of their program, and closely linked to these demands went an insistence on the authority of the Holy See as God's agent for the rule and reform of the church. Leo came from a background steeped in the traditions of Gorze and its offshoots; Gregory—wherever he may have been a monk[12]—counted St. Hugh of Cluny among his few close friends; and his successor Urban II (1088–99) had been a monk of Cluny under St. Hugh. These links were important; but more important still was the close union between the reforming popes and many leaders of monastic reform, their share in the ascetic fervor characteristic of the age. The papal reformers were practical men; but they were also dreamers, theologians and, after a measure, lawyers, for their program aimed to combine spiritual revival with the enforcement of major elements in ancient canon law, such as the law of clerical celibacy. Thus the revival in the study of theology and law was an essential companion to the papal reform, as it was of the monastic movements of the age.

The eleventh and twelfth centuries were exceptionally creative. The advance of Mammon greatly increased and diversified the resources available for monastic endowment, and the papal reformers encouraged investment in monastic communities, both by the fervor of their own belief in divine judgment on human, and especially on lay, sinners, and by their efforts to gather spiritual endowments in religious hands. In the tenth and early eleventh centuries the bulk of monastic wealth had lain in land. But already from the days of Charlemagne on, and increasingly in this period, substantial resources were being collected for ostensibly spiritual purposes under the guise of tithes. Payment of tithes was now compulsory, anyway for landowners, and in principle a tenth of every man's income went to the charitable purposes organized by the church—to relieve the poor and sick and (by this date) to support the clergy. In practice landowners who owned churches or who built churches in order to add to their property as well as provide for their own and their tenants' spiritual well-being frequently gathered back into their own barns a substantial proportion of the tithes. To stop this abuse was one of the aims of the papal reformers; but like much else in the old system of proprietary churches the practice was deeply rooted in custom when they came to weed it out, and direct appeals proved of little effect. Furthermore, the charitable purposes that the church wished to support were becoming increasingly diverse, and a large place in them was allotted to the monks, God's poor—even if the monasteries they served were often corporately rich. In origin it had been held that monks, as landowners, should pay tithe, and since they were neither impoverished nor engaged in the cure of souls, should not receive them. In the eleventh and early twelfth centuries this doctrine was reversed, not without protest or difficulty. The papacy came increasingly to see that the only cure for secular control of spiritual things was to place control in the powerful hands of monastic leaders. Furthermore, for a time, the attempt to make all clergy monks or quasi-monks also often involved monks joining in the activities of the rest of the clergy—serving parish churches, perhaps, even engaging in cure of souls. In the long run this was reckoned no

part of a monk's work: the monk's place was the cloister.[13] But
in this period the practice was accepted and widespread, so far
as we can tell. However this may be, tithes and grants of churches,
with the offerings that were laid by the faithful on their altars,
frequently came into monastic hands. These offerings reflected
the enormously increased use of money—of silver coins—
throughout western Europe in the eleventh century. The
resources that were mobilized could be astonishingly large. A
great fire swept Saint-Benoît-sur-Loire twice in the eleventh
century; twice the monks set to work to rebuild a large part of
their church and other buildings to withstand the flames; and
so far it has withstood them.[14]

To us it seems an astonishing thing that such a religious
community, however well endowed, could sustain the vast
expense of rebuilding its church twice in a century—especially
as the abbey lived on through the centuries that followed and
the church was scarcely altered after 1200. Even more surprising perhaps is the total aggregate of new abbeys and new
churches in this period, which would strain the resources of a
highly developed economy at the height of its prosperity, so
one would suppose, and yet was the product of developing
societies suffering ups and downs, good weather and bad. The
concentration of resources on such buildings as these has astonished many modern observers. Some have condemned them as
wasteful, since they meant spending on stone, paint and reliquaries money that might have gone to feed the poor; others
have been the more impressed by the dedication of funds and
skills to a sacred cause. In an agricultural society, there may be
very few who are wholly unemployed, but great numbers who
have little to do outside the harvest season; thus great building
works, then as now, can provide much-needed employment.

We do right to remember this, and lay some emphasis upon it; the point has been unduly neglected. Yet it was clearly not the first thought in men's minds when they planned these enterprises, not even the first material thought. The question must commonly have been asked: How can such an enterprise be paid for? Not only the number, but the size of these buildings is astonishing. Of the greatest of all, the third church at Cluny, only a fragment remains; yet this fragment still lords it over the little town.

Lay Offerings

In the later years of St. Odilo (994–1049) and the early years of St. Hugh (1049–1109) the abbey's economy depended almost entirely on its estates.[15] From those near at hand came food and rent; from all came money renders of various kinds. A substantial community was amply but not luxuriously provided for (see pp. 179–80). In the mid– and late eleventh century numerous dependent houses were presented to the mother abbey, and so formed what we call the order of Cluny, and although each of these had to run its economic affairs in effective independence of the great abbey, they all sent tribute and offerings. Above all, there was a steady flow of presents to the abbey, offerings from visitors great and not so great, offerings and pensions from all over Europe. Cluny lies in the east of what we call France, although it had special privileges of exemption from secular control (see pp. 63, 68). The kings of León-Castile sent it especially rich offerings, and in the early twelfth century King Henry I of England competed with them. When the third church was finished (1088–1121)—and the nave had fallen and been rebuilt (c. 1125–30)—Abbot Peter the Venerable could say that the kings of Castile and

England had contributed to it more than anyone else.[16] Henry had done this partly because (though commonly mean) he loved the grand gesture, partly because he was aware of terrible sins, partly because Cluny contained one of his favorite nephews, the son of his sister, Adela countess of Blois. The young Henry of Blois was presently removed to England, to become abbot of Glastonbury. He was soon promoted bishop of Winchester, but retained his abbey and so was provided with the income of a multimillionaire. He never lost his affection for Cluny, and later in life his enormous wealth and financial ability helped to save the great abbey from penury and reduce its debt. By the 1140s and 1150s—indeed, even before this—the flow of gifts had dried up, the wealth of the abbey was reduced, and the scale of building and size of the community had saddled it with debts. Abbot Peter the Venerable (see pp. 82–85), a man of great diplomatic charm, panache and wisdom but not a great financier, struggled manfully but unsuccessfully against them until the return of the prince-bishop Henry of Blois set the abbey on the path to recovery. Economically, they were back in the eleventh century; they had to learn to live off their large estates; the days of the overflowing treasury had passed forever.

Innumerable houses of the eleventh and twelfth centuries enjoyed the rich offerings especially characteristic of this age. Those who made offerings to these houses sometimes came as pilgrims to a shrine, sometimes as visitors to a church or monastic community; sometimes they did not come at all, but sent their messengers. In any event, the offerings presupposed that they could be received as honored guests, if they wished. A pleasant fashion made it possible even for the great to lend a hand in building a church. The flow of offerings and the enormous richness of the result reflect the fact that there was an intimacy between the secular society of the day and the monastic order of a degree unique in the Middle Ages.

Of this the first St. Dominic, Santo Domingo (c. 1000–1073) who refounded the great house at Silos, is an excellent example. He was a protégé of King Ferdinand I of León-Castile (1037–65) and also for a short time an adviser to his successor Alfonso VI (1072–1109). Domingo set the pattern of monastic observance and of relations between the monasteries and the king. In 1041 he was put in charge of the small, poor, struggling community at Silos; when he died it was flourishing and had a community of about forty—quite a substantial number for this date and for Spain, even if small compared with the greatest of twelfth-century communities. Its customs were Cluniac, and Domingo was one of those who inspired his kings to take the close interest in Cluny from which many of the monastic developments in Spain before the coming of the Cistercians were to spring. He himself frequently went on preaching tours; he encouraged the development of a scriptorium and of various crafts at Silos—it is no accident that it remains a noble monument of Spanish craftsmanship, even though the author of the sculptures that survive is quite unknown. Domingo combined the life of a fervent monk with frequent visits to the royal court; and he showed his involvement in the world by so notable a concern for the treatment of slaves—numerous in Spain, as in all Mediterranean countries, throughout the Middle Ages—that he was remembered as the saintly patron of slaves and of those who freed them.

The art of Silos was to have some influence on painting and sculpture over a wider area; the saint himself inspired his royal masters to indulge in generous patronage to monastic houses far and near. It was Domingo's patrons, Ferdinand and Alfonso, who first provided St. Hugh of Cluny with the royal benefactors needed to set the masons of the third church of Cluny to their task.

The ups and down of Cluny's economy faithfully mirror its relation to its estates and the people among whom it lived. It greatly affected their material and spiritual life. The enormous numbers of candles needed to light a great church encouraged the beekeepers of a wide area; the wine that flowed into its chalices and on its refectory tables played a part in fostering the vineyards of Burgundy (see p. 80). The huge monastic community and its large household of servants ate their way through the produce of many villages. The large estates of Cluny, as of many abbeys in this age, were organized to provide for the multifarious needs of the community—some manors to bring bread, others the cash or materials to provide candles, the vineyards wine, and so forth. In this activity some monks joined as "deans" over groups of manors and administrators of part of the empire within and without the abbey walls; all this was characteristic of the age and of the traditional pattern of monastic life. But the tilling of the fields was for the most part the work of peasants and organized by peasant reeves and lay bailiffs. The Cluniacs were not involved themselves in agriculture as were the members of the new orders by the end of the eleventh and increasingly in the twelfth century. In the reclamation of land and technological advance the new orders and the Cistercians in particular were, in the twelfth century, to play a crucial part. The Cluniacs remained old-fashioned, deeply affecting their tenants, but still themselves living as landlords.

Abbey and City: San Zeno, Verona

Advancing wealth was chiefly expressed in this period by the rebuilding, extension and beautifying of cities. The cathedral and monastic churches often became the supreme status symbols of rich cities, as well as providing a spiritual counter to the growth of Mammon.

The western prospect of the abbey church of San Zeno Maggiore at Verona is in a sense the image of Verona, a great Italian city of the late eleventh and twelfth centuries; within, the church reflects the way the life of a city and a great monastic community mingled in this age. That this should be so in a building essentially of the early twelfth century, completed c. 1138, is hardly surprising. The continued devotion of the people of Verona to their saint and his church is shown by the considerable embellishments that took place later in the century, along with the rebuilt cloister, which was not finally finished till 1313. Essentially we are looking at what Verona thought fitting as an expression of piety and civic pride in the early twelfth century.

The first age of civic pride in most of Italy since the decline of ancient Rome occurred in the eleventh and twelfth centuries. At first the local bishop was commonly the effective ruler of the city. His demotion was sometimes the result of violence, more often a gradual process, outwardly peaceful. Lay magnates first placed their own relations or friends in the see, then step by step removed them, as it were, to a more spiritual sphere. In the process much heat was sometimes generated, and no doubt a great deal of anticlerical feeling; but it was also an age, in Italy as elsewhere, rich in generous feelings toward the saints and their shrines. Growing material wealth flowed to the adornment of cities, above all with beautiful churches. Even in a city like Florence, dominated by later buildings, San Miniato sits on its little mount and smiles at the great churches of the *trecento* and *quattrocento* in the heart of the city. Elsewhere it is often Romanesque that is most in evidence; so it is in Pisa and Lucca and Bologna, in Modena and Parma and Piacenza; and so it is in Verona. The inside of San Zeno is heavily restored, but retains the essential features of the twelfth-century church. Our view is not impeded, nor our attention diverted, by such massive screens as divide up Canterbury Cathedral into a series of quite separate mansions.[17] San Zeno is one large room, set (as it might be) for an opera in form comparable to the final act of Aida: that is, with a large auditorium all on one level (the nave) and an ample, though not very big, stage with crypt below and stately choir above. High aloft is a great crucifixion in fresco; more commonly, in Italian apses, one meets Christ in Majesty. This is, as it were, the part of the church which is God's alone, too lofty for man to walk there. Next below is the monks' choir and sanctuary, the home of the mortal community. Finally, in the crypt, but now so arranged as to be fully visible from the nave—in a way one commonly meets in central and north Italy and southern Germany—the shrine of the saint, and an ample arcaded lower church in which pilgrims can gather or be led round in orderly procession to pay tribute to St. Zeno in money and prayers.

In such an arrangement it was not at all easy for a layman, unless specially invited and conducted, to stray into the monks' choir. But the monks had no privacy; their offices and masses were conducted in full view of the layfolk in the nave, of the citizens, that is, of Verona, and of those who came to visit this fair city, set between the upper Adige—and so the Brenner Pass in the Alps and Bavaria and Austria—and the plain of Lombardy.

Verona had been a strategic center in Roman times; in the heyday of the medieval Empire, in the tenth, eleventh and twelfth centuries, it became one of the greatest strategic centers in Italy; and such it could be again, from time to time, down to the days of Napoleon. Of this the outward and visible sign is to be seen in the sculpture surrounding its western portal and in the bronze panels of the western doors. The panels represent two periods and styles of craftsmanship, whose date has been much disputed. The view that seems most probable is that the first stage in the bronze panels belongs to the last stage in the main building program, c. 1138—though an array of earlier dates has been propounded. These and the later panels, along with the stone sculpture that surrounds them, make this west front a delightful storehouse of narrative art. The whole ensemble, though a strange jumble in some ways, sits amiably together, its reconciliation symbolized by the famous figure of the sculptor in stone represented in bronze. Yet the sources are very diverse. Here are many scenes from the Old Testament, and an outline of the life of Jesus. The style of the first bronze period is strongly reminiscent, crude though it is, of the splendid bronze panels at Hildesheim; there is little doubt that this is German work and that German craftsmen, along with merchants and Bavarian knights, came over the Brenner Pass and down the Adige to hammer the bronze into shape. The stonemasons have given us, as well as biblical subjects, the death of Theodoric the Great, Theodoric the Ostrogoth, who became, in Germanic legend, Dietrich von Bern, that is, Dietrich of Verona, and the legend of his last hunt, which ended in hell. Dietrich von Bern was taking his place in the poems that culminated in the *Niebelungenlied* in Germany at much the same time that he was taking shape in stone on the walls of San

Zeno. Thus the west front broke into speech, in a tongue intelligible both to native Italian and visiting German.

We have explored a number of paths and byways leading to various explanations of the concentration of men and money into the monastic communities of the eleventh and twelfth centuries. If we put together what we have learned so far, we can say that for a host of reasons, from the fear of hell through the search for peace to the pursuit of the monastic virtues as an end both fervent and fashionable, recruitment soared. We have explored reasons social and spiritual, and it is not at all surprising, in view of the pace of the movement, that there were many bad monks as well as many good and indifferent, even some whole communities given over to bickering and brigandage. The traditional monasticism seems to have remained the monopoly of the well-to-do; the new movements, as we shall see, were sometimes more egalitarian. But within these limits, the older monasteries' power to attract recruits was evidently very strong; they gathered in men of the most varied character and talent. It is this variety of talent that provides the monasticism of the late eleventh and early twelfth centuries with one of its most striking marks. In this period one finds an unusual concentration of men of great business gifts, of great gifts as thinkers and writers, and of notable craftsmen, within the walls of monasteries. There is no period in the Middle Ages when there was not diversity of talent and personality in the cloisters, but it is at this time especially marked. The variety and range of talent declined after the mid–twelfth century; the rival opportunities open to men of an academic or peaceful turn of mind and the professional opportunities open to craftsmen greatly increased in the world outside; the monastic movements lost their first bloom, ceased to be avant-garde. They continued to draw throngs of recruits right through the thirteenth century and, in many places, beyond; but they no longer recruited among men of original mind or special talent to anything like the same degree. This is one of the reasons for the relative decline of monastic influence in the church in the late Middle Ages.

7.

The Monastic Contribution to the Twelfth-Century Renaissance

The movement of thought and culture that has come to be known as the twelfth-century renaissance began in the eleventh century at the latest and was scarcely extinguished, even in part, in the thirteenth. It was the artistic, literary and cultural expression of the great epoch of change of the central Middle Ages. It began as an ecclesiastical movement, with the improvement of clerical education and clerical learning at its core, and the revival and reorganization of ecclesiastical institutions as its first most obvious achievement. The creation of the universities on the one hand, and of the great churches of the Romanesque and Gothic periods, with their adornments and satellite crafts, were its most spectacular monuments. In this sense it always remained a movement clerically inspired. Yet as it grew it spread in all directions, came to include some very secular elements and some heresies, and inspired vernacular literatures of great variety, sophistication and worldliness.

Architecture and the Crafts

The twelfth-century renaissance was a cosmopolitan movement, and we shall wander over the face of Europe in our pursuit of it; but its characteristic centers lay in France and Italy. In Italy and Provence the physical presence of the remains of the ancient world was a constant artistic influence, coupled with frequent contact with Byzantium and (to a slightly lesser extent) with Islam. To the historian of medieval art, Italy is often confusing, because some of these influences were always present and could ambush the craftsmen of almost any age. Nonetheless, Italy is crucial, since through it there flowed both the Roman and Byzantine influence that provided so many of the themes of eleventh-and twelfth-century art and architecture, and one of the routes of Islamic influence that inspired some elements of Gothic architecture, especially in the form of the Gothic arch. Provence at this time was part of the Italian cultural world, and if one wanders in Nîmes and observes the barrel vault and the fluted columns of the ancient Temple of Diana, or in nearby Saint-Gilles, where twelfth-century architects and sculptors contrived a building alive with classical entablatures and friezes, one may see something of the history of Romanesque architecture and sculpture in a small compass. Yet for clarity of vision and a lucid chronology of the development of Romanesque, it is the rest of France to which we must chiefly look. The term itself has been given many meanings, and various subdivisions of time and country have been proposed to confuse the layperson. For our purpose, it is in its essence the architecture of the great churches of the eleventh and early twelfth centuries, the sculpture that came increasingly to adorn their portals and doors and the capitals of their arcades, the stained glass, the painting of their walls—and all the attendant arts and crafts which hung the walls with tapestries, laid occasional small carpets on their floors, laid against the altars splendid frontals, upon the altar finely wrought patens, chalices and pyxes of silver and gold and splendid service books, and on or behind the altars reliquaries of precious metals inlaid with stones or adorned with enamels. The most durable material used was stone, and thus it is the architecture that most fully records the arts of the period; much sculpture has survived where the weather or changes of fashion or religious iconoclasts have not defaced it. The illumination of books is also richly recorded in numerous surviving manuscripts. Almost all the tapestries and carpets of the age have gone; of the other ornaments and wall paintings only a small part remains to show us the splendor of a great church in this age. But in some treasuries, especially in the Catholic areas of Germany, in parts of France and Spain, and in Italy, collections of early treasures survive, and many more are gathered in the world's museums.

Thus the word *Romanesque* is most commonly applied to a style, and also to a scale of building—above all, to the fashion for building large churches with ambitious vaults. The style was first detected by the historians of architecture in Lombardy in the ninth and tenth centuries, and then, in the tenth and eleventh, over a wide area that includes southern and central Germany and the Rhineland, the basin of the Rhône and large parts of France and Catalonia. In early days the determination to build on the monumental scale was most evident in Ottonian Germany; it spread in all directions in the eleventh. Few major churches of the tenth century survive in Germany, but one may still see what they were like in the abbey church of Gernrode. German Romanesque became so conservative that the shape and pattern develops little through the Mittelzell at Reichenau, or Worms or Speyer Cathedrals, mainly tenth and eleventh century, or Maria Laach, mainly of the twelfth, or Mainz Cathedral (as it now is) of the twelfth and thirteenth centuries. In scale and number combined, the most spectacular efforts were made in the Anglo-Norman kingdom after the Norman Conquest. Every English cathedral and almost every major abbey were rebuilt in the French and Romanesque fashion within a generation or two after the Conquest, and the effort was equally conspicuous in Normandy itself. The impression intended by these great churches is still conveyed on the grandest scale by the abbey of Jumièges. Contemporary with it were the two abbeys at Caen, for men and women, founded by the Conqueror and his wife. The plan and design of Jumièges, and even more of Saint-Étienne, the Abbaye-aux-hommes, at Caen, provided models followed by the Norman masons in England. At Caen the first ambitious attempts were made to provide a complete groined vault over a great church, and it was at Durham in the first quarter of the twelfth century

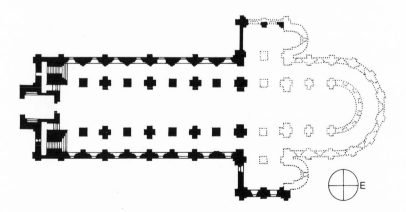

Plan of Jumièges abbey church, mid–eleventh century; only the nave and part of the transept survives, and the layout of the apse is partly conjectural.

that the next major technological advance was made, in the vaults that still span the great nave of the Cathedral. The Durham masons had discovered that a more secure vault could be built and the tremendous thrust of its weight more effectively transmitted to the arches and walls below, by a pointed vault. Thus, technologically, the pointed arch found its place in the repertoire of the most advanced masons of the day.

It had meanwhile arrived from another source in a house of even greater fame than Durham. The pointed arch had long been part of the idiom of Islamic architecture, especially in parts of what are now central Turkey. The aesthetic attraction and architectural advantage of the pointed arch very likely penetrated before the end of the eleventh century to St. Benedict's own abbey of Monte Cassino; it was certainly used in the third church at Cluny, from 1088 on. Of eleventh-century Monte Cassino no trace remains, and of the third church at Cluny only a fragment; but sufficient of that fragment and of various imitations of it survive for us to see the way the pointed arch established itself in a setting otherwise conservative.[1]

More striking, and more widely influential, was the meeting of Romanesque and Gothic at the abbey of Saint-Denis, outside Paris, under the patronage of Abbot Suger, whose work stretched from the 1120s to the 1140s.[2] Here were to meet the developing techniques of Durham and Monte Cassino, with the tradition of sculpture of Santo Domingo de Silos and Moissac. From the crude sculpture that survives of c. 1000 to the reliefs of Silos and Moissac is a large step, imperfectly recorded. What is clear is that technical expertise, though fairly widely spread, had a crucial meeting with a new and exciting iconographical tradition in the north of Spain and the south of France at the turn of the eleventh and twelfth centuries. The tradition grew from the Spanish fashion of providing copies of the commentary of Beatus of Liebàna (died c. 798) on the Apocalypse with lavish pictures in the Spanish style of the age, in which Islamic and Mozarabic influences (that is, cultural themes derived both from the Muslims and the Christians under Muslim rule in Spain) help to give a vivid and exotic flavor to the visions. At Toulouse and Moissac they were translated into stone, and at Moissac in particular we witness one of the fundamental inspirations of twelfth-century sculpture. In the world of cosmopolitan artistic influences of the early to mid–twelfth century, flourishing schools of sculpture sprang up in many parts of northwestern Europe. The most sophisticated and vivid were those of Cluny, Vézelay and Autun, the centers of Burgundian art, and that of Saint-Denis. Abbot Suger of Saint-Denis has left us his own account of his building works, in which the practical concerns of a great man of affairs mingle with the romantic, imaginative vision of a notable patron of the arts. In particular, he loved to see the beauty of God's house—his church—adorned with color and light; and in the jewels of the most beautiful of the ornaments he saw reflected the precious stones out of which the New Jerusalem in the Book of Revelation was constructed (21:18-20), based on the roll call from the prophet Ezekiel of the glory of humankind in the Garden of Eden (Ezekiel 28:13):

> Every precious stone was thy covering, the sardius, the topaz, and the jasper, the chrysolite, and the onyx, and the beryl, the sapphire, and the carbuncle, and the emerald.

In a measure all the arts and crafts in this period were related so that one can often see metalwork influencing manuscript painting, painting influencing sculpture and so forth. But there are nonetheless some surprising differences between the geography of painting and architecture. In book illumination, France is less important and Germany and England relatively more important than in other arts. There is also a pervasive influence from Byzantium much less apparent in other arts. Part of the reason for this is admittedly accident of survival. Thus a variety of reasons of which climate is one has left us far more wall painting in and from the churches of northern Spain than anywhere else; yet no one who has visited the great abbey church of Saint-Savin-sur-Gartempe near Poitiers could fail to regard it as one of the most impressive monuments of medieval art. Partly it is because in England and Germany there were powerful traditions of painting, which had made them principal centers of book production in the tenth century already. The Byzantine influence may be explained in a measure by the profusion of small movable objects coming into western Europe through the crusading world and Sicily, which could influence painting more readily than sculpture or building, and by interest in Byzantine ways of presenting the human body. Nonetheless, the difference from other crafts and from literature is striking. The most flourishing school of northwestern France was the Norman, product of the conjunction of English and French, which actually had preceded the Norman Conquest in this area. One of the most flourishing in Burgundy was at Cîteaux of all places, founded by the English St. Stephen Harding, the third abbot, and showing clear English influence.[3]

Monks and Romanesque Art

The first phase of the twelfth-century renaissance, by a simplification at once crude and drastic but not wholly false, might be dated from 1050 to 1140 and be defined characteristically as the monastic phase. The middle of the twelfth century saw the capture of the initiative in learning, literature and art by secular masters; from about 1170 the monasteries rarely provided new thoughts or new inspirations—though in the thirteenth century the new religious, the friars, played a crucial role in the intellectual and artistic world and in the organization of the church. But from about 1170 arts and crafts once characteristically monastic had become, partly or largely, the possession of professional craftsmen, mostly secular.[4] Monks never had a monopoly of any craft, nor of learning, but it may be said that the art and architecture commonly labeled Romanesque were characteristically monastic, and Gothic art and architecture the mirror of the secular church. This is a bold saying, perhaps a desperate one. Many a great Romanesque cathedral, Mainz, Speyer, Worms, and dozens more in Italy, France and England, rise up to rebuke it. Nor will it stand confidently up against the mass of Gothic art and architecture in countless monasteries. Yet there is something to be said for it. From the first rude traces of Romanesque sculpture at Dijon, through the reliefs and the paintings at Santo Domingo de Silos, to the sculpture of Moissac, Cluny and Vézelay, Saint-Gilles and Saint-Trophime at Arles, the history of Romanesque can be traced in great monasteries, but not without gaps, since if we may contemplate Cluny and Vézelay, in a book on monastic history we must leave aside the supreme triumph of Romanesque sculpture in the secular church of St. Lazarus at Autun. Yet as a crude measure, the link of Romanesque with the monks survives, and if we inspect the countless examples cited in Emile Mâle's great book on French religious art in the twelfth century, a large majority down to and including Abbot Suger's later work at

Saint-Denis, of about 1140, is monastic. His book on French religious art in the thirteenth century, which runs for his purpose from c. 1150 to the early fourteenth century, is almost exclusively based on Gothic secular cathedrals.

Monastic Involvement

The word *monastic* in this context is doubtless ambiguous, and for two reasons. First, it came in the late eleventh and twelfth centuries to cover a wide variety of new fashions and orders apart from the traditional Benedictine and Cluniac monasticism. The second ambiguity in the word *monastic* arises from the doctrine once held that medieval monasteries were built and adorned by the monks themselves. Many a romantic page in Montalembert's *Monks of the West* (1860–77) bears witness to that faith, and it took practical shape when the monks of Buckfast and Maria Laach of the late nineteenth and early twentieth centuries themselves set to work to restore and rebuild their abbeys. As applied to the masons and craftsmen of the Middle Ages, it was dismantled by G. G. Coulton and his disciples nearly eighty years ago. They showed that, so far as the evidence goes, the bulk of what we see is the work of professional masons and professional craftsmen. They made hay with the old, romantic view, and in the process, as so often happens when the pursuit of truth becomes trapped in controversy, they carted away more than they should. R. E. Swartwout's *The Monastic Craftsman* (1932) represents an intelligent exposition of the doctrine that had first been expounded at length in Coulton's *Art and the Reformation* (1st edition, 1928). Swartwout cited fairly some of the most telling evidence for monastic craftsmanship, and saw that one must take careful note of chronology. It has come to be increasingly realized, first, that the bulk of precise evidence comes from the thirteenth century or later, and second, that by then lay professionals were producing the majority even of finely written books, the most characteristically monastic of all the crafts before the twelfth century. The pendulum has swung back a fair distance—not perhaps quite far enough—but it is safe to say that in the eleventh and early twelfth centuries monastic involvement was common in many crafts, and played a crucial part in some. Also, in the same period, monastic inspiration and patronage played its most vital role even where monks themselves were not engaged in artistic work. Equally, it is clear that there was no period when secular men did not play a large part in every craft. In the tenth-century monastic revival in England, St. Dunstan and St. Ethelwold were personally involved in the artistic work characteristic of their age, and of many of the eminent Norman monks of the eleventh century Orderic Vitalis notes that they had special skills, commonly in music and the chant. These are samples, but they can be multiplied sufficiently to show that in that nonspecialist world, craftsmanship of various kinds was as normal inside as outside the cloister; that in communities dedicated, in some measure—even in the traditional monasticism of the tenth and eleventh centuries—to work, those whose talents lay in that direction had nothing to hinder them, and much to give them encouragement.

No doubt monastic involvement in heavy industry, that is to say in the building of enormous churches, was less common. The whole subject becomes more subtle and sophisticated in the early twelfth century. Multitudes of new monasteries needed buildings and furniture and (for the less austere) products of every kind of craft, and thus made unprecedented demands on the human resources even of that expansive age.

They must have called on talent from within when it was available; though it could not always have met the need.

We may ask: Was there a Cluniac style or a "school of Hirsau" in the eleventh or twelfth century? Or a style developed by the Augustinian canons? The short answer must be no. Great patrons with wide connections, like Cluny, could by the normal exercise of patronage influence trends and movements over a wide area. Yet it is interesting to observe that in the sphere of Cluny's influence, the sculpture of Moissac and Vézelay had more children than the architecture of the third church of Cluny; that in many parts of Europe, Cluny's churches and their decoration differ no whit from other local buildings[5]; that it is rare for us to be able to tell by looking at a building to what order it belonged or, in the case of churches manned by canons, whether they were regular or secular. To this the Cistercians are the major exception (see esp. pp. 179–86 ff.).

When all is said and done, even before the mid–twelfth century, it can never be taken for granted that a monastery could find a wide range of craftsmen within its own community. Sometimes a fine craftsman bred up a school of followers, especially in the days when communities were mainly recruited by children; sometimes these schools lasted for two or three generations. When a community or an abbot needed books or painting or building, they turned to the best talent available; within, if it was to be found there, outside, if not. The new choir of Canterbury Cathedral, built to house the shrine of Thomas Becket in the years following the fire of 1174, is a monument to the zeal of the monastic community, and some of them were in a measure at least involved in collecting money, and in organizing the masons' work. But the architect was chosen by competition, and once they had selected

William of Sens, they accepted with him a professional design based on various contemporary French, early Gothic models. Canterbury is exceptionally well documented; in other respects it may well represent what had often happened before; it certainly represented what was to be the norm for the future.

Theophilus

Thus the first half of the twelfth century saw monastic involvement at its height, and it is not by chance that it has left us some of the most sensational memorials of monastic craftsmanship. In early twelfth-century Germany the monk Theophilus, in his treatise *On the Various Arts,* laid out detailed instructions, very much in the manner of a renaissance manual, for illuminating books, making glass vessels and stained glass and creating ornaments in metal; on metalwork he is especially elaborate and thorough. It is highly technical, but shows us also something of the mind and spirit of the author.[6]

> Theophilus…unworthy of the name and profession of monk—wishes to all, who are willing to avoid and spurn idleness and the shiftlessness of the mind by the useful occupation of their hands and the agreeable contemplation of new things, the recompense of a heavenly reward.

> In the account of the creation of the world, we read that man was created in the image and likeness of God and was animated by the Divine breath….Wretchedly deceived by the guile of the Devil, through the sin of disobedience he lost the privilege of immortality, but, however, so far transmitted to later posterity the distinction of

wisdom and intelligence, that whoever will contribute
both care and concern is able to attain a capacity for all
arts and skills, as if by hereditary right.

He goes on to say, indeed, that a craftsman who refuses to
ply his trade is liable to God's judgment like the man in the
Gospel parable who failed to "restore to his master his talent
with added interest."

Theophilus sees craftsmanship as a divine gift and places his
treatise in a theological setting. But it is also an extremely practical statement of all that he could tell from his own experience, or learn from others, on these crafts.

If you will diligently examine it, you will find in it
whatever kinds and blends of various colours Greece
(Byzantium) possesses; whatever Russia knows of
workmanship in enamels or variety of niello; whatever
Arabia adorns with repoussé or cast work, or engravings
in relief: whatever gold embellishments Italy applies to
various vessels or to the carving of gems and ivories:
whatever France esteems in her precious variety of
windows: whatever skill Germany praises in subtle
work in gold, silver, copper, iron, wood and stone.

No doubt he exaggerated his knowledge of Russia and
Arabia somewhat; but he was right to emphasize that his skill
was genuine and cosmopolitan. He writes from within the
cloister, but his vision was far from narrow. He neither assumed
that his audience was monastic nor suggested that it was not; it
is clear that the book was written for men who could read
Latin without difficulty, both within and without the cloister,
and that its early circulation was largely in monastic libraries.

There is little doubt that he wrote in a west German monastery of the traditional mode, presumably one of the houses modeled on Gorze, and he has been identified with considerable probability as Roger, monk of Helmarshausen and noted craftsman in metal at the turn of the eleventh and twelfth centuries.

Work and Books

Of the religious orders of the twelfth century, the most cosmopolitan—and the one that has left an architecture of striking uniformity—was the Cistercian. Their involvement sprang essentially from two facts: that their egalitarian method of recruitment opened their gates in a unique degree to craftsmen of a wide variety of skills, at least in the first generation or two of their existence; and second, that they insisted, as no monastic order had done to anything like the same degree, on the importance of work. All medieval doctrines of work derived from the Book of Genesis, and it could only be seen as the consequence of the Fall, which obliged Adam to dig and Eve to spin. Even after the Fall, Jesus himself observed that the lilies of the field owed their beauty in no measure either to digging or spinning. St. Benedict had prescribed work for the good of the soul, and to ensure that necessary tasks were accomplished; the Cistercians took him to mean that all the work of the community should be performed by monks or lay brothers (see pp. 172–74).

This was not a wholly new idea. In the traditional monasticism the hours set apart for work were often eroded to make time for more elaborate liturgy, and it has never been difficult to find excellent ways of passing time allotted to manual labor without unduly soiling the hands. It was official Cluniac doctrine that reading was equivalent to manual labor; nonetheless it is clear that even at Cluny much labor of various kinds was done. Several of the new orders at the turn of the eleventh and twelfth centuries followed the ancient and hallowed tradition and set their choir monks to work copying books. This was commonly regarded as monastic labor par excellence, and thus the new orders came rapidly to acquire libraries that could vie even with some of the oldest houses.

Books indeed were of great importance to all the new orders, and it is in their copying and reading that the most characteristic influence of the monasteries on the renaissance of the twelfth century can be discerned. It is because the books that were studied most frequently were found in monastic libraries and the largest network of active schools lay in the cloister—and their pupils were mainly prentice monks—that the early stages of the intellectual revival were predominantly monastic in inspiration. There were always secular schools as well; and they came to flourish alongside the monastic. The old cathedral libraries had always rivaled the monks' libraries, and came into their own again as the revival developed in the cathedral schools. In the first half of the twelfth century ideas that had grown up among monks were being developed far beyond their ken in secular schools.

Books and the Apostolic Life

The ascetics and reformers of the eleventh century read the classics on the spiritual life of earlier days: They were inspired by the literature of the desert, and above all by Cassian, to go out into the wilderness, to live as hermits or to form new kinds of communities. They read the Rule of St. Benedict, not in the context of the mass of custom in which it lived in the monasteries of traditional observance, but as if it had just been written, fresh and new. Cassian had found the origin of the monastic life in the New Testament, and every religious reformer, every Christian idealist, looked for his inspiration or justification in the Bible. At the heart of almost every monastic rule lay an echo or quotation of the words in the Acts of the Apostles that defined the life of the apostles and early disciples: men and women "united in heart and soul…" who had "everything…in common" (see p. 27). Thus the monks began once again to study the life of the apostles, to find their own root and inspiration in it. But the consequence of such study was to lead far beyond its original devotional intent. For some monks observed differences between the life of the early disciples and themselves that they felt were not wholly to their advantage, and critics of the monks from outside advanced the opinion that quite a different mode of life was more truly apostolic. It was out of this controversy and the ferment of ideas which it produced that the leading principles of most of the new orders were formed. It was an ancient idea that the active clerks in the world, those engaged in evangelism, popular preaching and pastoral work, were leading the lives of the apostles, that the apostolic life was essentially active, whereas the monastic, the life of the desert or of the community, on the other hand, was contemplative. Now many arguments arose as to whether the truly apostolic life was not the better, or whether the two lives could not and should not be mixed and mingled, or as to whether the monastic life was not after all truly apostolic. By a curious irony, these speculations led many monastic leaders of the age to believe that stable enclosure within the monastic precinct and a wandering life without, preaching and teaching, or setting up new communities, were both somehow simultaneously expressions of the truly apostolic life. Thus Robert of

Molesme wandered from house to house and eventually founded Cîteaux. Thus St. Anselm's disciple, Honorius Augustodunensis, wherever he may have sprung from, wandered between Germany and England, gathering and spreading his master's and his own ideas among monks and secular teachers, and his ideas included some of the symbolic, biblical schemes most influential in the artistic iconography of the day.[7]

Biography and History

Throughout the twelfth and thirteenth centuries history and biography were the two fields of literature in which monastic preeminence survived. Orderic Vitalis, Eadmer and William of Malmesbury were characteristic monastic authors of this period: characteristic both in the range of their interests, centering on history and hagiography, and in their devotion to calligraphy. Of all three we possess autograph copies, carefully and beautifully written, of some at least of their works. The interest in history was specially characteristic for a time of the Anglo-Norman monastic world, and the revival of an interest in the past and in English and Norman traditions was one of the inspirations that affected all three. In any case it was only in communities tenacious of their memory, with records and books giving some basis for historical study, that history could begin seriously to flourish. William of Malmesbury, the most acute historical student since Bede, inspired others no less acute to copy his methods in writing and inventing histories more secular than his. Bede had written the *Ecclesiastical History,* and Orderic's great ramble of a chronicle was also ecclesiastical, though it strayed into every path of interest to a Norman community: the settlement of the Normans in England, and the wanderings of the family of the founders of his monastery and their colleagues in the south of Italy and on Crusade. Eadmer wrote biography and history; his best works were his *Life of St. Anselm,* and his *History of Recent Events,* which is a second life of Anselm in a different key—his part in public events. William was chiefly inspired by Bede; but he divided his major works into two: a history of the English bishops and a history of the English kings, for he wrote for secular as well as monastic patrons, and it suited him to provide for their secular interests. His most distinguished imitator was Geoffrey of Monmouth, a secular clerk who wrote the most secular of twelfth-century chronicles, first for the same patron as William, then for whoever would read it. The rich tapestry of good tales that he provided, and especially the elaborate account of King Arthur that he invented, ensured him the widest audience of any medieval chronicler. His account of Arthur also provided one of the crucial links between the learned Latin world of the cloister and the secular world of vernacular literature.

St. Anselm, Theology and Humanism

St. Anselm himself was an Italian (c. 1033–1109) who settled in Bec in Normandy and was already about sixty when he became archbishop of Canterbury. His philosophic insight and power to express his most abstruse thought in language both subtle and simple made him the greatest theologian of his age. He did not command a large audience, but it was sufficient, in that peripatetic age, for some of his seminal ideas to spread. Thus he came to be the central figure in the devotional and theological revolution which set aside the majestic Christ characteristic of earlier images and placed the human Jesus and his Virgin Mother at the center of the religious sentiment of the twelfth and thirteenth centuries. This sentiment united the world of devotion, of literature and art, with the world of learning. Adumbrations of the growing interest in the human Jesus, and the growing appreciation of human values that went with it, could be found in many parts of western Europe, perhaps especially in Italy. Anselm was austere and ascetic; but in the hands of those influenced by him, his notion that God became man not to cheat the devil of his rights, but to establish a relation between God and man, became the basis of the Christian humanism of the twelfth century. No one would have been more surprised by the roads down which his concept led the academic and popular theologians of the century than Anselm himself. In the next generation the great secular teacher Abelard carried the line of thought on to the point of saying that Jesus came to give men a human example. Abelard coupled in his own thought and life a deep involvement and belief in human emotion that is a part of the story of his affair with Heloise. Later, in a moment of bitter penitence, Abelard became a monk, and he died eventually a monk of the community of Cluny. This illustrates how close the classroom and the cloister still were; it does not make Abelard himself a monastic theologian.

The cult of the Blessed Virgin was firmly established centuries before 1100. Nonetheless, in the same meeting of Italian and English traditions in the circle of Anselm, it began to take on a new complexion. Not Anselm himself, but his nephew and namesake, who was a monk at the Sagra di San Michele (or Chiusa) and later abbot of Bury St. Edmunds, was the center of a circle with a special interest in the conception of the Blessed Virgin. Out of this circle, in which William of Malmesbury and Eadmer were much involved, came the doctrine and the cult, the first substantial collections of miracles of the Blessed Virgin, and the interest in her coronation by her son in heaven, which was first represented, so far as the record goes, at Reading Abbey in the 1120s, then taken up at Saint-Denis by Abbot Suger, and so entered the mainstream of Gothic iconography.

The characteristic of the twelfth-century renaissance of greatest moment to us was its variety. Not everyone accepted the view that the human Jesus looked kindly on human feelings and failings; not everyone agreed that the exuberant techniques of painting, sculpture and jewelry were appropriate for the adorning of churches. In the early twelfth century some heretics were burning churches, some puritans arguing that they should be plain and unadorned, while Abbot Suger and the monk Theophilus saw God's glory revealed in the most sumptuous ornament and the most brilliant jewel. The stern asceticism characteristic of many monastic leaders went hand in hand with a view that the world was almost wholly evil, even though at first created by God and good. The narrowest of margins separated some eminent monastic thinkers, most notably the Italian Peter Damian, from the view that the world was evil even in its making, which was heretical, and the basis of the most success-ful of twelfth-century heresies, that of the Cathars. Yet it was within the walls of monasteries and among monastic leaders that the love of God's creation was at first most evidently fos-tered. If we ask what unites St. Basil in the fourth century, the Irish hermits of the sixth and seventh, St. Bruno in the eleventh, Bernard of Clairvaux and Francis of Assisi in the twelfth and thirteenth centuries, the first answer might be their love of nat-ural beauty—though one might equally find it in their devotion to the ascetic life. Plants and fruit begin to creep over the pages of herbals about 1100, and frequently entrance us by the vivid observation shown in the craftsman's eye in minor sculpture a century later. Love of nature is equally evident in the situation of the Grande Chartreuse, of countless Cistercian abbeys and of the Carceri above Assisi. All these places were the homes of ascetics, who renounced the world while rejoicing in it. Yet we can hardly wonder that in the same world of Bernard and Francis we meet in Latin and vernacular lyric and romance copious evidence that a love of natural beauty and a delight in the world as God's and as good went hand in hand with an ever more consciously accepted hedonism, sometimes quite pagan in inspiration, sometimes devout. Clear traces of the doctrines of St. Bernard have been found in Wolfram von Eschenbach, the great German epic writer of the early thirteenth century, who was a thoroughly secular knight.

In the early twelfth century the fame of St. William, the Carolingian count of Toulouse who had founded Saint-Guilhem-le-Desert, was spread far and wide, as Orderic Vitalis noted, in the chanson de geste on Guillaume d'Orange. Its main theme is the slaughter of Saracens; it is one of the bloodiest of crusading epics. In the early thirteenth century, when the leaders of the Albigensian Crusade were slaughtering heretics round Toulouse, Wolfram issued his version of St. William's legend, the *Willehalm,* whose theme, contrariwise, is a plea for tolerance. Wolfram had probably never seen a Muslim, nor even Orange or Saint-Guilhem. But human kindness was a deep part of his nature, and his doctrine of God's love for man shows how deeply he had drunk from the stream that flowed from the devotional and theological treatises of the twelfth century.

The sense of human values here portrayed comes most directly from St. Bernard, but also makes Wolfram the heir of a wider tradition of twelfth-century humanism. In biography, autobiography and personal letters a few sensitive writers of the eleventh and twelfth centuries added greatly to the literary tradition of their age by revealing a capacity to express and expound human personality quite exceptional for the Middle Ages. Perhaps its most brilliant expression is in the letters of Heloise and Abelard (see pp. 209–11); but more characteristic, and nearer the heart of our subject, were the more modest endeavors of the biographer of St. Anselm, the monk Eadmer, and the autobiographical efforts of the Norman chronicler Orderic. Eadmer was inspired to write in an original way by the extraordinary personality of Anselm, and especially by his conversation. In a famous passage he tells how Anselm, as abbot of Bec, tried to impress his idea of the monastic life on the boys of the cloister in a manner less fierce than some of his fellow abbots employed. "What, I ask you, is to be done with them? They are incorrigible ruffians," grumbled one of his colleagues. "We never give over beating them day and night, and they only get worse and worse…." "You never give over beating them? And what are they like when they grow up?" "Stupid brutes," he said. To which Anselm replied, in effect, that this was no more suitable treatment for spiritual monks in the making than it would be for tender plants in the garden, and that even the goldsmith did not form his leaf of gold or silver by blows alone. "He now presses it and strikes it gently with his tool, and now even more gently raises it with careful pressure and gives it shape. So, if you want your boys to be adorned with good habits, you too, besides the pressure of blows, must apply the encouragement and help of fatherly sympathy and gentleness."[8]

The education of the cloister was for a whole way of life. Here, in the monastic schools, much of what was most charac-teristic of the eleventh and twelfth centuries met, and the best of traditional monasticism is summed up in the devout and moving—yet quite unheroic—survey of his own life that concludes the life's work of Orderic Vitalis.

> On Easter eve I was baptised at Atcham, a village in England lying on the mighty River Severn....When I was five I went to school at Shrewsbury, and dedicated my first lessons to you in the church of St. Peter and St. Paul....It did not please you that I should lead my life there longer...in case I ran the danger of failing to follow your law owing to the human affection of my parents. And so, O God of glory, who ordered Abraham to leave his country, his father's house and kindred, you inspired my father Odeler to give me up and surrender me wholly to you. Weeping, he gave a weeping child to Rainald the monk, and sent me into exile for your love—nor ever after saw me. A small boy did not presume to contradict his father, but I obeyed him in all things, since he promised me that I should possess paradise with the innocent...; and so I left my country, my parents, all my kindred and my friends....At ten years old I crossed the Channel, and came, an exile, to Normandy, knowing no one, known to none. Like Joseph in Egypt, I heard a tongue I knew not. Yet by your grace I found among the strangers every kindness and friendship.

He describes his reception by the abbot of Saint-Évroult; how the monks gave him the name Vitalis so that they would not have to use his barbarous English name; how he had lived there fifty-six years,

...by your favour, loved and honored by all the monks and all who lived here much more than I deserved. I have suffered heat and cold and the burden of the day...and I have awaited my penny wage with confidence....Give me the will to persevere in your service, unfailing strength against Satan's crafty malice, until I may receive, by your gift, the inheritance of eternal salvation. And what I ask for myself, here and to come, I desire too, merciful God, for my friends and benefactors, and for all your faithful children according to your providence. Our own merits do not suffice to obtain things everlasting, for which the perfect ever ardently long....May the glorious intercession of the holy Virgin mother Mary and all the saints help us in your sight...."[9]

Part Two

NEW ORDERS

8.

The Augustinian Canons

The Apostolic Life

The inspiration for the new monasticism flowed through two channels, which met at the turn of the eleventh and twelfth centuries in what some historians have called "the monastic crisis"—*la crise du monachisme*. Yet perhaps it was not so much a crisis as the stirring of the waters, a whirlpool with ripples and eddies, with a noisy center and still pools out of the flood's reach, such as one may find where two strong currents meet.

The first stream brought down from the early church and the old monasticism the Rule of St. Benedict, the hermit ideal and the rules or regulations for a common life for canons. In the eleventh century all three enjoyed an enhanced prestige, partly because of the intellectual revival—our second stream—which led many to read these texts and interpret them afresh. The Rule of St. Benedict was now firmly established as the basis of the traditional monasticism, which enjoyed the height of its prestige at Gorze, Cluny, Hirsau and many other notable centers. The hermit ideal enjoyed a renaissance, prepared in Italy at the turn of the tenth and eleventh centuries, blossoming both in Italy and in France in the second half of the eleventh century. Out of the papal reform in the eleventh century came a movement to convert all clergy who were not monks into canons living under a rule, and the rule to which they were subjected was the Rule of St. Augustine.

In the ferment of social, religious and intellectual life of the eleventh and twelfth centuries, it was natural that there should be argument and controversy about every aspect of the Christian life. No dispute is more characteristic of the age than the debate about the apostolic life, the *vita apostolica* (see pp. 141, 221–23). It had been the traditional view of all monks, and especially those under the Rule of St. Benedict, that their life was apostolic. Yet it was an undeniable fact that one of the main functions of the apostles had been to preach and to evangelize; they were missionaries. So too had been many of the monks of early centuries, and there never perhaps was a time in the history of monasticism when the community and the world were in closer rapprochement than in the late eleventh and early twelfth centuries. This was the age when large numbers of churches were given to monks, which they seem commonly to have been expected to serve; this was the age when they defended their enjoyment of tithes on the ground that the laborer was worthy of his hire.[1] This was the age when the citizens of Verona and Milan poured silver and gold into San Zeno and Sant'Ambrogio (see pp. 121–24, 252–60), and harmony, not the bitter conflict which was later to be common, was the norm between townsfolk and the monastic communities nearby.

Yet there were many who thought that the monastic life was angelic not apostolic, one of prayer rather than activity, the monks' role that of Mary, not Martha.[2] And it is precisely in this same period that the distinction between the active and contemplative became once more strongly urged. Ascetics and hier-

archs agreed from time to time to forbid monks to serve
parishes, and to foster alternative ways of providing for clerical
service to the world. In their different ways St. Peter Damian,
hermit, monk and cardinal bishop (c. 1007–72), and St. Anselm,
a retiring monk and abbot who found himself one day, to his
sorrow, archbishop of Canterbury (c. 1033–1109), served and
fostered the growth of canons regular to rescue the secular
clergy from their sins and the monks from the chores of Martha.

The canon living according to a rule was no novelty in the
eleventh century: Numerous communities paid service in some
degree to the *Institutio Canonicorum* of 816 or 817, which is an
anthology from earlier rules, especially those of Benedict and
of Bishop Chrodegang of Metz, who had legislated for canons
in the eighth century. In the mid–eleventh century the papal
reformers inspired a movement to draw clerics and canons into
a type of institute whose base was the Rule of St. Augustine.

The Rule of St. Augustine

The document that has passed under this name since the
eleventh century was not actually composed by St. Augustine of
Hippo in the early fifth century. He wrote down indeed some
principles of life for small communities of men and women; this
was adapted for the use of men. In due course both the male
and female versions were enlarged, and it is a version of this
enlarged rule for men that circulated in the eleventh century
as the Rule of St. Augustine and changed the face of the
monastic world. It prospered for three reasons: the prestige of
Augustine's name; for its combination of spiritual fervor, practical sense and vagueness, which allowed a pile of useful customs to be attached to it and several quite different ways of life
to be based on it; and because it came in due course to seem

to its adherents that it was closer to the life of the apostles than Benedict's Rule. Let us observe at once, then, its utility to the modern student: A monk was one who followed Benedict, a canon one who followed Augustine. There were orders of monks not strictly Benedictine, but even the Carthusians had great respect for Benedict, and there were orders vowed to the Rule of St. Augustine who were not canons, notably the Dominican friars (see pp. 230–31). But it is a decent working definition, nonetheless.

The early propagandists for Augustine's rule had no idea of setting it up as a rival to Benedict's. Many of them were devout monks who saw the Rule of Augustine as a thoroughly practical instrument for gathering into a regular, orderly, celibate and devout life all the many clerics who were not and never would become monks. But the inspiration for the spread of St. Augustine's Rule came also from men who saw it as something more powerful than this; and as adherents grew in numbers, this point of view was likely to have spread. It seemed to many who meditated on the apostolic life that Jesus had laid emphasis in his instructions to his disciples on poverty, simplicity and practical good works; these three elements were emphasised, in varying proportions, by most monastic reformers of the late eleventh and early twelfth centuries. The Rule of St. Augustine seemed to its own adherents to allow more space for these qualities; the followers of St. Benedict strenuously denied it. No doubt Augustine left rather more scope for the development of good works, and this was observed as much by ardent Benedictines like St. Anselm—who clearly regarded the regular canons as a thoroughly useful second best in the religious life—as by reforming bishops not attached to a particular mode or order, anxious for practical help or for the means to reform their clergy.

If ever there was a time when monk and canon were distinct, it was in the canons' heyday in the early twelfth century. Augustine's Rule formed the basis of the way of life of canons regular, Austin or Augustinian and Premonstratensian, and also, later on, of the Dominican and Austin friars—and of other orders of more recent date. This gigantic feat of comprehension was due to the vagueness of Augustine's Rule. It is reminiscent of what Ronald Knox said of William Temple (after Dryden):

A man so broad, to some he seem'd to be
Not one, but all mankind in effigy.

Just at the point at which our definition appears to be most precise, it lets us down: The difference between the allegiance to Benedict and to Augustine is of great importance, but it tells us little of the way of life of the canon.[3] That depended on a whole body of customs added to the Rule. These were inspired by the papal reformers of the mid-eleventh century, who were monks and devotees of the regular life.

The Movement in Italy, France and Spain

To cure the irregularities of the secular clergy, Peter Damian and Hildebrand (Gregory VII; see pp. 89, 114) fostered a movement for the conversion of secular clerks into regular clerks, for putting the clergy under rules. Its first successes came in Italy, in Rome and Lucca and elsewhere. At Lucca, the link with the papal reformers was especially close in the time of Bishop Anselm, Pope Alexander II (1062–73); in the second half of the eleventh and early twelfth centuries a whole group of churches were given communities of regular canons, including the cathedral. The center of the movement, however, lay in the priory of San Frediano, whose growth and influence were encouraged by Alexander himself and by later popes. The present church, mostly of the twelfth century, is a remarkable monument to the relations of the world, the city and the canons of San Frediano; the large nave provided shelter for the Lucchesi, and the sumptuous font, presumably, baptism for their infants. Meanwhile, the movement was spreading fast into France and Spain, and north into Germany and England.

The most notable community in southern France was at Saint-Ruf on the outskirts of Avignon (later moved to Valence). It was founded as early as c. 1039, and in the second half of the eleventh century became the motherhouse of a group of communities following the Rule of St. Augustine and the customs of Saint-Ruf. The rays of its influence, and of the movement in general, spread very wide over Provence and the south of France and down into Spain. There in the early twelfth century began the conversion of the cathedrals of Toledo, Osma and one or two others to regular canons[4]; before the end of the century the canons of Osma were to include St. Dominic of Caleruega in their number. In the 1140s the abbot of Saint-Ruf was an Englishman called Nicholas Brakespeare, who became Pope Adrian IV in 1154 and two years later wrote to the bishop of Toledo commending the canons of Saint-Ruf to him. Thus the influence of the canons from Saint-Ruf in the abbey of Santa Leocadia came to supplement those of the canons in Toledo Cathedral.

Germany, Austria and the British Isles

After France, the most notable center of Augustinian canons lay in Bavaria and Austria, where their early development was inspired and controlled by St. Altmann, bishop of Passau (1065–91), in close union with the reformed papacy. Over fifty houses were founded or reformed in this area, the most influential of them Reichersberg, established between 1080 and 1084 in Altmann's diocese, though not directly under his influence; for it was one of an increasing number directly under the archbishop of Salzburg. Here in the early and mid-twelfth century lived one of the notable writers of twelfth–century Germany, Gerhoh, author of many treatises on theology and the relations of church and state, of clerical and lay society.

Altmann himself suffered for his support of the pope against the emperor in the dispute between Henry IV and Gregory VII; many of the houses were centers of papal influence. The canons indeed were in touch with almost every spiritual movement of the age: Several houses grew from hermitages or were linked with hermits; many were in towns and served parishes; several canons appeared as archdeacons in the diocese of Salzburg. The variety of their activities mirrored many fashions of the age, and their life and inspiration could be as varied as that of the monks.

The same was in due course true over much of western Christendom. Many of the earlier houses of canons were founded by converting old churches or colleges of canons; these included a number of cathedrals, stretching from Cefalù in Sicily, via Spoleto and Arles,[5] on to Sées in Normandy and Carlisle on the northern frontier of England. All these lay in towns, as did the first great English houses, St. Botolph's outside the city gate at Colchester, and Holy Trinity within Aldgate in the City of London. Holy Trinity was founded by Queen Matilda, in 1107 or 1108; she was the chief patron of the order in the British Isles in early days, inspiring in due course her brother, King David I of Scotland, a connoisseur of every religious order of the age (see pp. 271–72), and her husband, Henry I (1100–35), whom she taught to be a benefactor to the religious, and especially to the Augustinians, whose houses rapidly increased in his reign. By 1135 there were about sixty-five in England, over a hundred by 1154, when their grandson Henry II became king.

Many of these foundations lay in towns; but in the British Isles, as in Germany, the Augustinian foundations reflected a wide range of inspiration. No house could have had a site more remote than Llanthony in the south of Wales, under the Black Mountain. One of its founders was a hermit, the other a former royal clerk, and when Matilda and Henry offered him rich endowments, he refused them, for he wished his house to be poor and hidden from the world. In due course its poverty, and Welsh raids, forced his successors to search for new pastures. They founded a sister house in Gloucester, Llanthony Secunda, which became a notable town house and a center of learning with a fine library. But Llanthony Prima still remains a monument of Augustinian seclusion.

Many early houses were endowed with churches and expected to serve them. Soon after Toledo was conquered from the Muslims in 1085, the cathedral was restored and the nucleus of a community formed under Cluniac inspiration and perhaps partly of Cluniac monks. Not much later, however, it acquired a chapter of canons regular, and from 1156 Adrian IV's initiative in founding the abbey of Santa Leocadia with canons from Saint-Ruf made Toledo a center of Augustinian influence. In a similar way, shortly before 1100, the earl of Northampton gathered almost all the churches of that town to form the endowment of the Cluniac priory of St. Andrew. When his neighbor the earl of Leicester undertook a similar merger of the parish churches of Leicester into a religious foundation in 1143, it was for the Augustinian canons.

All manner of considerations may affect a founder: efficacy of prayers, a contemplative ideal, friendship with a group of monks or canons. Many Augustinian houses were formed in close association with hospitals, to serve all the various needs of the poor, sick and aged. The earls were clearly influenced by a wish to see effective pastoral care in the growing towns, but they were also doubtless glad to find a comparatively cheap form of endowment. The conversion of a large church into an Augustinian abbey or priory and its endowment with churches simply concentrated resources that were of no use to a secular lord, and an Augustinian house could be founded on a modest scale. By such means, and by putting pressure on lesser men, Henry I came to be called the founder of numerous houses.[6] It is evident that the patrons and canons whom we have met in recent paragraphs were following a fashion and knew what they were at. It is natural for us to suppose that this was always the case. Surely, we may think, the founders of the twelfth century understood these distinctions, however obscure they may be to us. For reasons that we shall discuss, it is doubtful if this was always (or perhaps commonly) true of founders of houses of nuns. For monks and canons, yes, one must concede that the founder knew what he was doing, up to a point. The proviso is important. Some founders were deeply involved and committed; but not all were so sure of the difference between one type of religion and another.

The founders of the tenth and early eleventh centuries were kings, princes, great nobles or bishops. A lofty status and great wealth were needed—and influence over lesser men who were expected to contribute lavishly but not to call themselves

founders. Nor was there any great range of choice: Down to
the mid–eleventh century it had to be a Benedictine house, of
monks or nuns, founded, refounded or dependent on another
house. But by 1100 already, and even more by 1150, the range
of choice had become bewilderingly great. Nor was it confined
to the rich. Poor men might found little cells or band together
to found a larger house.

Distinguishing between Monks and Canons: The Canon of Liège

In the 1120s, or soon after, a treatise called the *Libellus de
diversis ordinibus* ("On the Different Orders") was written by a
regular canon in the diocese of Liège, where canons regular
already flourished in great profusion at that date.[7] It is an
attempt to distinguish between the various orders of monks
and canons—not so much a guidebook for would-be postulants or patrons, as an olive branch, an attempt to quieten the
storm of controversy among the various orders as to which was
the most apostolic by suggesting that one and all had their
places in the sun and their justification in the Testaments Old
and New. It is cool, liberal and lucid; no one who has read it
can imagine that the difference between monk and canon was
necessarily of great significance.[8]

The author's intention was to show that all the species of
monks and canons were within God's providence, and it
never occurred to him that there was a profound or esoteric
difference between Benedictine and Augustinian or Premonstratensian. To him, there were two types of religious communities, those that dwelt remote from man's habitations and
those that lived in towns, surrounded by the secular world. He
has something too to say about hermits (whom he much

admires but treats quite briefly), and of the difference between monks and canons, and between canons regular and secular. The heart of his message is that those who dwell far from men are often more austere, more heroic in their prayers and their fasting, but that those who live in cities can combine contemplation with good works and practical influence. He simply takes it for granted that they engage in pastoral work and fructify the life of the city in quite a direct and practical way, and he makes little difference between monks and canons regular in this respect. If it had been widely read, which is unlikely, it might hardly have helped a doubtful founder to choose; but it would have brought comfort to any who had chosen, whatever his decision.

What is clear at once to the modern reader is that the good canon of Liège does not use the word "order" in the normal modern sense. To him it is a mode, a norm of regular life, not an institution. Today a religious order has a rule, often supplemented by customs and regulations: a unitary system of authority; a single head. In this sense there were no orders in 1120. By 1150 or so the Cistercian and Premonstratensian Orders were in full swing; early in the thirteenth century they were joined by the first orders of friars. But large Benedictine houses were by definition independent at this date, and even Cluny's dependencies formed an order only in a loose sense; they were all subject to the single head, but beyond that had no constitution and no separate rule.[9]

It is equally evident that the distinction between monks and canons that seemed so lucid to Peter Damian and Anselm was becoming rapidly less distinct. In due course canons ceased, over large areas of Europe, to serve churches and engage in pastoral work; they became more monastic.

Chaucer

Monks, canons and friars: We think we know the differences among these three types of men; or do we? May we not
honestly confess, whether we are novices or veterans of the
subject, that we have often been bemused by the distinctions?
If so, we may take comfort from the thought that our medieval
predecessors were equally confused.

Let us take Chaucer to witness. His monk is evidently a
Benedictine, in some sense of the term, for he refers at the out-
set to the Rule of St. Maurus, Benedict's companion, and to St.
Benedict (Benet or Beneit) himself.

> The rule of Saint Maure or of Saint Beneit,
> Because that it was old and some-del streit,
> This ilke monk let olde thinges pace,
> And held after the newe world the space.[10]

He thought nothing—not a "pulled hen"—of the saying
that hunters were not holy men, and he conducted the cell of
which he had charge as a hunting lodge. He thought equally
little of the text that likened to a fish out of water a monk out
of cloister: He thought it not worth an oyster. "And I said; his
opinion was good"—why sweat and toil, with a book, or with
his hands,

> As Austin bid? How shall the world be served?
> Let Austin have his swink to him reserved.

What is Austin doing here—St. Augustine, lord of the
Augustinian canons and of many other orders that did not follow St. Benet (Benedict) or St. Maurus? Many indignant critics have pointed out that he could not have been both monk

and canon; and that, in a strict sense, Chaucer himself knew as well as anyone. He made the figures of the Prologue to the *Canterbury Tales* so exceedingly precise and lifelike that the temptation to identify them with living characters was irresistible. The game still continues, and some scholars have delighted to claim that this or that of the pilgrims was based on so-and-so. Yet a moment's reflection should surely reveal to us that the irony and satire of the Prologue collapses if it is taken simply as a collection of portraits. It is the union of individual and type, so that the reader is kept on a knife's edge between saying—"of course this is only one individual" and saying "of course, this is what monks were like"—that makes the Prologue still such delectable reading. By the simple trick of making it ambiguous whether the monk was indeed a monk or a canon regular, Chaucer gives him a hint of universality. It is indeed possible that this had also the effect of helping to remind his readers of one of the great huntsmen of the day, William Clown, abbot of Leicester, an Augustinian.[11] But essentially he is surely enjoying an ambiguity that no modern student would dare to use: to confuse monk, canon and friar now is to commit a howler.

If we ask the question, what was the difference between a monk and a canon regular?—the final answer we should give, if we are honest with ourselves and with the evidence, is: "I do not know."

9.

The Cistercians

Cîteaux, Clairvaux and St. Bernard

Cîteaux was founded in 1097 or 1098 by one of the restless aspiring wanderers of the eleventh century.[1] St. Robert had been a leader among one of the amorphous groups of hermits of the late eleventh century from which several new orders sprang; in the forest of Colan, St. Bruno, founder of the Carthusians, had studied under his direction. Then Robert moved off to found the abbey of Molesme in accordance with the ascetic principles developing in his mind. After some years Molesme seemed to him too well established and becoming set in its ways, and he moved on with a group of his monks to found yet another new monastery, which later was given the name *Cistercium,* Cîteaux. The monks of Molesme complained that he had gone without their leave; the benefactors of Molesme complained that they had lost the prayers they had provided for. Robert was forced to return, and the new community seemed to be struggling for life. It contained some notable talent and monks of strong conviction, but it is doubtful if it would ever have made much mark on the history of the religious orders but for the intervention of Bernard of Clairvaux.

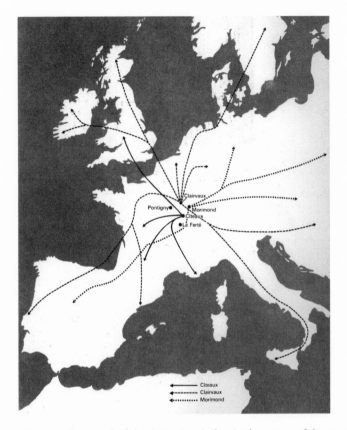

Map showing the spread of the Cistercian Order. At the center of the map lie Cîteaux and her four eldest daughters, La Ferté, Pontigny, Clairvaux and Morimond (founded 1115). It was from Cîteaux herself, from St. Bernard's Clairvaux, and from Morimond that the greatest number of daughter houses sprang. The arrows give some idea of the direction of the order's growth.

St. Bernard was born in the Burgundian village of Fontaine-lès-Dijon in or about 1090, one of the younger members of the large family of a landowner of moderate resources. Among Bernard's exceptional gifts was a power to influence people, not just by eloquence, nor just by force of character or moral strength, but by a combination of these qualities with a sense of urgency and spiritual adventure that proved almost irresistible. One greater than Bernard had observed that a prophet is not without honor save in his own home and among his own kin, and the most striking mark of Bernard's gift is that when he came to Cîteaux he brought almost all his brothers with him. Their arrival doubled the community and transformed its prospects. He had one year as a novice and two years as a simple monk, then was sent out to be abbot of Cîteaux's third daughter, Clairvaux, and an abbot he remained till his death in 1153. An abbot, and more than an abbot, for in due course not only did his fellow-monks at Clairvaux and his colleagues in the Cistercian chapter enjoy his eloquence, but he was heard by bishops and cardinals and kings and popes. Bernard felt called to help settle the schism in the papacy in 1130 and had no hesitation in making his intention plain to the hardheaded and difficult monarchs of England and France; he also allowed himself to be summoned to the preaching of the Second Crusade. He saw a disciple elected to the papacy in the person of Eugenius III (1145–53) and wrote an open letter to him—*De consideratione*—instructing him on how pope and curia should conduct themselves. No man insisted with more vehemence than he that a monk's place was in the cloister. If monks and canons ceased to do pastoral work in the second quarter of the twelfth century, if orthodox preachers disappeared behind the walls of monasteries, if every new religious order had something of Cîteaux stamped upon it, that was in a measure due to the extraordinary influence of Bernard. Yet he himself was never in his cloister for very long at one time. He preached stability but was in practice a wanderer.

In his early years at Cîteaux, Bernard was a disciple of the English abbot, Stephen Harding, whose clear head and kindly nature formed a vital contrast to the tempestuous, ruthless Bernard, and perhaps taught Bernard that charity which he nearly always showed even to those whom he had at first severely trounced.[2] Stephen had been a monk of Sherborne in Dorset, and it seems that he set off in the 1090s in search of a house more austere, yet he always retained an affectionate and grateful memory for his former home. One of the most attractive of the early Cistercian documents is the letter Stephen wrote to Sherborne between 1122 and 1134 expressing his humble gratitude and asking for the community's prayers:[3] It is an extraordinary contrast to the strident tones of Bernard's denunciation of the traditional monasticism, written at much the same time. Quite as striking, and as attractive, are the gay and humorous initials in the early Cistercian manuscripts painted under Stephen's eye.

Stephen's chief monument is the *Carta Caritatis,* the Charter of Divine Love, the constitutional foundation of the order,[4] a succinct and simple statement of the basic arrangements of the Cistercian life. In recent years it has been shown that some provisions, especially those for the general chapter or parliament of the abbots of the order, are a later addition to it, that some reflect the order's growth and Bernard's heyday. But the basis probably remains a genuine product of the era of Stephen Harding. In different ways and different measure, the charter, the initials and the letters of St. Bernard reveal a vision of spiritual adventure, and in the order's buildings we find it, in some ways strongly and unexpectedly, translated into stone.

The Cistercian Program: Choir Monks and Lay Brothers

The Cistercians were dedicated first and foremost to the Rule of St. Benedict, literally interpreted. They accepted from

the traditional monasticism a monastic plan and a way of life
essentially communal; they pruned the liturgy, but it remained a
major part of their life. They accepted from the hermit tradition
that prayer and spiritual reading should have a larger place in the
daily round and the raison d'être of a community than could be
squeezed out of the customs of Cluny; they inherited something of the ferocious asceticism of the Italian hermits. Above
all, their early leaders were exceedingly well educated and had
grasped the basic principle of the intellectual revival of their
day—to study ancient texts as fresh and living books composed
for their benefit. They took the Rule off the shelf and read it as
if it had just been written; they tried to forget the accretion of
customs that had gathered round it elsewhere, and to follow
Benedict to the letter. They found too, in his epilogue, a call and
a challenge to something beyond the routine of the common
life. They read the Old Testament and the New, as Benedict had
instructed them. St. Bernard frequently imitated an Old
Testament prophet denouncing the world about him as literally
as he imitated St. Benedict; he also reckoned that he and his
monks were walking in the path of the apostles, as did every
monastic leader of the day. Above all, the Cistercian leaders
found in the writings of Cassian and other early fathers the
most advanced and sophisticated literature on prayer and on the
individual's approach to God that then existed. Bernard has a
major place in the history of mysticism, but hardly a very original place. He absorbed the doctrine of the fathers of the desert,
infused it with a mystical theology derived from the Latin
fathers, especially from St. Augustine and St. Gregory the Great,
and laid it out in his immaculate prose to inspire and edify his
monks. What was new here was not the idea of contemplation
or of the mystical life, but that they should be offered to large

numbers of monks as an attainable ideal. In the full sense of the word the Cistercians produced few mystics,[5] but they produced a multitude that no man can number of monks who tried to live a life with spiritual aspiration at its center. That is the first mark of their originality.

They followed St. Benedict *ad litteram*; they were extremely austere; they pursued an ideal based on the personal pursuit of perfection. They aimed too at seclusion and self-sufficiency; they were the puritans of the Catholic Church in the twelfth century, and they developed a new kind of organization aimed to keep a measure of uniformity undreamed hitherto in a spiritual empire so diffuse and scattered. The puritanism and the constitution were written into the order's early statutes and directly reflected the personality of Bernard. But their supreme document is the order's surviving buildings, which reflect almost every aspect of the Cistercian adventure.

The buildings were designed to house two kinds of monks; choir monks and lay brothers. In the *Book of Life* of the New Minster at Winchester, one can see already, in a Benedictine house of the tenth and eleventh centuries, that a high proportion of monks ended as priests and almost all the rest as deacons. By the twelfth century advancement to the priesthood was becoming normal (see pp. 106–7). At the same time the practice of daily celebration by every priest was also on the way—though far from general, and even further from being a rule. These changes had two notable consequences. First of all, ever more lavish provision of altars to accommodate these private masses was needed. The Cistercians from the first placed several chapels in their transepts and, doubtless, altars elsewhere.[6] But the plain, blunt east end gave no space for more than the main altar.

The other consequence, likewise, was a general feature of the monastic movements of the eleventh century shown at its most complete and most highly organized in the Cistercian Order: the growth of a class of monks not suited for or aimed at the priestly calling, the lay brothers. One notable attraction of the Cistercian movement was that the doors were open to men from every walk of life. In theory this was already true of many communities and groups of houses in the eleventh century; the Cistercians, however, gave it an enormous extension. Already before Cîteaux was founded, the word *conversus*, the convert or converse, which had formerly meant any grown man turned monk (see p. 107), came to have also the special significance of a layman turned monk: a man who (in theory, if not always in practice) was illiterate and would always remain so—age or temperament having rendered him impervious to book learning and the cane. There has been much argument as to where and when the *conversi* first appeared; at the end of the day we cannot be sure, nor does it matter. The idea grew out of the religious climate of the eleventh century, out of the demand for wider opportunities and a richer variety of experience. In the group of houses reformed, with the aid of Cluniac customs, by the abbot and monks of Hirsau in south Germany in the late eleventh century, it was the practice to incorporate in a semimonastic garb laymen living away from the abbey who administered its estates, a characteristic arrangement in the heyday of monastic offerings and involvement in the world. But more commonly the *conversi* everywhere were monks exempt from learning, who took a greater share of the manual work of the community in return for having a lesser share in the *opus Dei*.

Seclusion, Self-Sufficiency and Manual Work

It was the lay brothers who enabled the early Cistercian communities to be self-supporting, to be separate islands cut off from the world. The Cistercians were inspired by the vision of self-contained houses of monks cut off from the world described in the Rule of St Benedict, and by their knowledge of the way of life of the monks of the desert—the ultimate inspiration of medieval monasticism. So they sought "desert places," by which they meant peaceful and secluded homes, not dry and sandy wastes. On the contrary, they had a very practical idea of the basic needs of a community living on its own: a narrow valley with ample water supply and a river to carry away their refuse—and, ideally, ample pasture land nearby for their sheep. They could not always hope for an ideal situation, but they could be very determined in pursuit of secluded and serviceable homes, even to the point of moving house if need be—or moving other settlers out of the way. The Cistercian dedication to the Rule of St. Benedict naturally involved them in manual work. They expected, for instance, to grow their own corn and to produce their own clothes. The Benedictines had traditionally bought their own cloth ready woven and dyed black. The Cistercians reckoned to rear their sheep, and spin and weave the cloth for their habits from the undyed wool, which at first seems to have turned out brown or grey when they had finished it, but was later somewhat bleached to make them "the white monks." In point of fact St. Benedict himself seems to have assumed that agriculture was mainly—though not exclusively—the work of lay peasantry, and that manual work normally meant the chores of the enclosure: washing up, sweeping and gardening, and a few simple crafts. The Cistercian lay brothers were farmers, shepherds and masons; they were also millers, fullers, weavers and what-have-you. The rapid development in the twelfth century in the use of mills for purposes other than grinding corn owed much to them. The noise of the mill wheels echoes through the description of the rebuilding of Clairvaux in St. Bernard's first *Life*. The author described how the monks and hired craftsmen worked together to rebuild the abbey of Clairvaux after it had been moved to a more ample site; how some of them "divided the river, set it in new channels and lifted the leaping waters to the mill-wheels; fullers and bakers and tanners and smiths and other artificers prepared suitable machines for their tasks, that the river might flow fast and do good wherever it was needed in every building, flowing freely in underground conduits; the streams performed suitable tasks in every office and cleansed the abbey and at length returned to the main course and restored to the river what it had lost,"[7]—no doubt with interest. Anyone who has closely inspected a Cistercian site where conduits and drains can still be traced knows how ample and how carefully planned the plumbing was; and the mill-wheels emphasize the technological skills involved. Nothing so elaborate had been seen in Christian Europe since Roman times. The extreme simplicity and austerity of their life and their efficiency in all these crafts, and especially in rearing sheep, enabled the Cistercians to amass wealth in early days, which helped their benefactors to pay for their tremendous building programmes, and tempted kings and princes to mulct them.[8] As the generations passed, recruitment became less varied and gradually fell off. After the Black Death in the mid–fourteenth century, the recruitment of lay brothers ceased, and the Cistercians finally melted into the monastic landscape.

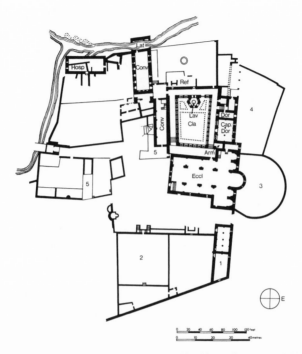

Plan of Le Thoronet, to show the medieval buildings, begun c. 1146 when the abbey was moved from Tourtour, and mostly of the late twelfth and early thirteenth centuries. 1. Tithe barn. 2. Vineyard. 3. Cemetery. 4. Garden. 5. Later buildings.

Of the place of the lay brothers in early days, Le Thoronet in Provence and Buildwas Abbey in Shropshire tell us as much as any documents; in particular they reveal the careful segregation of choir monks and lay brothers. Buildwas, like the houses in Provence, is an impressive monument to the determination of the Cistercians in early days to see that adequate, convenient and commodious buildings were provided. It was always a small house and gives a good idea of what the order thought fitting for a community never expected to grow larger than a dozen to twenty choir monks and perhaps up to forty or fifty lay brothers. Few benefactors providing for the needs of a

community of less than a hundred souls in the opulent societies of the twenty-first century would conceive of building on
this lavish scale today. It is odd to reflect that this was thought
appropriate for a group of men called to an extremely harsh,
severe, ascetic, cold and silent way of life—cold in a physical
sense, that is, in the Shropshire winter, for there must have been
warmth of another kind to bring recruits flocking to these
houses in their early days. However that may be, Buildwas is a
large house for a small community, and as the community
never grew larger than originally expected, its arrangements

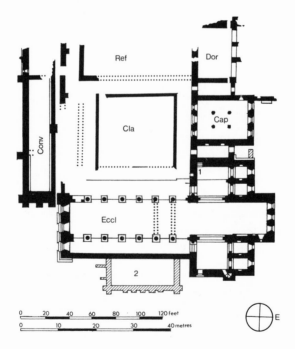

Plan of Buildwas. It lies to the south of the River Severn, hence the church
is on the south, the cloister on the north. 1. Night stair. 2. Chapel added c.
1400, probably for lay parishioners. The rest of the buildings are twelfth to
thirteenth century.

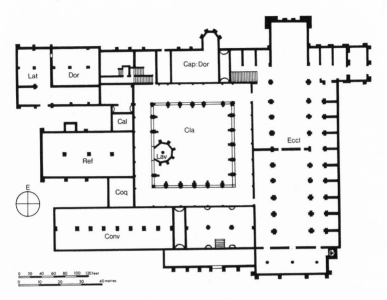

Plan of Maulbronn.

were never altered. The lie of the land at Buildwas affected and exaggerated one peculiar feature of the plan: the original separation, commonly lost by later expansion and rebuilding in the late twelfth century, of western range from cloister. At Buildwas this is still clear. The lay brothers' quarters start at a lower level than the cloister and some feet away; they form a separate block, narrow, owing to the way the land lies, but unusually high, three storeys in all. Within the church there are striking roughnesses on the piers of the nave, which can only be due to some arrangement for linking the piers to the screens and primitive furnishings of the church in early days.[9]

At Maulbronn in Germany there still survives, though heavily restored, the screen that separated the main choir from the choir of the lay brothers—that is, in the church of any other community, the nave. The choir and crossing were allotted to the choir monks for their masses and offices; then came a screen, at Buildwas approximately six feet high, at Maulbronn somewhat higher, separating off the nave, which was the lay brothers' choir. They attended mass and their simpler round of offices within the nave, in a box west of the screen, enclosed on both sides by wainscoting (at Buildwas) approximately five feet high. This separation continued outside the church. At Le Thoronet and Silvacane, also in Provence, substantial remains can be seen of the lay brothers' buildings; and in particular, at Le Thoronet, the separate door by which they entered the church. At Buildwas the lie of the land dictated a building entirely separated from the cloister.

Puritanism and Efficiency

Reflected in the Cistercian miniatures of c. 1100 is a gaiety such as one might expect in a young community clambering up the ladder to heaven. Artistic flair and a love of nature seem to have lived at Cîteaux before Bernard, and in an odd way he fostered them. Odd, because he was an extreme puritan who succeeded in ignoring everything in the world that he regarded as inessential, including the physical setting provided by nature and by man. As a novice, we are told, he spent a year in a chamber at Cîteaux and had no idea at the end what sort of ceiling it had. In later years he rode for a day by the Lake of Geneva and claimed not to have known the lake was near. This could reflect a nature indifferent to physical things, but it is possible that the opposite was true. There is no doubt that he thought ornament of any kind in a church a distraction. He makes this abundantly clear in his attack on rival orders, and there is copious literary evidence that his puritanism was of an extreme kind, and one of his own contributions to the Cistercian customs. It may have been partly due to a temperament naturally sensitive to his environment, and there was one striking flaw in it. Bernard's Latin prose is among the most ornate and rhetorical of the century. It shows us that he was an artist.[10] But Cistercian architecture reveals with abundant clarity that the ruthless enforcement of puritan values all over Europe—or at least among the daughter houses of Clairvaux, for there came to be more variety elsewhere—involved an obsession with this basic notion, that ornament and striking proportions distract. Abbot Suger, in a famous phrase, claimed to see the divine light reflected in jewels and glowing ornaments. To Bernard they distracted, and it is natural to see in the relative uniformity of the Cistercian idiom a reflection of this doctrine.

There is nothing in Bernard's writings to suggest that he was himself an architect. The Cistercian documents occasionally tell us, when a new foundation was in the making, that this or that monk of Clairvaux, often a close companion, sometimes a brother of Bernard, was responsible for establishing the order or customs of the Cistercians here or there. This has sometimes been taken to mean that these eminent choir monks directed the planning of the buildings. Everything about Cistercian buildings of the mid– and late twelfth century, however, suggests the professional hand of trained masons. At first sight, we seem to be faced with a paradox. The quality of the work is often extremely good, and they seem to have relied on first-rate masons. Local varieties of style show that the work was often executed by local craftsmen. The documents tell us from time to time that monks and local layfolk lent a hand, and there is no reason to doubt the truth of this, but key building work, the uniform plan and idiom were the work of experts. This can only mean that the Cistercians had their own team of expert masons, presumably lay brothers, who traveled with the

senior choir monks and instructed the local masons who executed the work. There is, indeed, an occasional hint of this in
the documents, and it is not in itself at all surprising. Thousands
of laymen of every walk of life were recruited as lay brothers;
it is characteristic of the tremendous success of Cîteaux, and of
the rhythm of monastic movements in general, that a wide
range of talent and craft should be recruited in early days.

There are indeed grounds more positive than those already
displayed for discerning Bernard's influence behind the work
of the lay craftsmen. The developed plan and idiom were not
formed in a day: they were hammered out in the 1120s and
1130s; like the constitution of the order, they were the products of experience and thought.[11] One of its marked features
was the shallow, square east end to the church; it has long been
noticed that this is more commonly to be found in daughter
houses of Clairvaux than in other branches of the Cistercian
tree. In 1953 a remarkable chart of the eastern limbs of all
churches built for Clairvaux's daughters in the twelfth century,
whose shape is known, was published by K. H. Esser.[12] This
suggests that the shallow square east end was a feature of all the
known churches down to Bernard's death in 1153, and of a
large number built throughout the century. It also shows that
after 1153 there could be variety, that there were indeed a number of apses, that even Bernard's own Clairvaux acquired an apse
when he was securely dead. (In 2002 we must enter two caveats:
square east ends were by no means rare in *non*-Cistercian
churches, and the precise nature and dating of many of the plans
is not wholly secure.) To a man like Bernard a large apse could
represent the essence of contemporary traditional Benedictine
fashion: a semicircle of alluring light and color—or dark mysterious painting—that provided a frame for a glistening altar and

Saint-Martin-du-Canigou, France:
The main church looking east, eleventh century

Sant'Ambrogio, Milan: The atrium of the eleventh/twelfth centuries, from which can be seen the monks' tower on the right, ninth century, and the canons' tower on the left, finished in 1144. (All that we see had to undergo elaborate restoration after bombardment in 1943.)

Assisi, Italy: Looking down from the east

perhaps a glorious shrine, the essence of distraction. In a Cistercian church a plain wooden altar sat in front of a plain stone wall, with windows round to let in the light so that the priest and the sacrament could be seen. No doubt variety would have come in any case; what is most surprising is that so great a degree of uniformity seems to have been preserved so long. No doubt one must not insist too precisely on the coincidence of dates. Yet when all is said and done the outbreak of apses is eloquent testimony to the urges Bernard had held in check; a remarkable example of the space that lies between the written record and the documents in stone.

Uniformity, Architecture and the Cistercian Constitution

Everything we have seen so far might suggest a degree of uniformity of a somewhat heartless kind; there is something, at first sight, impersonal about it. Yet this cannot be our final impression. First of all, it reveals a measure of communication somewhat surprising in an age when news traveled at the speed of a galloping horse at best, often by sailing boat, pack horse and mule. It reveals the cosmopolitan culture of the twelfth-century renaissance, the possibility of communication in a clerical world that was Latin-speaking; above all, the nature of Cistercian organization. When the order began to grow beyond the number of a few houses, it devised a constitutional structure that made it (in fact if not in name) the first order in the modern sense. In the twelfth century every abbot of the order was expected to visit Cîteaux every year for general chapter, and (when the constitution was fully integrated) every abbey was visited in theory by the abbot of its motherhouse. At the moment when he performed this duty, the abbot of the motherhouse was a "visitor" with supreme power in the daughter community. Nor was the abbot of Cîteaux himself exempt from surveillance, for the abbots of his four eldest daughters came annually to Cîteaux to act as a committee of "visitors" (see p. 11). The general chapter was the supreme governing body of the order, under the pope, and it passed constitutions that the abbot could report to his community and the visitor (if necessary) enforce. Negatively, there are stories of visitors presiding over the demolition of new building works not according to the rules. In the late twelfth and early thirteenth centuries this uniformity broke down: there are signs of a breach even sooner. The breakdown in control over style and plan coincided with the breakdown of the annual chapter. It became increasingly difficult for all the abbots to gather every year. Compromises were tried, with local meetings and triennial general chapters, but the unity of the first two generations was never revived. For it represented more than any formal machinery could provide; the abbots were drawn to Cîteaux as to the gate of heaven, by a zeal that defies analysis, and the call to chapter and the energy with which the program was inspired and enforced in every corner of Europe would strongly suggest, even if we knew nothing of Bernard, a tremendously powerful personal influence in the center. He represents in the religious world of the twelfth century what St. Francis was to represent in the thirteenth, the cult of personality, the living saint whose individual characteristics and eccentricities molded an order and more than an order.

The constitution and the buildings clearly in a measure reflect Bernard's personality. This is not to say that he personally devised them, which is improbable: He inspired the men who fashioned a parliament suited to his eloquence and buildings suited to his principles and tastes. Nor is the uniformity of a mechanical character, like the military architecture or the town planning of the Romans. What is strikingly reminiscent of the Romans is the universal insistence on high standards of building. This is illustrated in Cistercian remains in every part of Europe. Whether baked by the sunlight of central Italy at Fossanova, or the Catalonian plain at Poblet, or in the duller northern climates of Maulbronn, Eberbach or Buildwas, the standard of workmanship is always high and, even more striking, it is as much sustained for small houses as for large.

The visitor to Sénanque is quickly reminded that he is in Provence. The abbey is splendidly sited in a steep, narrow valley,

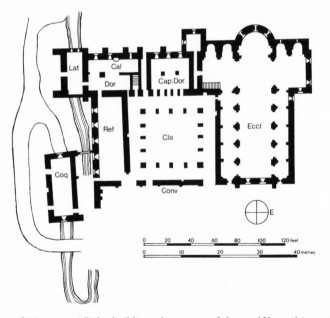

Plan of Sénanque. All the buildings shown are of the twelfth to thirteenth centuries; the modern buildings replacing the lay brothers' quarters, and those beyond the dormitory, have been omitted. The identification of the kitchen is doubtful.

at one of the few points where this little cleft in the hills is broad enough to permit the laying out of a Cistercian complex—thus far an ideal Cistercian situation, such as one might find in any land. But the scenery is Provençal, and so is the water supply; and it is not at all clear how the Cistercians faced the challenge.[13] Within the monastic buildings the first impression is of peace, plainness and practical good sense. The pattern of the cloister is repeated elsewhere in Provence—with three arches under a single head, repeated four times to make twelve openings on each walk of the cloister, representing perhaps the twelve apostles and their more recent imitators, the twelve monks who set out to found any new Cistercian house. A simplified pattern may be found at Silvacane and Le Thoronet, the Cistercian neighbors of Sénanque. These cloisters are at once Provençal and Cistercian. Similarly with the church: The plain cross, the aisled nave, the transepts with their chapels all reflect the normal Cistercian plan, but the apses at Sénanque and Le Thoronet and the cupola over the crossing at Sénanque are of Provence. Far from Bernard, affiliated to Mazan and Cîteaux, not to Clairvaux, they felt no need to seek the plain square end of Bernard's Clairvaux, such as one may see, however, at Silvacane. The proportions are plain, and the comparatively squat effect of most early Cistercian churches is faithfully reproduced, in marked contrast to the great height of many Provençal Romanesque churches. Thus, once again, the monks of Sénanque lived in Provence and in Cîteaux too.

The chapter houses give a similar impression. A risqué note is struck by a twisted column at Silvacane; otherwise they are almost identical, and the shape and height, and the form of the vaulting differ very little from the northern houses, Fountains, or, particularly, Buildwas. Round a square room that feels like a cellar were set stone steps on which the community could sit[14]; the whole is surmounted by a low ribvault resting on piers in the middle of the chapter house. It seems designed for common meditation—suitable for monks who spent the greater part of their lives in silence, but a surprising setting for the flow of eloquence of Bernard's sermons. The chapter house was the only part of the Cistercian design that seems now confined, even mean. Other types of community adapted the plan to suit an awkward site; the Cistercians were determined to make the site suit the plan. Even for a small community of choir monks like that at Buildwas, it was felt necessary that they should be able to walk out of the transept of the church, up a flight of steps straight into the dormitory—and along the floor of a dormitory large enough for separate mattresses for every choir monk the community might have in the foreseeable future, that is (as they envisaged it) until the day of judgment. It had to be possible for a monk returning from the night office, with only rudimentary lighting or no light at all, to walk up the night stairs and along a level floor. In Benedictine houses he went (most commonly) from church to cloister and up the stairs from the cloister; but the Cistercians in all things planned the most convenient arrangement they could devise consistent with extreme austerity. Thus the whole plan of this walk of the cloister at Buildwas is modified to keep the floor of the dormitory level. The night stairs go to only half their usual height, into a dormitory not much above ground level. This makes the chapter house more cryptlike than ever. But beyond it the land falls away, so that presently the dormitory is farther from the ground than usual, and at its extremity it was built so high in the air that even the parlor underneath it was raised on stilts.

The difficulties of the site at Buildwas and the problem of water supply at Sénanque were somehow overcome. But it is easy to see why in many cases the early Cistercians became dissatisfied with their sites and moved. Sometimes it was the small and struggling houses that wandered, like Kingswood in Gloucestershire, which moved four times in its first thirty years. Sometimes it was the very large houses that found they needed more ample sites, as happened to Clairvaux herself in the 1130s.

Rievaulx and St. Ailred

It is rare, even among the Cistercians, for a well-preserved site to be richly documented. Bernard's Clairvaux has disappeared; and even if the church that grew on its site immediately after his death can be studied in a faithful copy at Alcobaça, we are nonetheless somewhat remote from the building described in Bernard's *Life*. To fit the written and material evidence together, Rievaulx remains the inescapable choice, and it has the added attraction of a great abbot deeply influenced by, yet in some ways quite independent of, Bernard.

The setting of Rievaulx today is very much as it appeared to the first recruits, a group of English monks who were sent by Bernard from Clairvaux in 1131–32.[15]

> They set up their huts near Helmsley, the central manor of their protector, Walter Espec, a very notable man and one of the leading barons of King Henry I. The spot was by a powerful stream called the Rie in a broad valley stretching on either side. The name of their little settlement and of the place where it lies was derived from the name of the stream and the valley, *Rievallis*,

Rievaulx. High hills surround the valley, encircling it like a crown. These are clothed by trees of various sorts and maintain in pleasant retreats the privacy of the vale, providing for the monks a kind of second paradise of wooded delight. From the loftiest rocks the waters wind and tumble down to the valley below, and as they make their hasty way through the lesser passages and narrower beds and spread themselves in wider rills, they give out a gentle murmur of soft sound and join together in the sweet notes of a delicious melody. And when the branches of lovely trees rustle and sing together and the leaves flutter gently to the earth, the happy listener is filled increasingly with a glad jubilee of harmonious sound, as so many things conspire together in such a sweet consent, in music whose every diverse note is equal to the rest. His ears drink in the feast prepared for them, and are satisfied.

"Such was the story—and a true story"—that was told to a young steward of the king of Scots called Ailred, who happened to be visiting the archbishop of York about three years after the first settlement there. He was told more, for the Cistercians were still unfamiliar even in the court of King David I of Scotland, soon to be their greatest patron in Britain. They were white monks, their habits being made

…from the pure fleece of the sheep. So named and garbed and gathered together like flocks of sea-gulls, they shine as they walk with the whiteness of snow. They venerate poverty…are welded together by…firm bands of charity.…Trampling the flowers of the world with the foot of forgetfulness, counting riches and

honours as dung, beating with the fist of conscience on
the faces of mutable things, spurning fleshly desires and
vain glory in food [and drink]. If they sup, the remnants
of their former meal are dished up again, except that,
instead of the two cooked dishes, fresh vegetables, if
they are to be had, are served. When they rest on their
beds, each of them lies alone and girdled, in habit and
tunic in winter and summer. They have no personal
property; they do not even talk together; no one takes
a step towards anything of his own will. Everything
they do is at the motion of the prelate's nod and they
are turned aside by a like direction. At table, in procession, at communion and in other liturgical observances,
all of them, small and great, young and old, wise and
ignorant are subject to one law. Personal standing is
merged in the equality of each and all, there is no
inequitable mark of exception....The only test of
worth is the recognition of the best....Women, hawks
and dogs, except those ready barkers used to drive away
thieves from houses, do not enter the gates of their
monastery. By their exceeding love they stifle among
them the bane of impatience, and every growth of
anger and the smoky emanations of pride.[16]

The enthusiasm of this account of the early Cistercians can
still communicate to us the message that inspired Ailred's biographer, Walter Daniel, as it had inspired Ailred himself. It helps
us to understand how in one generation the small community
at Cîteaux had come to spread all over Europe, and to count
many hundreds of houses and many thousands of monks in its
allegiance.

The special emphasis on the beauty of the scene clearly answered something in Ailred's mind and in his friend's, and can leave no doubt that for some Cistercians this beauty was accepted without puritanical qualms as part of the joy of life in a Cistercian solitude. The passage also shows that the life itself was hard, and as is here implied, uniform, disciplined and monotonous well beyond the Benedictine norm.

What is abnormal about Rievaulx is the spirit of Ailred, visible in some traces from his time of the scale of the place. The chapter house is large and spacious; it allows for much more communication, monastic conference—sermon and discussion—than most. It lacks the central pillars common in Cistercian chapter houses; in plan and scale it closely resembles that at Durham Cathedral priory, where Ailred's father had spent his last years. It suited the eloquence and expansive goodwill of Ailred; for in his later years Rievaulx held the largest community in England, perhaps, after Bernard's own Clairvaux, in the order, with 140 choir monks and 500 lay brothers.[17] The exceptional numbers at Rievaulx were due to Ailred's deliberate act of charity in opening the gates. Bernard, his master, had savaged the abbot of Cluny because the vocation of recruits there was inadequately tested and there was even at times no novitiate. That the Cistercians themselves put any close check on the quality of their recruits in this period of rapid expansion is hard to believe; it was evidently not so at Rievaulx.

> He turned the house of Rievaulx into a stronghold for the sustaining of the weak, the nourishment of the strong and whole.…Who was there, however despised and rejected, who did not find in it a place of rest?…And so those wanderers in the world to whom

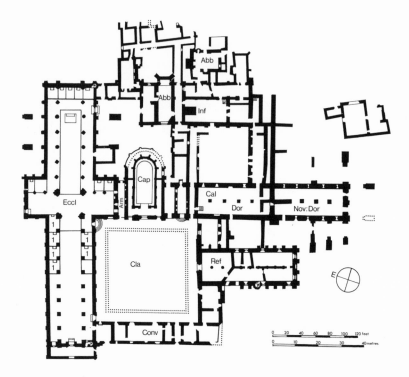

Plan of Rievaulx. The buildings are still mainly twelfth century, the chief exceptions being the thirteenth-century refectory and choir, which is today the dominant feature of the church and is in fine mid-thirteenth century English Gothic. In the fifteenth century there was much remodeling, especially of the infirmary, abbot's lodging and chapter house, which was shortened, though the shape given it by Ailred in the mid–twelfth century can still be discerned. At the end of the dormitory farthest from the church the ground falls away: hence the flying buttresses whose foundations are shown in the plan. 1, 1 etc. Chapels partitioned off (see p. 310, chap. 9, n. 6).

no house of religion gave entrance, came to Rievaulx, the mother of mercy, and found the gates open....If one of them in later days had taken it upon himself to reprove in angry commotion some silly behaviour, Ailred would say, "Do not, brother, do not kill the soul for which Christ died, do not drive away our glory from this house. Remember that…it is the singular and supreme glory of the house of Rievaulx that above all else it teaches tolerance of the infirm and compassion with others in their necessities."

And so we can understand how Ailred came to double

…all things in it—monks, *conversi* [lay brothers], laymen [servants], farms, lands and every kind of equipment; indeed he trebled the intensity of the monastic life and its charity. On feast days you might see the church crowded with the brethren like bees in a hive, unable to move forward because of the multitude, clustered together, rather, and compacted into one angelical body.[18]

The Adventure and Its Victims

The spiritual adventure of the Cistercians was inspired by Bernard in a very obvious and direct way. For all his wanderings he could not be personally known to the greater part of his confrères; no doubt to most of them Cîteaux or Clairvaux was known first and foremost as a way of life. Yet even strangers met Bernard in his writings. This was one secret of his immense influence. There were times in his life when his many illnesses and intense physical suffering made him physically repulsive to those who lived with him—he even had to live in a separate hut at Clairvaux for a time. But for the most part his presence was effective and compelling; it is said that when he preached the Second Crusade in Germany his audience was more moved by his own sermon in French than by the same sermon repeated by the interpreter in German. Yet he lives now, and always lived for most of his fellow monks, in the written word. At every point in this story we have seen links between the austere Cistercians and the far-from-austere movement we call the twelfth-century renaissance. Here it is at its most striking. Every trick of Latin rhetoric was known to Bernard: the capacity for self-expression, for revealing his emotions, which is characteristic of what we call the "humanism" of the twelfth century, was preeminently his (see pp. 143 ff.). He used his mastery of Latin for various purposes: to comfort those in sorrow, to help monks whose spiritual lives had shriveled, to settle a dispute, to keep in touch with friends; but also to trounce an enemy of the church (as he saw it), to destroy Peter Abelard. We cannot readily forgive him for the persecutions he mounted, owing (as we are bound to think) to his giving undue credit to his own divine inspiration. But every historian must be grateful that he devised, or perfected, a mode of communication that we can still understand today.

No doubt he communicates more directly with the modern scholar than with many of his own day and order. The lay brothers were (in principle at least) illiterate, and segregated from the choir monks; so far as we know, they had little or no opportunity to hear Bernard's letters read, nor would most of them have understood his Latin. In other respects the Cistercians were egalitarian; in this they chose and maintained a rigid class distinction. Nor was this the only way in which the delectable adventure revealed in Bernard's and Ailred's writings hid a harsher reality. The empire they built so rapidly was won at a cost; villages were moved out of their way, peasant holdings dismembered, small proprietors eased from their inheritance. Many early Cistercians were ambitious and arrogant; sometimes their arrogance took a spiritual form and opened them to the charge of being Pharisees; sometimes material, and their enemies charged them with acquiring land and riches by force and fraud. No doubt the picture can be painted unduly black: Some of their victims received compensation (we have little idea how many); others invented or enlarged their wrongs. Cistercian remains enforce the lesson that the order grew swiftly large and prosperous, and this was not done without large movements of men and property. In such a process some will suffer and many will nurse a grievance. The claim that the kingdom of heaven is advanced thereby is little consolation to those who suffer. Yet within the order, and among its friends, Bernard and his colleagues spread a message of charity and joy.

In his letters he tried to make his audience feel that he was present in person; his tone is by turns friendly and intimate to one of his monks, stately and respectful to a king, a waterfall or torrent to the cardinals if they are slow in condemning the church's enemies.[19] His informal conferences in the chapter house at Clairvaux were revised so that they could be circulated and read in all the chapter houses of the order and outside the order too. Cluny in its heyday had stood for a grand communal life, represented by vast liturgies and huge processions, amid the splendor of light and color and magnificent architecture. Cîteaux provided a framework of common life and work in which above all the monk as a person could find his way to God, with all distractions stripped away. Some human emotions are trounced and excluded. But human friendship, the love of man for man, was a feeling that for Bernard reflected God's love. When his brother Gerard died, Bernard was heartbroken, and uttered a famous lament in one of his sermons on the Song of Songs; then let it pass from

house to house for choir monks everywhere to meditate in the
dim half-light of their chapter houses on his message:

> Rather would I have risked my life, Gerard, than lose
> your presence—who zealously roused my studies in the
> Lord, a faithful helper, shrewd examiner. Why, I ask,
> have we loved, have we lost one another?[20]

And so down the ladder into the vale of misery; then up
again, up the steep slope that leads from human friendship to
the love of God, and to a triumph of life over death whose
echoes still linger in every surviving Cistercian building of the
twelfth century and help to give these buildings an eloquence
equal to the eloquence of St. Bernard of Clairvaux.

The Knights

The Cistercian adventure was a genuine expression of the religious ideas and ideals of the late eleventh and early twelfth centuries, but it was only one example of the ways in which monastic ideals spread into every corner of life in that age. The rapid pace of change and the spread of new ideas led to a deep and searching malaise as to the true function of the religious life, and in the process some strange excrescences appeared on the monastic mansion.

In 1099 Jerusalem was captured, at the dénouement of the First Crusade. This notable success (from the Christian point of view) enhanced the popularity of the pilgrimage to the Holy Land, but only slightly diminished its dangers. To protect the pilgrims and provide them with shelter, groups of pious folk of a practical turn of mind were formed early in the twelfth century. Some of these groups gradually became more military, as the need for defense became more apparent, and also more monastic, as they fell under the spell of other religious orders of the day, especially of Bernard and the Cistercians. In 1118 the first house of Templars was formed in Jerusalem, and in 1128 the Knights Templars took counsel with Bernard and accepted a rule that had many Cistercian features. Much more slowly, the guardians of the Hospital of St. John of Jerusalem, who had in origin been hardly distinguishable from canons regular, came also to have castles in their hands, and ultimately, under their grand masters Raymond du Puy and his successors in the mid– and late twelfth century, to develop military symptoms. In the second half of the twelfth century they grew into the Order of Knights Hospitallers, and by 1200 the two orders had closely similar functions and consisted of professional knights, supported by chaplains, sergeants, peaceful brothers and teams of servants—but now essentially military in function.

Their way of life retained a strong monastic and ascetic base. Full members of both orders took vows of personal poverty, obedience and chastity; and when not on campaign they were expected to attend the monastic hours as well as to engage in private prayer—150 daily Pater Nosters was the special fare of the Hospitallers. In the west they lived in small communities, called commanderies or preceptories, each with a chaplain or a group of chaplains, provided by the order. As with the Cistercians, the majority of knights were lay brothers; but unlike their Cistercian colleagues, the lay knights gave the orders their raison d'être. We know little of their daily life in western Europe, but a monastic routine, varied by military exercises and a large amount of estate management, seems to have been its core. The more military they became, the more they were involved in the social distinctions of their world. The knight was becoming an increasingly expensive, socially distinct type of cavalry officer in the late twelfth and thirteenth centuries, and so there developed class distinctions within the orders. Among the Hospitallers the brothers knight, by the mid–thirteenth century, had to be recruited from the knightly class; lesser warriors were brothers sergeant; peaceful hospital

brothers and the like were brothers at service. Round the
orders gathered a large penumbra of friends, benefactors and
lay supporters, similar to the third orders, the Tertiaries, among
the friars (see chapter 12).

In Spain and Portugal the Templars and Hospitallers were
only two among a number of military orders: They included
the large Order of Santiago and half a dozen other congregations, smaller but by no means negligible.[1] Spain, like the Latin
kingdom of Jerusalem, lay on the frontiers of Islam, and the farther south one went, the more one passed into the frontier
lands, the more military the religious life became. In the Latin
kingdom, in the late twelfth century, Templars and Hospitallers
came to have increasingly similar functions; even the Hospitallers spent more of their resources and energy in warfare and on
their castles than on their hospitals. As the two orders grew
more alike, so an intense rivalry developed, and it proved
extremely difficult to prevent them from fighting one another
rather than the supposed enemies of Christendom.

In the twelfth century, the kings of almost every kingdom
of western Christendom and a multitude of noblemen as well
were sooner or later called on to lead contingents to the
defense or reconquest of the Holy Land, or to some other crusading enterprise against the perceived enemies of Christianity.
Many went, but many more searched eagerly round for any
possible excuse not to go. A vast number commuted their call
or their vow for a gift in money or kind. This created a very
interesting challenge to the economic techniques of the age. A
rich German or Englishman might commute his vow for cash;
one not quite so rich—or rich in land but not in silver—
might wish to give an acre or two, or a manor or two, toward
the good work. It was hard enough to transport the silver

thousands of miles to the eastern Mediterranean to pay for the crusading effort; how to transport the acres was a pretty problem indeed. Thus modern banking was born; for the Templars and Hospitallers set about gathering resources in the west and disbursing them in the east on a scale unprecedented in the history of medieval Christendom.

The first site of the Templars in London lay in Holborn. But they rapidly grew so rich and the inmates so numerous that they needed more space in a more salubrious quarter. By 1185 their removal to an ample riverside enclosure, which has been known ever since as the Temple, was accomplished; and the greater part of the present circular nave of their church had been built. The Latin patriarch of Jerusalem, visiting England in a desperate attempt to stir Henry II's conscience and recruit for the Third Crusade, was present at the consecration of their church and of the Hospitallers'. For the folk of London, the great round churches of Hospitallers and Templars provided an opportunity to worship in the gates of Jerusalem without leaving London. But they were also reminders, symbols of the earthly Jerusalem; to put the matter bluntly, they advertised the pilgrimage and the crusade. Henry II himself had no intention of going on crusade—that could be left to his more romantic, gadabout son, Richard I—but he was compelled to be generous in his benefactions and was thus duly impressed by the skill of the Templars in handling money and keeping it safe. The result was that he made the London Temple one of his principal treasure-houses, and it passes the wit of man to decide where in the Templar movement treasure on earth ended and treasure in heaven began.

In the end, their wealth was the Templars' undoing. The quarrels among the orders of knights undermined their prestige, especially when first Jerusalem fell (1187), then Acre (1291), in spite of (or as some thought because of) their efforts. Early in the fourteenth century Philip IV, the Fair (1285–1314), a king of France almost as greedy and egocentric as the English Henry VIII two centuries later, urged on the pope their many crimes real and imaginary, and other kings cashed in. The result was the suppression of the order. Much of their property went to the Hospitallers, much to the royal patrons of the "Process." Today the Temple Church is a splendid chapel for the lawyers who live and work around it. But the tombs attributed to William Marshal, earl of Pembroke, the knight errant who rose to be regent of England (1216–19), and his clan—none of them Templars, but all of them closely involved with the order—remind us that the Temple once enshrined an ideal that could inspire men of heroic stature and that played a part in English government.

The most popular of the pilgrim centers in western Europe were Rome and Santiago de Compostela; and on the roads that led to Compostela, from all parts of France across the north of Spain, lay a whole series of shrines themselves of great prestige. One route began in Tours, where was buried one of the patron saints of France, the fourth-century soldier turned monk and bishop, St. Martin; another from Vézelay, believed to hold the shrine of St. Mary Magdalene; a third, from Le Puy, passed by the church of Sainte Foy (St. Faith) at Conques; a fourth led from Arles through Saint-Gilles (St. Giles) at the mouth of the Rhone. It is no coincidence that great Romanesque churches at Tours (no longer extant), Vézelay, Conques and Saint-Gilles were among the most splendid and the most influential in the architectural history of the central Middle Ages.

But here and there about western Europe were churches, large and small, that were reminders of the greatest of all earthly pilgrimages. For modest churches of the Templars like the ones at Tomar in Portugal and at Laon in France, as well as the Temple Church in London, were directly imitated from the Church of the Holy Sepulchre in Jerusalem. Churches with circular, octagonal or hexagonal naves were built in different parts of Europe at different periods, especially in central and eastern Europe, where rotundas are or were relatively numerous.[2] Most of these were probably based, at one or two removes, on the palatine chapel of Charlemagne at Aachen. In the twelfth century a new fashion arose, based on the Church of the Holy Sepulchre, and disseminated mainly by the Templars—mainly, but not exclusively—for in England only half of the known examples from the twelfth century were Templar in origin. The Hospitallers built one in Clerkenwell, London, and one at least elsewhere. One or two were secular or attached to hospitals, and the earliest of all, the round church in Cambridge, was probably built for the ephemeral order of Augustinian Canons of the Holy Sepulchre.[3] Thus were the elements of several religious movements interwoven: crusading zeal, the love of pilgrimage, Cistercian austerity and the practical activities of canons regular and other founders of hospitals. The Temple Church in London is at once the monument of a local fashion and one of the most cosmopolitan buildings in Western Europe.

11.

On Abbesses and Prioresses

To the Eleventh Century

"A woman must be a learner, listening quietly and with due submission. I do not permit a woman to be a teacher, nor must woman domineer over man; she should be quiet." Thus thought the elders of the early church, as represented by the First Epistle to Timothy (2:11–12). Nonetheless, they allowed elderly widows to take special vows to lead an austere and ascetic life; to the young ones—with surprising abandon—they recommended that they marry as often as they wish. The group of elderly respectable widows became in time, especially in the circle of ladies harassed, harrowed and inspired by St. Jerome (see p. 37) in the late fourth century, one of the primary institutions of early monasticism. St. Augustine probably wrote a rule for such ladies, and St. Cesarius of Arles in the sixth century provided the community in his own city with another.[1] Yet in the long run, patrons or founders of monasteries in the early Middle Ages tended to neglect the nuns, so that by the mid–eleventh century there were four monasteries for men in England to every one for women, and in France the disproportion was probably even greater.[2]

There were exceptions. In seventh- and eighth-century England, for example, a succession of princesses of strong

character and powerful aversion to marriage provided a principal impulse in the monastic life. Such were Hilda, great-niece
of King Edwin of Northumbria, who presided over the famous
abbey of women and men at Whitby in the mid– and late seventh century, and Werburga, daughter of King Wulfhere of
Mercia and presiding abbess over a group of Mercian convents
a century later, which were in their turn ruled by abbesses
younger or less eminent in birth and sanctity than Werburga
herself. At much the same date as Hilda, an Anglo-Saxon slave
in France called Balthild had risen by character and charm to
be first a queen and then an abbess. These instances reflect a
society in England, and in a measure too in the Frankish kingdoms, in which women could hold their own and achieve a
status rare in the central Middle Ages. It also bespoke a society
in which it was fashionable for aristocratic ladies to take to the
religious life. In the tenth and eleventh centuries we have to
look to Germany for an interest in convents and nuns at all
comparable. The various monastic documents issued in
816–17[3] included a rule for canonesses. Houses of both nuns
and canonesses flourished in Germany in the centuries that
followed. The Saxon dynasty looked with favor on these
houses, and so did its daughters: Matilda, daughter of Otto the
Great, was abbess of Quedlinburg, where her father died (973)
and is buried. In the next generation, Otto II's daughter
Adelaide was abbess of Quedlinburg, Gernrode, Vreden and
Gandersheim; nor did the line end with her.[4] Among this
group, Matilda's cousin and namesake, Matilda abbess of Essen
(from before 974 to 1011) has left us the most remarkable
memorials of any abbess of the age. She was descended from
both the German and the English royal lines. She was a granddaughter of the Emperor Otto the Great, who sent her to

Essen with a dowry consisting of one of her own estates, and of his English wife, Edith, sister of King Athelstan. She was sufficiently interested in her English ancestors to write to a distant cousin in England demanding some account of them; the reply took the form of a Latin translation of the Anglo-Saxon Chronicle made by the same relative, the Ealdorman Æthelweard. She was also the patroness of fine craftsmen, and the collection of crosses, the tiny crown and other rich ornaments that still adorn the treasury of Essen Cathedral (as it now is) are the most perfect collection of the age to survive. Matilda was one of a line of aristocratic princesses who presided over Essen in its golden age and who won protection and patronage from local nobles and from the emperors, as well as admiration from the local bishops, so that the convent prospered spiritually as well as temporally. As we should expect, high patronage flowed to the aid of these great ladies, and in Germany nuns were by no means as neglected as in France and England.

Even in Germany far greater funds and estates were at the disposal of the men. Yet in France and England neither patrons nor princesses altogether ignored the convents of nuns. The Princess Christina, sister of Edgar the Atheling and of St. Margaret of Scotland, and so a member of the Old English royal line, presided over a school for young English princesses at Romsey and Wilton, and attempted to keep them safe from the lust of the Normans. One Norman princess meanwhile was dedicated at birth to the abbey at Caen which her mother, Queen Matilda, had founded, and grew up to find herself abbess; her sister Adela became in due course dowager countess of Blois and a nun at the Cluniac priory of Marcigny.

Marcigny was a very significant phenomenon of its age.[5] The abbots of Cluny of the eleventh century, like most of the

great monastic organizers of the eleventh and twelfth centuries, were averse to nuns, arguing that they distracted monks
from their proper tasks and lay difficulties and temptations at
their gates. Such men set their faces sternly against the double
monastery, though a few survived and a few more were
founded; small communities of nuns attached to male houses
were by no means rare.[6] The holy and importunate widow
could not be held indefinitely at bay, especially if she were rich
and strong of will. Such a lady sometimes set up house in a
male community and became a mother to the community as
did Eve Crispin at Bec in St. Anselm's time. Marcigny was
established by St. Hugh, abbot of Cluny, in 1055, to provide a
home for his mother and sister and a group of like-minded
persons. His biographer notes his success in converting women
from the world—"not an easy task," he observes—but the nuns
of Marcigny were noted for a way of life more austere than was
general among their menfolk. Nonetheless, St. Hugh insisted
that it remain firmly under his own rule, although the Blessed
Virgin was elected perpetual abbess.

The comparatively small part played by women in some
countries in the religious movements of the eleventh and
twelfth centuries is puzzling, and the explanation is not fully
revealed to us (but see pp. 17–22). Clearly, it owed something
both to the prejudices of monastic reformers and to the patrons
who provided funds for new buildings and endowments for
monasteries. Endowments were provided as never before or
since, but chiefly by male patrons for men. No doubt this
reflects a society in which the reins of power were in men's
hands: In some sense, as we shall see, this was the heyday of
male dominance in medieval social history. Furthermore, if you
lavish a substantial part of a large patrimony on investment in

heavenly treasure, you must be sure that the treasure is of the best metal. None doubted that women could lead holy lives, but they could not sing mass, and there were a number of reasons, sensible and absurd, for supposing their prayers less efficacious than those of men. In Germany the monasteries played a crucial part in imperial administration, and their lands were the recruiting grounds of armies. Needless to say, the monks themselves were not expected to fight, but it could readily be assumed that it was normally more satisfactory to have male communities and male religious working with the lay "advocates" and recruiting officers. At the social level, furthermore, a man who was well enough off to imagine his children entering religion would certainly not be expecting to pay very substantial dowries for his daughters. The lavish endowment of a great house like that of Queen Matilda at Caen might be occasionally possible for a queen of exceptional wealth; her foundation was a part of the penance imposed by the church in its strictness for a marriage of doubtful legality. Most of the new houses of nuns of this age and the next struggled into existence on a very modest scale; often they were small and poor, little more than depositories for daughters with moderate dowries. Sometimes even the poor houses grew to considerable wealth if they were near great cities and the dowries and legacies fell thick upon them.[7] Sometimes they were the lineal descendants of great houses of the past and had a stately existence, like Essen. They were commonly served by chaplains from one order or another; and it sometimes happens that the documents fail to specify to what order the nuns themselves belonged.[8] The explanation may be that they obeyed the rules provided by their chaplains or followed the rites that they performed, and that these themselves varied from time to time when chaplains of one order were replaced by a group from another.

The chaplains were an essential feature of any house of nuns, since the sisters could not be in holy orders, and so could not perform the sacraments. In most houses there were a number of male officials and servants, besides the multitude of maidservants that attended any flock of well-to-to ladies. Even very poor houses must have had some menservants, to act as porters and guardians of the house, and there was usually a male steward to represent the nuns in business affairs and litigation. In court and counting house women were reckoned at a disadvantage, although there were doubtless plenty of women of shrewd business sense and ability in the Middle Ages as in every age.

The Twelfth and Thirteenth Centuries

In most parts of Europe, the nucleus of the convents consisted of ancient houses like Essen, some of which continued to flourish and prosper, especially if they preserved their noble connections. In the twelfth and thirteenth centuries they were joined by a much larger band of smaller houses. But every age saw one or more really notable exceptions.

No stranger exception could be found than that which appeared about the year 1100, in the Forest of Craon on the borders of Anjou and Touraine. Shakespeare in imagination peopled the Forest of Arden and Windsor Forest—or the Athenian Forest of *A Midsummer Night's Dream*—full of folk. When one reads of all the people who lived in the Forest of Craon at that time, one gets a similar impression. From the monks and hermits who settled there sprang no less than three quite different religious orders.

Robert of Arbrissel was born about 1047 in the diocese of Rennes. After a career as a student, archdeacon and schoolmaster, he found his true vocation and became a hermit and wandering preacher. This seems to us at first sight an odd combination, but we have met it already in Peter Damian and some of his Italian colleagues, and we shall meet it shortly in St. Francis. Robert was evidently a preacher of enormous impact. He helped Pope Urban II to preach the First Crusade, and he went on preaching tours till shortly before his death in 1117. But the major effort of his life went into organizing the groups of penitents who gathered round him from which sprang orders both of monks and nuns. Over one of these he presided himself for a time. Over another he set Vitalis de Mortain, another preacher turned hermit, and in one of the various groups was a preacher of almost equal eminence, Bernardus Grossus. Vitalis founded the abbey of Savigny in Normandy, Bernard that of Tiron in Le Perche, also in Northern France. Both were to grow into ascetic male communities very similar to Cîteaux in her early days; and Savigny, with her progeny, which included numerous English houses—Buildwas among them—was to merge with the Cistercian Order in 1147.

Robert of Arbrissel was dedicated, like so many of the reformers of the day, to the apostolic life, to the direct imitation of the apostles. In the Gospels he read how Our Lord from the cross had given St. John to the Blessed Virgin as to a mother, and Robert took this to mean that John and the other apostles were set (in some sense) under her authority. In 1096–99 he established a church and a community dedicated to the Blessed Virgin, and as her earthly representative he chose a lady of great piety and noble birth, Petronilla, widow of the baron of Chemillé. As time passed, the new monastery, which

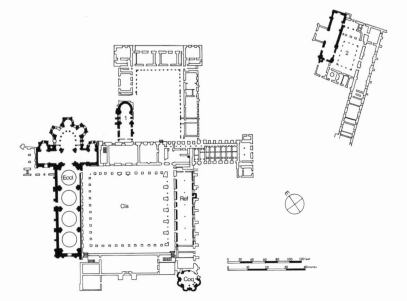

Plan of Fontevrault, with the twelfth-century buildings—church, kitchen, etc.—outlined in black; the rest are of the sixteenth and later centuries. 1. Chapel of St. Benedict. 2. Priory of St. Lazarus (S Lazare).

presently came to be called Fontevrault, became more highly organized, more feminine, more wealthy and, above all, more aristocratic. So strange is the reversal of the values of the world that placed earnest male ascetics under female control, that elaborate theories have been propounded linking it to the origin of courtly love, or of the Provençal lyric.[9] It is indeed a fact that the first of the troubadours, William IX, count of Poitou and duke of Aquitaine, was very friendly with Robert and that his granddaughter Eleanor, widow of Henry II of England and a celebrated figure in the courts of love, is buried there. Perhaps it is best simply to say that the devotion to the Blessed Virgin, so signally represented in Robert, and the popular concept of courtly love both reflected, in very different ways, fashionable reversals of the order of the world and that contemporaries saw as clearly as we do the analogy and the contradiction between them (see p. 21).

At Fontevrault the fine church, with its northern apse and its southern cupolas, still survives; in its transept, though heavily restored, is a row of royal tombs. Here are Queen Eleanor, her husband Henry II, her son, Richard I and a wooden effigy wrongly identified as Isabel of Angoulême, widow of King John. The first two tombs are the work of Eleanor, who brought here, after his death in 1189, the husband with whom she had so bitterly quarrelled; ten years later she laid her son beside him, raising tombs to both of them shortly before her own death in 1204.[10]

In the world of chivalry most literature was composed by men—though often in women's honor—and so we have comparatively little direct contact with the nuns of the Middle Ages.[11] It is possible that the inferior education offered to women at this date reduced the number of vocations. It was assumed that monks could read Latin, and nuns too, it seems, in the tenth century; but instructions for nuns in the twelfth and later centuries were commonly in the vernacular, like the famous *Ancren Riwle* and *Ancrene Wisse* for English anchoresses,[12] and the French inscriptions that appear in the illustrations to some of the most magnificent of twelfth-century psalters, such as those of Winchester and Shaftesbury—both of which were at Shaftesbury Abbey in the late Middle Ages. These seem to be due to the needs (real or supposed) of nuns for whom they were composed. To this there are striking exceptions.

The surviving letters of Heloise to Abelard were written in the 1130s, when she was abbess of the Paraclete, near the road from Paris to Troyes, a house on the way to becoming the center of a small order similar to Fontevrault. They are famous for

their intensely moving account of her relations with her former lover and husband, but the greater part of them is taken up
with the life of the nuns of the Paraclete. From their pages we
can conjure a vision of a remarkable personality, Abelard's
humble servant, yet as forthright, and masterful in her own way,
as he, and fully able to hold her own in intellectual debate with
the greatest master of logic of the age.[13] After she had spent her
passion in describing to Abelard how her love for him was as
intense as ever, she submitted to his will as her lord and master
and, as many a submissive wife has done, set him to work. She
asked for some account of the origin of the religious life for
women, and she demanded a rule. At this date, he was a very
unsuccessful abbot, while she was already a widely respected
abbess. She can hardly have been unaware that she knew more
about the monastic life than he did. Partly for this reason, no
doubt, she took the precaution of telling him what to say in his
rule: especially, that he was to make up for the deficiencies of
St. Benedict, who had written for men and took no account of
women's special needs in clothing and so forth, nor of their
physical weakness: "…who lays such burdens upon an ass as he
deems fitted for an elephant?" she asks. She sought for a retired
life, free from the inconvenience of having to entertain men,
who were dangerous company, and gossipy women of the
world, who were worse. Her demands were austere and practical, though occasionally eccentric. St. Benedict, she explains,
though a holy man and spiritual adviser, was occasionally silly:
Thus he refused to allow meat although everyone knows that
fish is often more luxurious and expensive than meat, and
allowed wine, which is dangerous stuff—"Wine and women
make the wise to fall away," she quotes from Ecclesiasticus
19:2—even if women can hold their wine better than men. In

later years, it seems, she became more conventional and rejected meat; meanwhile her letters reveal a brilliant mind critically at work on the role of nuns and their traditional manner of life.

Heloise was in every way an exceptional figure; and we shall not be surprised to find more evidence of an intellectual tradition among nuns in Germany. There a notable creative writer appeared in Hildegard, abbess of Bingen (1098–1179), poetess, philosopher and mystic; and at Saint-Odile in Alsace (then also in Germany) was composed the famous illustrated encyclopedia of Abbess Herrad, the *Garden of Delights*.

There is copious evidence, furthermore, of a strong demand for greater opportunities for women in the religious life in the twelfth and thirteenth centuries. Early in the twelfth, Norbert of Xanten found himself head of a mixed order centered in Prémontré (see pp. 217ff.), which was alleged in the middle of the century to include ten thousand women. Significantly, the canons who won control of the order soon put a stop to the recruitment of women, so that the female element presently withered away. Meanwhile, in the 1130s and 1140s, the English St. Gilbert of Sempringham succeeded in founding a double order, similar in conception to Norbert's and similarly influenced by the Cistercians, with the blessing of the hierarchy and of St. Bernard of Clairvaux. No doubt Bernard felt relieved that these importunate women should be managed in someone else's order. Yet his path was not altogether smooth; for in spite of repeated and plain refusals by the Cistercian general chapter to countenance nuns within the order, convents of Cistercian nuns began to spring up all over western Europe in the twelfth and thirteenth centuries, and even, in Spain, to rival the men in influence, and in Germany, greatly to outnumber the communities of men.

Here again is a puzzling but significant movement. The ladies of the twelfth and thirteenth centuries rebelled against their lack of opportunity. While the age of the twelfth-century renaissance saw the enrichment, in all manner of ways, of the choices and professions open to men, respectable women had to accept marriage to whomsoever their overlord or father chose, or hope for one of the scarce places in a convent (but see pp. 17–22). They expressed rebellion in ways carnal as well as spiritual; but their pursuit of a Cistercian vocation is one of the most characteristic of the age. Nonetheless, it remains puzzling. The abbesses of Las Huelgas near Burgos, for instance, were ladies after the fashion of the abbesses of Essen and Fontevrault. Queen Eleanor's daughter, Queen Eleanor of Castile, was one of their founders, and she lies there amid a galaxy of royal tombs. The abbesses insisted that they were Cistercian, and they insisted that they would not obey the general chapter at Cîteaux in which no woman sat.

The difficulties and frustrations—and ultimate success—of an intelligent girl who wished to find her own vocation as a nun are uniquely presented to us in the *Life of Christina of Markyate*, a contemporary of Heloise of the first half of the twelfth century.[14] She was the daughter of a well-to-do burgher of Huntingdon, near Cambridge, who felt the vocation to become a recluse. Such ladies and groups of ladies formed the spiritual nucleus of many of the new houses of the age, just as the citizens' dowries provided their temporal base. Christina won through to be foundress of Markyate Priory; and she inspired not only her remarkable biography, but the St. Albans Psalter, one of the notable works of art of the age. Her parents were decent and worthy people, but they thought it quite out of the question that Christina should choose for herself: Her vocation could only, in their eyes, be a childish fancy. The story of her struggle against her parents, of how she spent her wedding night converting her husband to her point of view, and of how, even so, she still had to face stiff opposition and the attempts of one of her spiritual advisers to seduce her, show quite starkly the difficulties encountered by young women who wished to choose their own way of life. One of the deepest of medieval prejudices was the view that women were incapable of conducting their own affairs and must be protected from the dangers and temptations of the world—or else they would themselves rapidly become part of those dangers and temptations. Even so original and imaginative a religious founder as Francis of Assisi accepted this view; not perhaps with complete consistency, for he allowed Jacoba of Settesoli to bring him marzipan as he lay dying, though women were not permitted in Franciscan convents. But "Brother" Jacoba was allowed to be an exception; the normal rule applied even to St. Clare herself, and so the Franciscan nuns were enclosed as strictly as any religious, in contrast to the male Franciscans whose function was to wander (see p. 227).

Yet the powerful urge to the religious life evident among the ladies who flocked to St. Norbert and among the nuns who sought to be Cistercian was not without influence. In the thirteenth century great numbers of new houses were founded, mostly Cistercian, especially in Germany and the Low Countries. Here they found a patron and helper in the abbot of Villers, the chief Cistercian house in what is now Belgium, who directed and encouraged the Cistercian nuns as they no doubt hoped and wished to be helped elsewhere too. The establishment of convents was only one segment in the religious movement for women of the age, which also witnessed

the formation of the informal groups of Beguines, ladies dedicated to a religious life but without any elaborate rule of permanent vows, who flourished first in Liège and Flanders, then
in Cologne and the Rhineland and ultimately throughout the
north of Europe in the thirteenth and fourteenth centuries.
Thus for the women, the thirteenth century saw the largest
number of new foundations, and worthy successors to Heloise
and Hildegard in St. Elizabeth of Schönau and the Blessed
Agnes of Bohemia. Yet the movement never had the same
impact in France and England as in Germany and the Low
Countries; in Spain, although a few houses, like Las Huelgas,
were large and influential, they were much less numerous.
Elsewhere, the glimpses we can obtain of the life of nuns in the
late Middle Ages suggest domestic comfort or discomfort
rather than any deep penetration of a religious movement
among women. Yet religion was not entirely cold in the fourteenth century—the age of St. Bridget of Sweden, founder of
the Bridgettines, and St. Catherine of Siena, recluse and hammer of the popes—and it was to enjoy a mighty revival in the
sixteenth, in the days of St. Teresa of Avila.

Lacock

In conclusion, to set beside Fontevrault and Essen, we have
chosen a small house that may be inspected as an example of
domestic comfort; a house of no great size, yet not poor; a
house not founded until the thirteenth century, whose buildings range in date over the late Middle Ages; a good setting,
that is, for one of the most famous of medieval nuns, Chaucer's
prioress. Of the history of Lacock we know little. It was
founded by Ela, countess of Salisbury, in 1232. She seems to
have wished it to be Cistercian, but in the event it became a

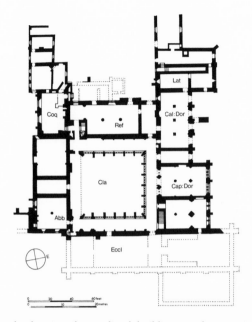

Plan of Lacock, showing the medieval buildings as they survive on the ground floor: later additions have been omitted.

community of Augustinian canonesses. It was moderately well endowed; it suffered no great scandals. It escaped the poverty into which some houses fell in the late Middle Ages through the drying up of dowries or by sheer mismanagement. The cloister was largely rebuilt in the fifteenth century, which reveals that there was still a flow of funds and that the nuns still lived and worked in the main monastic buildings. In 1535–36 there were still fifteen nuns—there had perhaps been twice that number in the thirteenth century—four chaplains, and nearly forty servants. At the Dissolution in 1539 the buildings were in such good order that they could be rapidly converted into the charming country house that still survives. Of the buildings of the 1230s only the chapter house and some other fragments of moderate size remain. But they are sufficient to show us how

closely the layout of convents of nuns was modeled on those
for men. The great difference was that nuns could not perform
the services themselves, were entirely dependent for mass (and
commonly for a part at least of their music) on the aid of male
chaplains, on the "nuns' priests" who had to be housed separately from the nuns. Chaucer's prioress, Madam Eglentyne, is
a striking contrast to Dame Petronilla of Fontevrault: a thoroughly worldly lady, imitating in a decorous and charming way
the life and standards of her secular counterparts. Yet we should
be wrong to make too much of this. She was no more worldly
than the monk, nor would the irony and the satire have its sting
unless Chaucer were setting her against an ideal and a practice
perfectly well known. We cannot tell whether the contemporary abbess of Lacock was more worldly or more spiritual than
Chaucer's prioress; all that we know for sure is that the abbess
lived in the world both of Chaucer and of St. Catherine and
St. Bridget; and that her life was led in the convent which we
can still inspect.

St. Norbert and St. Francis —the Premonstratensians and the Friars

Norbert of Xanten

The most original exponent of the apostolic life in the early twelfth century was St. Norbert of Xanten, and in the early thirteenth, St. Francis of Assisi. They were men, however, of very different achievement, and the contrast is exceedingly instructive. Norbert was a German, the son of the lord of Gennep (now in Belgium); his mother was related to the dukes of Lorraine and he, so it is said, to the Emperor Henry V himself. Certainly he was brought up as a courtier and went with the emperor to Rome in 1111, where he witnessed his master's kidnapping of Pope Paschal II. The events of 1111 made a deep impression on him, which was strengthened by what seemed a divine intervention some years later, when he was thrown from his horse during a thunderstorm. This led him to preach the apostolic life as he conceived it to the cathedral chapter of Xanten in Germany, north of Cologne, where he was a canon. The prophet was not well received among his own people, and he set off to Provence to call on the pope, Gelasius II, at

Saint-Gilles; Gelasius gave him a license to preach; his successor the next year set him under the direction of Bartholomew,
bishop of Laon. Thus was Norbert's career launched.

He was by instinct a preacher, a missionary rather than an
organizer. Bartholomew seems to be responsible for the idea of
forming the group of followers who gathered round Norbert
into a community, then into an order. In 1121 Norbert began
to take this vital step, and in that world a man did not lack good
advice as to how an order should be founded: Some recommended him to a hermit life, others to follow the path of
Cîteaux. Norbert was undoubtedly blown by every wind in the
religious life of the day, and this has caused much confusion
among his modern interpreters. The heart of the matter seems
to be that he wished to be free for practical good works, for
preaching and pastoral work, to lead the life of Martha, and also
wished to imitate the apostles in the most direct way, in poverty,
simplicity and preaching. Thus he preferred the Rule of St.
Augustine to the Rule of St. Benedict, because he regarded it as
more apostolic and more practical. Nonetheless, he knew
Bernard well and much admired him, and Cistercian influence
is evident at many points in the customs of Prémontré,
Norbert's foundation, and of the Premonstratensian Order.
Norbert, meanwhile, had not been forgotten by his friends in
Germany, and in 1126 he was invited to become archbishop of
Magdeburg, the natural center for missionary work and for new
fields of religious activity in twelfth-century Germany.

The translation of Norbert seems to have worked fortu-
nately for the young community at Prémontré. His canons
were left in the charge of men better equipped as legislators
and planners than Norbert, and they were free to develop the
young order as they chose, even though they traced a much

more definitely monastic pattern than Norbert seems to have intended, and in the long run his order of canons regular differed little from monks. Norbert himself, meanwhile, was able—rather briefly, since he died in 1134—to deploy his exceptional gift as a missionary and inspire missionaries in the area of eastern Germany and beyond where German settlers and Slavs met and mingled. His presence ensured that Premonstratensian canons and Cistercian monks played a leading part in German settlement in the east.

The Apostolic Life in the Twelfth and Thirteenth Centuries

It could be said that the most powerful evidence of St. Bernard's impact on the twelfth-century scene was a negative one. The most curious fact about the orders of the twelfth century is how very monastic they were: All save the knights settled down eventually within their cloisters. This is all the stranger because many of their founders were men of missionary urge. Thus Robert of Arbrissel remained a popular preacher to the end of his days, even when under the rule of the Blessed Virgin and the Abbess Petronilla. Indeed we may suppose that his promise to obey her had about as much effect as St. Francis's promise to obey the beasts of the field. But the point is that it was made.

It was natural enough that beside a cauldron in which so many new flavors of religion were cooking, there should be controversies both gentlemanly and bitter between the devotees of rival tastes. There were secular clerks who denounced all monkcraft and monks who replied in kind.[1] All manner of men interpreted and reinterpreted the apostolic life from which it was all supposed to come. For a long time, the free range of opinion on how the apostolic life should be imitated was checked by the prestige of the monastic vows. A place was found for laymen living in the world—and in the long run for groups of married penitents—within the spectrum of the religious life; but in the early twelfth century movements of this kind usually ended in some kind of orthodox monasticism—or else in heresy.[2]

After Bernard, the most inspiring figure in this world in the early twelfth century was Norbert of Xanten, and when he gathered penitents and clergy around him and set them to follow a way of life that was ascetic and apostolic, he himself clearly continued to feel a strong call to be a missionary. Yet the order that he founded soon became almost indistinguishable from the Cistercian. He was a personal friend of Bernard and deeply influenced by him; one cannot but think that the disciples of Norbert who converted his inspiration into institutional form were even more influenced by the Cistercians. It seems exceedingly paradoxical that Norbert, of all these founders the most devoted to practical ends, should have founded an order that became enclosed, austere and remote. Some of the German houses still show their relation to the extensive new settlements in Germany east of the Elbe characteristic of the *Drang nach Osten*—the Drive to the East—of the twelfth and the thirteenth centuries. The remoteness of a house like Blanchland, hiding in a little valley amid desolate moors just to the south of the border of Scotland, or the beauty of Dryburgh, a little to its north, perched in an angle of a great river, surrounded by splendid trees and water, tell us still that Norbert and Bernard were friends.

Yet in its own context all this is quite intelligible. Bernard preached stability, put down practical good works, built large

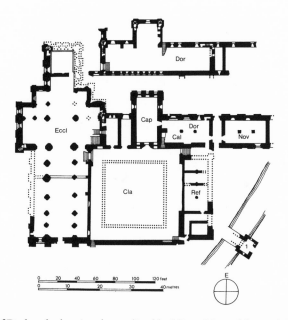

Plan of Dryburgh, showing the medieval buildings. Most of those which survive are twelfth to thirteenth centuries. The west end of the church and the gatehouse (1) are fifteenth.

walls round his enclosures and himself wandered about outside, answering almost every call to practical action that came. Norbert felt the austere authority of the Cistercian life and wished to follow it; the inspiration of the world in which he lived led him to Cîteaux and Clairvaux. He felt too, as an intellectual deeply read in the ancient and modern literature on the Christian life, that the rule of St. Augustine was more apostolic, more biblical, than St. Benedict's. Meditation on the life of the apostles led him to Augustine, to practical good works, to the mission field.

In spite of the prestige of Bernard and his ideal, the view that the apostolic life should still involve practical aid to ordinary Christian folk and missionary work within and without

Christendom retained its strength throughout the twelfth century. From time to time little groups of penitents or wanderers gathered into a community; poverty and good works were their aim, or else they wished to live mainly withdrawn from the world. There was much diversity. Many of them developed into communities of monks and canons; one—the followers of the English St. Gilbert of Sempringham, like Norbert, an admirer of St. Bernard this side idolatry[3]—formed an order of nuns and canons living in double houses though carefully segregated. As time went on and the world became richer, reaction against growing interest in material goods led to a sharper emphasis on poverty. The merchant of Lyon, Waldo, who reacted against his own desire for wealth and formed a community of poor preachers in the late 1170s, was at first accepted by the pope on condition of swearing, among other things, that he did not believe all the rich to be in hell. Presently he passed beyond the pope's ken and became the founder of the Waldensian Church; many of these groups became "heretics" in the mid– and late twelfth century. The consequence was that orthodox hierarchs—especially the group of stern Cistercian bishops whom the popes placed in and around Narbonne to reform the church and stave off heresy—regarded all such poor wanderers as potential heretics.

Thus was Christendom making ready for St. Francis or, rather, one is bound to say, staving off the time when he should come. The prestige of the cloister and the fear of heresy were both very powerful at the turn of the twelfth and thirteenth centuries. They go a fair way to explain why the friars started no earlier than they did—though some of these earlier groups were not heretical and were almost indistinguishable from the friars in their way of life.

Francis of Assisi

Like Norbert, Francis of Assisi found his way to his vocation by what he was convinced was a direct, personal call to follow the way of the apostles in poverty and simplicity, but he gave a new meaning to the same words and rejected the model of Cîteaux that had dominated the monastic scene in the twelfth century. The son of a rich merchant of Assisi, Francis spent his early life restlessly searching for a more satisfying medium than the counting house for his adventurous nature. First, he tried to become a knight in a band of condottieri; then he became involved in the petty warfare between rival cities, but a year in a Perugian prison convinced him of the difference between knightly adventure as it appeared in romantic fancy and the cruel reality of war. Gradually, in his early twenties, he came to realize that spiritual adventure was his vocation, and in 1209–10 he began to gather followers and to compose his Rule.

In 1210 Francis's Rule was given informal, verbal approval by Pope Innocent III, and the final revised version was enshrined in a papal bull issued by Innocent's successor, Honorius III, in 1223. Verbally, this final Rule was a very different document from that presented by Francis and his small band of followers in 1210. But the founder himself always maintained that it was in essence the same Rule, describing the manner of life that God himself had revealed to him at the outset. It had a monastic element: The friars were vowed to chastity, obedience and poverty, and lived in simple and humble versions of monastic convents. It had an apostolic element: The way of life was literally modeled on Jesus' instructions to the disciples, that they were to go out two by two and without money or inessential possessions: Thus the friars were dedicated to wandering and to a poverty more complete than any

monastic order had hitherto conceived. Those who were educated or specially fitted to the task were to preach. But Francis
always reckoned that his friars would be simple, humble folk
and mostly lay brothers, and the majority were not expected to
preach, but to work among the poor or with everyone they
met, and teach the Christian life by living it.

To Pope Innocent, Francis and his followers must have
seemed in 1210 much like several other bands of dedicated
wanderers who had come to ask his blessing. With the knowledge of hindsight we can see that they were the beginning of
a large movement that was to lead to the creation of the orders
of friars. By 1220 there were two orders, the Franciscan and
Dominican, the "Friars Minor" and the "Preachers," as their
founders labeled them; by 1226, when Francis died, both were
on the way to becoming large and flourishing institutions, and
later in the century other orders joined them. In the religious
life the thirteenth century was as much the age of the friars as
the twelfth of the monks and canons. But if we ask the question, What was original in Francis's message, what had he to
offer which no earlier order or group or founder had conceived?—we shall find it surprisingly difficult to answer.[4] The
monastic influence, the inspiration of the apostolic life, the urge
to poverty and simplicity: All can be paralleled in the twelfth
century, and especially in the informal groups that proliferated
as it turned into the thirteenth. The best we can say is that in
the early years of the thirteenth century the inspiration of
Francis was able to meet and be merged with a tide such as had
flowed in with the Cistercians a century before, and that he
enjoyed the benefit of a sympathetic papal Curia. Equally
important, perhaps, he was joined in his enterprise before a
decade was up by St. Dominic.

So much we can say with confidence, but as for the nature of Francis's inspiration, that will always escape definition. Let us say at once that he had a gift to influence men and women akin to Bernard's, the insight and skill of a born teacher, and that he made of poverty and obedience positive, exciting, even romantic qualities. He created and made respectable the idea of the friar: a humble kind of monk based in a convent but not bounded by its walls, a man living his life in the public eye and inspiring all men to follow his example.

Franciscan and Dominican Friars

The friars are not the primary subject of this book, but the monastic life of the twelfth and thirteenth centuries is unintelligible without them. For Francis (c. 1181–1226) and Dominic (c. 1171–1221) derived much of their inspiration from the monastic world in which they grew up and yet showed all the more clearly for that certain striking marks of originality.

Francis and Dominic were very unlike one another. Dominic, the Spaniard, grew up an earnest, conventional Augustinian canon with a strong urge to preach and an even stronger urge to obey his superiors. This led him to years of work in the most discouraging mission field of the day, among the Cathar heretics in the south of France. He formed a group of fellow workers in Toulouse; he took steps to have it recognized as an order. But in 1215 Pope Innocent III had presided over the Fourth Lateran Council and had been compelled to allow the fathers of the council to pass a decree forbidding new orders—or rather, as the clause was interpreted by the curial officials, new Rules. Ironically, this deflected Dominic hardly at all: He took the Rule of St. Augustine, to which he was already professed, as his base, and its alluring vagueness once more served a religious

movement well. But a much more powerful influence com-
pletely altered the whole frame of his intentions. He suddenly
abandoned Toulouse, turned his back on the heretics, spread his
order (all sixteen of them) throughout Christendom and began
to organize a missionary, peripatetic movement; in short, he
made them friars. I have little doubt that the bouleversement
was in a measure due to meeting St. Francis.[5]

The apostolic life had always grown from fresh meditation
on the Gospels, and it is no chance therefore that it should be
the direct imprint on his mind and imagination of a passage
from St. Matthew heard one morning in the Gospel at mass
that directed Francis's thought and life. "As you go proclaim the
message: 'The kingdom of Heaven is upon you....Give without charge. Provide no gold, silver or copper to fill your purse,
no pack for the road...; the worker earns his keep.'" He felt
called, as by God's direct inspiration—"...the Lord Himself
revealed to me" how to live and form an order of men living
and working in the world. Francis was naturally fastidious, he
had a dislike of beggars, a horror of lepers. He taught himself
to conquer this, but their lot remained one of the central facts
of his view of life. Why had the apostles been sent out poorly
dressed and even more poorly provided? On this question
learned men were to write many treatises in the thirteenth and
fourteenth centuries. To Francis it seemed obviously to answer
a fact of experience: To help the poor to find Christ's path in
their grim existence one must be as poor as they; only so could
one hope to show them by example that poverty was a holy
thing, even an exciting thing. He was a teacher of genius, yet
always reckoned example far in advance of precept: He
recruited all manner of different kinds of folk and expected
only a small minority to be able formally to preach. Example

was the basis of his way of life, and when called on to preach to the college of cardinals he danced a jig to show them how God's love should be conveyed. In the long run, indeed, he embraced every walk of life in his "religion": celibate friars formed the First Order, nuns strictly enclosed his Second—for even Francis could not countenance wandering women as a religious order (but see p. 20)—and married folk living according to a simple rule of life the Third Order, the Tertiaries.

The life of the friars itself showed an equally catholic appreciation of the traditions Francis had inherited. We can see this in the churches in Assisi in which he still lives: in the tiny chapel in the Portiuncula, so long as we can shut our eyes to the later church that surrounds it; in San Damiano without the walls; in the Carceri, high on the hillside above the town; and in his own shrine, the magnificent basilica that stands at the city's edge. St. Dominic's monument is in Bologna, but in quite a different sense. It stands in the city to which the ageing *déraciné* founder came to renew his own and his order's youth by recruiting among the university students. Bologna and Paris were his headquarters. Francis had originally spread his activity more widely than Dominic, and he accepted no frontiers. He himself traveled to Egypt to visit the sultan, and throughout Italy, visiting Rome on several occasions. But from time to time he came back to Assisi, which was always the center of his life, and they brought him to Assisi to die.

The Carceri is an enchanted place, where the Peter Damian of the fifteenth century, San Bernardino, founder of the Observant Franciscans, restored the ancient home of Francis and his closest companions. Their cells may still be seen and visited, each with a traditional attribution to one of the well-known names—Francis, Leo, Rufino and Masseo. "Those who wish to lead the religious life in hermitages," said the saint in one of his writings, "let them go in threes and fours at most. Let two of them be the mothers and have two sons or one at least each; let the former lead the life of Martha, the latter of Mary."⁶ This is most characteristic: first in expression, for everything Francis wrote was succinct, simple and yet subtle; second in its doctrine, since this most gregarious of religious founders loved and cultivated the hermit life as well. The spirit of the Italian anchorite movement lives at the Carceri, and one of Francis's strongest temptations was to stay there for good. He often felt the call to be Mary himself, and sit at Christ's feet, and never underestimated the value of this call in others. When considering what this or that friar should do, he always faced the problem as a human and personal one; not as an administrator planning a scheme of work, but as a spiritual director considering with sympathy and subtlety what was best for an individual soul. Looking back, it must seem to us now that he sometimes preached and practiced a sublime anarchy. He showed this attitude toward the administrator's lot by writing to one much bothered by the importunities of some of the friars: "…and show your love for them by *not* wishing them better Christians!"⁷ Yet Francis the spiritual adviser and hermit also felt a very powerful call to preach, and to prepare his friars to work in the towns of Umbria and the world.

And so we go down with him to the convent not far from the city gates, to San Damiano, where he lived in the early days of his conversion. It then became for a time the home of the nuns, of St. Clare and her early companions, but it still gives a living idea of the way of life of the early friars once the order began to grow. But what shall we say of the basilica? Here is a splendid building, made famous by the frescoes that encrust its walls. Many a devotee, from early days down to the present, has denounced its magnificence: a rich monument to the apostle of poverty is either a sublime paradox or a scandal.

> One day while St. Francis was lying ill at the bishop's palace at Assisi, one of the friars who was pious and saintly said to him joking and teasing: "For how much will you sell all your sackcloth to the Lord? Many rich brocades and silken cloths will be put on to cover this little body of yours which is now dressed in sackcloth." For St. Francis had at that time a leather bandage because of his illness, which was covered with sackcloth, and a habit of sackcloth. St. Francis replied, not himself, but the Holy Spirit through him, with great fervour of spirit and gladness: "You say true, for so it will be."[8]

But Francis's vision was of paradise, not of the Basilica of San Francesco.

When he was dying, the citizens of Assisi sent soldiers to guard him and bring him home, for they knew that when he died his body would become a collection of relics of infinite value and that all the cities of the neighborhood would try to seize him. So after his death they hid his body in the rock, in the lowest level of a tremendous church of three storeys, and they set about it a large convent, so that the final effect is of a fortress looking defiantly out toward Perugia, the greatest of Assisi's rivals, in whose prisons Francis himself had once spent some unhappy months. He would have preferred to be buried without fuss at the Portiuncula, yet the grandeur of his shrine is not wholly inappropriate. For all his love of simplicity and humility, Francis recognized that he was the center of a personality cult, and welcomed the fact.

If Dominic turned his missionary canons into friars in imitation of Francis, he showed by almost all his other dispositions a shrewd appraisal of the difficulties that the Franciscans must encounter. He wished his order to be a collection of trained and disciplined preachers, drawn from a select class—the aspiring university students, chosen not for their learning but because to be a student in the incipient universities of the day, one had to combine sound education and a love of adventure. In place of the loose-knit structure of the Franciscan Order—always in ferment, always in crisis—he began, and his successor Brother Jordan of Saxony completed, the erection of an orderly structure of committees. Francis made his own inspiration and example the standard, the stabilizing point of his order; Dominic hid his own personality, and is indeed as a man, compared to Francis, still comparatively obscure. In its place he set a framework for development and discussion from which an order that did not depend on the divine spark in a single breast could grow. It was extraordinarily successful and compels our admiration, even if we feel at best a doubtful gratitude to the apostle of committee government. Thus two contrasting personalities combined to bring to birth the apostolic order from which the twelfth-century founders had so often turned away; and in this story the personality of Dominic is as crucial as that of Francis, for each contributed to the other's success, and when the founders were gone the two orders were free to grow more like each other, even if in the process they sometimes drew away from the intentions of both their founders.

The basis of the Dominican way of life was taken by St. Dominic from two previous rules. His order was founded on the Rule of St. Augustine. The regulations that Dominic drafted for the daily round within the convents of his order were adapted from those of Prémontré, which themselves owed much to Cîteaux. Thus the ascetic, monastic traditions of the twelfth century still lived and reigned, but a clear limit was set to their kingdom, for the Dominican constitutions were at all points adapted to suit the practical needs of an Order of Preachers.

In two ways the friars were in evident contrast to monks and canons as they were in the early thirteenth century: It was their specific task to wander, to preach or to set an example in the secular world, and they were beggars, seen to live wholly on such alms as they could collect. Monks and canons could take round the begging bowl, and many a building was partly financed by a begging tour undertaken by a group of religious and the relics of the saint whose church was about to be rebuilt. But the friars lived wholly by begging: They had no property.[9] They were and are the Mendicant Orders. The abuses to which this could lead have been made notorious by Chaucer's portrait of a friar in his Prologue, perhaps the most cruel of all his gallery. The satire presupposes that it was well known that such abuses could exist; it is always a mistake to judge any order solely by its ideals and its saints. But if all friars were like the princely beggar of Chaucer's imagination the joke would fail and the satire become a bore—and the friars would not have survived. It is equally false to judge a religious movement by its notorious failures. Few men have enriched the world more evidently than Francis and Dominic.

Yet that is not quite the last word; for our present concern is especially with their relations with the monastic orders. The friars provided a calling for those who wished to wander and preach as well as to lead a regular life; they were for a century or more leaders in the avant-garde religious movement of the age. They stole the initiative that the Cistercians had enjoyed in the twelfth century. The monastic orders were never quite the same in the later Middle Ages. They survived; they kept a way of life in being; here and there appeared local revivals of exceptional fervor. In the sixteenth and seventeenth centuries, and again in the eighteenth and nineteenth, more general renewals changed the nature of the religious orders as the friars had done in the thirteenth. But the orders of monks and canons have never since held the place in Christendom that they enjoyed in the heyday of St. Bernard and the Cistercian movement in the middle of the twelfth century.

Part Three

GATHERING
THE THREADS

13.

Three Visits

We have traced the history of the religious life from the New Testament to the thirteenth century. As we draw the threads together, the first and most challenging question facing us is: Can we fit our narrative together with the visible remains of medieval monasteries? Can we draw "oil from the hardest stone" and make these buildings reveal their story? If not, the attempt to weave together text and pictures has failed. This is a real challenge, and it would be wrong to answer it lightly; the answer lies in the reader's mind and imagination. Yet something may yet be suggested by taking a variety of samples rich both in history and in remains, which can show us in depth the sort of answers we can hope for. It is for this that we set off to explore three of the most evocative monastic sites in Europe.

I. *Fountains*

Fountains Abbey in Yorkshire sits at the end of a fair lawn, framed by the wooded banks of a narrow vale, set off by a chattering stream: the greatest of eighteenth-century romantic ruins or, to see it another way, a thoroughly functional monument of twelfth-century Europe. Here is a strange alliance between the most practical aspect of the twelfth-century renaissance and

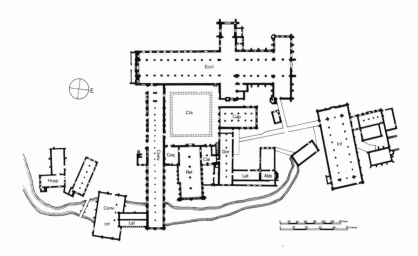

Plan of Fountains. Most of the church, chapter house, dormitory and lay brothers' wing are late twelfth century; the refectory was rebuilt and the lay brothers' quarters extended in the early thirteenth century, and the first phase of building was completed with the Chapel of the Nine Altars, finished by the middle of the century. The abbot's lodging and infirmary are mostly fourteenth century; the tower above the north transept is of the sixteenth.

the most romantic aspect of the Gothic Revival of the eighteenth century; a piquant contrast, which stirs the mind and the imagination and urges us to ask many questions about its history.[1]

At first sight, the comparison between the two ages that conspired to give us Fountains Abbey as we know it seems nothing more than an intriguing contradiction. The Cistercian monks who built the abbey in the twelfth century chose the site because it was comparatively remote from towns and villages, and they wanted to be alone. They chose the valley because it provided the two things they most needed: a convenient flat space on which a great complex of buildings could be constructed, and plentiful running water to fill their wash-basins, to flush their drains and to turn their mill-wheels. They built a large abbey, solid, commodious and practical, but neither comfortable nor ornamental—save for the mid-thirteenth-century Chapel of the Nine Altars at the east end of the church and the fine sixteenth-century tower. The rest of the buildings are mainly of the twelfth and early thirteenth centuries, a striking monument to the efficiency of the Cistercian architects of the order's early generations.

In contrast, it is the well-kept lawns and the trees that give the scene its romantic charm, and these are of the eighteenth century. As far as we know, the valley was only modestly wooded in the Middle Ages, and the park to which it is appended was pasture and grazing land. The eighteenth-century landlords beautified the European landscape and added something of permanent value to our civilization. In the late twentieth and early twenty-first centuries, when so much of what they created is in danger of destruction, we are learning to value their creative appreciation that produced this beauty of landscape of a special kind—owing as much to man's improvements as to nature's raw deposit. There was another side to their work, however, for they sometimes treated the human inhabitants of their landscape as cavalierly as its natural lineaments. Many a contemporary and many a modern historian has commented on the activities of eighteenth-century improving landlords who enclosed fields and laid out parks, something as follows:

> They proceed to raze villages, they overthrow churches, and turn out parishioners...level everything before the ploughshare, so that if you looked on a place that you knew previously you could say, "and grass now grows where Troy town stood."

But these actual words come from the pen of a twelfth-century satirist writing about the Cistercians; and although the tone is that of satire, not cool appraisal, the basic facts have been shown to be true. "…It is prescribed to them that they are to dwell in desert places, and desert places they do assuredly either find or make.…"[2] Walter Map wrote, it must be admitted, with the freedom of the satirist who does not really expect his satire to be read—nor was it read till the nineteenth century—and some of his cruder charges cannot be checked. However it is now clear that the Cistercians not only insisted that their founders give them sites and fields untrammelled by peasant settlers or tenants, but in some instances connived at and joined in large-scale expropriation.[3] Fountains was not such a case: The valley was a wilderness when the monks first settled there, but they presently removed peasants from cottages not far away to the south.

They dwelt in desert places because their rules were inspired by memories of the root and source of the monastic ideal: the life of the Egyptian and Syrian desert in the days of St. Antony and St. Pachomius (see pp. 28–33). What this meant in practice was that they dwelt in the wild countryside of western Europe. "Believe one who has proved it," wrote Bernard of Clairvaux, whose disciples Fountains' early monks became; "…you will find among the woods something you never found in books. Stones and trees will teach you a lesson you never heard from masters in the school. Think you that honey cannot be drawn from the rock, and oil from the hardest stone? Do not the mountains drop sweetness and the hills flow with milk and honey, and the valleys abound with corn?"[4] Doubtless, the phrases carry overtones today that were quite foreign to its author. Yet it cannot be urged that men were indifferent to natural beauty in the twelfth century. More than one herbal or bestiary already anticipated a flair for portraying natural objects all the more striking for being contrary to the normal artistic fashions of the day.[5]

Whatever the overtones, Bernard's essential point was that silence and solitude were a monk's best teachers. If his thought be a little adapted, it may serve as a theme for this book. In the stones of the abbey and the trees that line the glade in which it lies are the key to much of Fountains' history. If the view from the east reveals most clearly the modern setting of the abbey among the trees planted by landscape gardeners, the western range introduces the modern visitor most directly to its original function. Passing Fountains Hall, which was built at the turn of the sixteenth and seventeenth centuries of stone quarried from the abbey, and passing the foundations of the ancient mill, bakehouse and guest house, one is confronted with the immense length of the lay brothers' quarters. With their refectory and offices below and the floor of their dormitory above, the west wing still reveals the great numbers expected to live there in early days. It was built perhaps for about two hundred, at a time when it was assumed that many would live on the outlying farms, or granges, as they were called. The wing lies between the church, an immensely heavy and solid building set on the firmest ground in the valley, and the river, which was harnessed to every practical task of the large community. It provided a head of water to turn the wheels of the mill, and a supply of water for the kitchens of lay brothers and choir monks. It also served drains to carry away the refuse from the guesthouse, the lay brothers' latrines and kitchen and, a little further east, first the kitchen and then the latrines of the choir monks, finally reaching the infirmary and the abbot's lodging.

The center of the main monastic complex, the cloister, is 125 feet square, and the buildings are on a scale to match. Yet refectory, calefactory, novices' quarters, chapter house, large as they are, differ only in size from other Cistercian buildings of the twelfth century. The choir monks' dormitory, estimated to have been designed for fifty monks and perhaps for seventy-five, is not so well preserved as the lay brothers' but it ran, as usual, over the eastern range, over the chapter house, giving the monks direct access to the church.

Portions of the buildings had to be rebuilt after a raid by the abbey's enemies in 1147, and the bulk of what one sees today dates from the period 1150–1250. So solid and substantial was the building effort of that period that most of it never needed to be redone; nor may it have been easy to afford major changes in the fabric in later times. Fountains had numerous granges and extensive properties, especially sheep runs, yet it was never comparable in resources to the ancient royal foundations, like Glastonbury and St. Albans. For two centuries at least its community was substantially larger than theirs, while its revenues remained considerably lower, and after the great building period it may not have found offerings and alms for the fabric so readily available. Thus only two substantial changes took place later: the reconstruction, on a far larger scale than before, of the abbot's house and infirmary, mostly in the fourteenth century; and the building of the handsome bell tower, in defiance of earlier Cistercian custom, by Abbot Huby in the early sixteenth century. Many changes were made in the abbey's furnishings in the later Middle Ages, but these have disappeared, leaving the abbey ruins essentially a monument to the Cistercian model as it had been in the twelfth and early thirteenth centuries.

It has often been disputed in recent years whether the Cistercian model was something essentially new: How original was the order and how great was the break with traditional monasticism? These are questions Fountains can help us to answer: documents and ruins are in perfect accord. The documents have been subjected to ruthless criticism, and the romantic story of the flight from St. Mary's Abbey, York, the painful winter sojourn under the rough shelter of a great elm tree, is threatened with demolition.[6] But no one doubts that the story begins in York, in an abbey built deliberately to combine the finest monastic inspiration of the late eleventh century in northern England with the other most notable type of community of the age, the rising town. Essentially, St. Mary's at York represented traditional monastic ideals into which some new ideas had infiltrated.

After a generation a group among the monks were unsettled by the passage through their midst of English disciples of Bernard of Clairvaux on their way to found the first of the major Cistercian houses in the north, the abbey of Rievaulx, in 1131–32. Next year they presented reforming proposals to their aging abbot, Geoffrey, and it seems that it was his incapacity to handle the human problem involved in a divided community that precipitated the real crisis. The archbishop of York, Thurstan of Bayeux, came to make some inquiries, and the result was a riot, from which the archbishop narrowly escaped without a beating, carrying off the reformers with him. Presently a few melted back to St. Mary's, and for some months the rest lived on the archbishop's hospitality and wondered what to do. Eventually they decided to join the

Cistercian Order. They were settled at Fountains, on the archbishop's estates, and Bernard sent one of his monks, Geoffrey
of Clairvaux, to complete the transformation into a Cistercian
abbey. From this group came some of the most distinguished
Cistercian leaders of the middle of the century. In some
respects their careers and actions reveal that they thought their
world very different from the traditional world of St. Mary's,
York; but they had hesitated for some months, perhaps for a
year or two, before joining the Cistercians, demonstrating that
they were not in the first instance aware that the Cistercian
challenge could not be fully met within the precincts of an
older house.[7]

Similarly in the buildings: There are plenty of elements
that Fountains, along with virtually all Cistercian houses of the
day, shared with traditional abbeys. The basic model—the large
and stately church; the cloister garth and walks forming the
center for the monks' domestic life; the common rooms for
day and night, chapter house, refectory, parlors, dormitory—all
are essentially in the same situation in Benedictine and
Cistercian houses, or in those of other orders. Some peculiar
features all Cistercian houses show: an unusual measure of uniformity and a large wing devoted to housing the lay brothers.
But it is in the style and fashion of the church building that
the contrast shows most clearly, and must indeed have been far
clearer in the twelfth century than now, for Cistercian churches
always avoided rich sculpture, sumptuous paintings, stained
glass, shrines and grandiose vistas. Plain glass made them far
lighter than most churches, and plain or whitewashed walls
made them far duller; even the proportions were deliberately
lumpish. Thus the buildings, like the documents, enforce what
at first sight seems mere confusion: The Cistercians were at

once very much like and utterly unlike the other monastic communities. Yet this is as true to human nature and human experience as it is tiresome to tidy minds, and it is reflected in the personal tastes and friendships of many eminent monks. Among the leaders and the rank and file of monasteries old and new were many who engaged in controversy, but even more who made close and lasting friendships. The man who made possible the founding of Fountains, Archbishop Thurstan, thus became a notable patron of the Cistercians; he died a Cluniac, at Pontefract Priory. He was also, it may be noted, sprung from old corruption in the sense of being the offspring of a married canon of St. Paul's in London. From a similar dynasty in the north came the greatest of the English Cistercians, St. Ailred of Rievaulx, and Ailred's friends included the eminent Cluniac Gilbert Foliot, bishop of Hereford and London (1148–87), who counted other Cistercians among his closest friends, and one of whose nearest relatives died clothed in a Cistercian habit.

An academic cannot fail to notice the analogy with some modern universities and colleges. From within, the differences may appear profound and be the subject of much keen observation. To the outsider the same institutions may seem utterly indistinguishable and if he has penetrated into them, bewildering as well, for the mark of some modern academic communities is a strange combination of a spirit humane and liberal and cosmopolitan, with a spirit sometimes almost equally narrow, parochial and intolerant. It was the same with the medieval religious orders, and it is this that gives them a special fascination, if we have the patience to sit amid the ruins and look closely at the stones, and to read both the stones and the books.

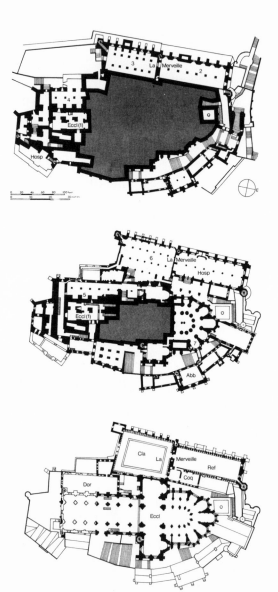

Plan of Mont Saint-Michel, at low, middle and high levels, as in c. 1500.
1. The ancient church, "Notre Dame sous terre." 2. Almonry. 3. Cellar. 4. Old
Almonry, Salle de l'Aquilon. 5. Monks' parlor or *promenoir*. 6. Calefactory,
later Salle des Chevaliers.

II. *Mont Saint-Michel*

The famous house of Mont Saint-Michel, of "St. Michael in peril of the sea," commands our attention first of all because it successfully withstood the assaults of men and of the elements for many centuries. Its foundation[8] in 708 represented the first peak in the cult of the militant archangel; it only ceased to be an abbey at the time of the French Revolution.[9]

The cult of St. Michael showed its first bloom in the seventh and eighth centuries, then flowered as never before or since in the eleventh and twelfth. Its chief center in western Christendom has always been Monte Gargano in Italy, but many a hilltop was adorned in the Middle Ages with a chapel or a shrine dedicated to the archangel, who led the angels to war in heaven against the Devil, according to the vision in the Book of Revelation (12:7–9)—which perhaps helps to explain why his cult flourished in lofty places. In 708, according to an early legend probably with an authentic base, St. Aubert, bishop of Avranches, translated relics—whatever they may have been—from Monte Gargano to the spectacular small hillock of rock that juts into the sea where Brittany and Normandy meet. Doubtless it was in early days the spirit of Breton or Celtic monasticism that reigned on the mount, and we may suppose it the home of a small group of hermits at most, living in a cell or group of cells round the chapel on the peak, surrounded by the sea and the seabirds like their brethren on and off the west coast of Ireland. But in the ninth and tenth centuries the diocese of Avranches became part of the new Viking Norman principality, first pagan, then reconverted under new influences. Pilgrims continued to flow to the mount, and the Vikings brought trade. Thus in the tenth century there grew up a small town with its center in the little church whose nave

survives now within the crypt—the oldest part of the present
monastic buildings (see p. 327). In 966 Duke Richard I converted this church into an abbey, bringing monks from Saint-
Wandrille. Of its early history we know little until, at the
beginning of the eleventh century, it joined the mainstream of
Norman monasticism, was put under the custody of St.
William of Volpiano and became one of the notable centers
of the flourishing monastic world of eleventh-century
Normandy (see pp. 65–66). The transepts, their crypts and a
part of the nave show clearly that it flourished in the early
eleventh century. They are indeed among the earliest monuments of eleventh-century Norman monasticism to survive. In
the temporal sphere the abbey undoubtedly flourished; like
the seafaring community that nestled at its feet, it took to the
sea,[10] received rich endowments in Jersey and, after the
Norman Conquest, in England. These included, most appropriately, the Cornish St. Michael's Mount, the nearest equivalent in Celtic Britain to the Mont itself.

Abbot and monks must often have been in peril of the sea,
but their own needs combined with the fame of their church
as a pilgrim center to keep them perched on their narrow plat-
form of rock. The site of the abbey of Le Mont Saint-Michel
is a dramatic illustration of the triumph of religion over common sense. One can scarcely imagine a more awkward situation for the two expressions of medieval communal living:
town and monastery.

The town still bears witness to the close links between
monastic life and secular society, even in so isolated a place. The
way these links worked is more precisely revealed in the monastery itself. As the great church occupied the whole of the top of
the little hill, the monastic buildings had to perch precariously

on its clifflike sides. Thus a series of two- or three-storey buildings set one on top of another contain the elements of the
monastic complex normally spread out over a level plain, and
the way order came out of the disorder of the scene is fascinating to observe. To the north lies the sea, separated from the
monastery by a small wood and steep slope. Here between the
sea and the solid bulk of the church on the summit of the hill
lay the monastic buildings, as secluded as the site allowed from
the human throng, from all distractions save the sound of the
gulls and the waves. To the south, between the church and the
town, lay the abbot's lodgings, the buildings of the lord of
Mont Saint-Michel, where the head of the community met
important visitors and the leading townsfolk. The main stair-
case still leads up from the town between the abbot and his
church, crossed by a charming fifteenth-century bridge. Here
in the mid– or late twelfth century the historian-abbot Robert
of Torigny recorded in his chronicle the history of Normandy,
and incidentally of his abbey, and added to the abbey's cartulary a register of the charters of his own abbacy.[11]

The monks' quarters north of the church lie in two complexes, the smaller of the eleventh and twelfth centuries, the
larger, "La Merveille," of the thirteenth. La Merveille includes
some of the most beautiful monastic buildings in Europe, but
the first thing we must say about it is that it hides and disguises
the original layout of the cloister of earlier times. The smaller
group consists of the old almonry, where the poor were fed and
humbler guests received in the Salle de l'Aquilon, the monks'
parlor (with the old kitchen and refectory) and the monks'
dormitory (or as some think, their chapter house) on the two
floors above. Thus from the original entrance one proceeds
from the most to the least public rooms in the house.

Behind the old almonry lies the remnant of the tenth-century church, now a crypt dedicated to the Blessed Virgin, Notre-Dame-sous-terre, with the surviving portions of the Romanesque church of the eleventh and twelfth centuries around and above it—for most of the church is of this period, save for the choir and western end, both of which collapsed at various later dates.

The patron of Robert of Torigny was Henry II, king of England, duke of Normandy, count of Anjou and duke of Aquitaine. In 1204–5 Henry's youngest son, King John, was driven from Normandy and Anjou by King Philip II, Philip Augustus, of France. In the course of this conquest, an attempt was made to defend the Mount, a natural fortress of great strength, and Philip's vassal, Guy de Thouars, burnt the town and some of the monastic buildings in his efforts to reduce it to surrender. The efforts were successful; but King Philip, determined to reconcile the Mount and its lord and chief inhabitants to the new regime, gave his patronage to a splendid rebuilding. From this stems the Merveille, which in its present form is almost a complete monastic complex in itself. At its base is a large storeroom, such as any abbey needed—for a sizeable medieval household reckoned to keep imperishable goods for long periods, since transport was (by our standards) exceedingly expensive and the monks of the Mount were never unmindful of the possibility of a siege, especially in the early thirteenth century. Also on the ground floor lies the new almonry, the hall for receiving the poorer guests and for dispensing the abbey's charity. The community were the lords spiritual as well as temporal of their town and seafaring kingdom, and the functions of the welfare state, insofar as they were performed at all, were squarely laid on the church in the

Middle Ages. The building, like the treatises on canon law that enshrined the rules of the welfare church, is a dramatic reminder of the monks' duties; how they performed them it cannot in its nature tell us.

La Merveille symbolically represents the hierarchy of medieval society. The second storey contains (like the first) two large chambers. In one, the ordinary guests of the abbey were entertained, fed and put to sleep: the guests not poor enough for the almonry nor grand enough for the abbot's table. The second chamber was originally the calefactory, the monks' warming room and winter parlor. It is now called La Salle des Chevaliers, after an order of knights founded in the late Middle Ages and based for a time at Mont Saint-Michel; and the present name of the Salle des Chevaliers may serve to remind us of the knightly element in the hierarchy of the Mount and the militant nature of the cult of St. Michael. In the thirteenth century an abbot, in Normandy as in England, was a baron as well as the head of a monastic community, and for his own and his duke's defense he had to be able to mobilize a platoon of knights; these would have gathered, however, not in the Salle des Chevaliers, but in the abbot's hall. On the third storey of the Merveille, the monks ate and worked, in refectory and cloister; and above the cloister looms the great church in which the monks and their visitors worshiped, the home of St. Michael himself, where God was his guest at the altars when mass was celebrated, and yet also, in his nature, present everywhere and all the time—the all-pervading summit of the living hierarchy of mortals and immortals.

The cloister is one of the most delightful products of the Gothic architecture of Normandy. No doubt it carries reminders of the cradle of Gothic not far away in the Île de France, from which King Philip sprang. But its style indicates still more the paradox of Norman Gothic: that in the years when the French king became, not merely the distant suzerain, but the immediate overlord of Normandy, the Gothic masons of the duchy developed a style of their own with closer links to England than to France. Something of its quality may be seen in Rouen Cathedral; it is at its best and most lucid at Coutances, since the destruction of Avranches Cathedral the nearest of the Norman cathedrals to the Mount. The shape of the arches, the deep moldings within them: both are strongly reminiscent of Coutances.[12] There are many reminiscences of Salisbury Cathedral, too, but the foliage of the cloister at the Mount has a richness and a fantasy all its own. It also illustrates the religious sentiment of its age in quite a direct way. Should Jesus be viewed as a suffering human or as a king? King and judge he still was, and as such appears in one of the scenes on the western walk in the cloister. But he is portrayed as human too; another scene depicts a suffering Christ upon the cross. The great apostle of the human Jesus in the early thirteenth century was Francis of Assisi, and near the crucified is a representation of St. Francis, now almost worn away, dated to the year 1228, informing us that he was canonized in that year. This gives us a vital clue to the date of the whole building and shows that traditional monasticism could still flourish when the new monasticism of the twelfth century had passed its prime and the apostolic life of the friars had risen to challenge it. It is interesting, too, to reflect that it should be in France that we find the earliest known picture of the saint called the Frank, the Frenchman, Francesco, though by birth, life and death he was a man of Umbria.

Throughout La Merveille one may study the development of Norman Gothic, but in the church itself one is back with traditional monasticism in its heyday. In the crypt of the choir and in the nave we have solid, rather plain monuments of the eleventh century. In the ruins of Jumièges, the most notable survivor of that first group of large, solid Romanesque monastic churches in northwestern France, we see the moment in the eleventh century when the fashion for enormous churches first broke through to the sea. Soon after, the largest of all the building explosions of the age took place in Norman England and in Normandy together. Jumièges and Bernay and the Mount were followed by the abbeys at Caen, Winchester, St. Albans, a multitude of others and finally by Durham. Durham is mainly of the early twelfth century, when the west end and the west front of the Mount were rebuilt. To the modern observer it makes little difference whether the churches were originally secular cathedrals, monastic cathedrals[13] or abbeys—that is to say, whether their choirs were expected to provide homes for communities of secular canons or monks. Both needed space for a full round of offices, and stalls for a large community. In the abbey or monastic cathedral the community was more regularly present in force; there were more priests to be provided with altars every morning (anyway in the twelfth and thirteenth centuries), and there remained certain liturgical differences between monastic and secular uses. But architecturally the differences were never very conspicuous. These enormous churches represented fashion, generosity, religious sentiment—the efforts of the Norman layfolk, bishops and clergy to win the approval of Christ the judge. They were also built large so that they could house within them lay pilgrims and visitors, the monks, St. Michael and God himself.

Of Michael's presence the chief reminder today is the great image above the lofty spire. Many centuries divide the nave from choir and spire. By the fifteenth century the abbots of the Mount were absentees, great men enabled to maintain their princely state by accumulating the revenues of abbacies and other dignities. One such was the Cardinal d'Estouteville; he was not, however, so forgetful of his abbey that he neglected to help rebuild the choir, which had collapsed in 1421. The choir was finished and the spire added in the following century.

At Fountains we saw a world apart: a community as cut off from its neighbors as circumstances and human affairs allowed. At Mont Saint-Michel we see the traces of a community much more intimately linked with the burgesses of its little town and with the pilgrims. This contrast brings us face to face with one of the greatest issues in monastic history: Is the life of the monk and of his community inward looking, interior, concerned with its own affairs and its own salvation, or outward looking, concerned to help the world outside in practical ways as well as by prayer? If there were a single answer to this question, then either Fountains or the Mount would be unintelligible. Fountains reflects an urgent desire to escape from the world, the Mount to be in it and yet not of it or, rather, to keep one's hands in reach of earth and heaven at once: an awkward acrobatic feat, symbolically represented by this strange pile of buildings precariously perched on a rock jutting out into the English Channel.

III. Sant'Ambrogio, Milan

Our third visit is to a house securely placed in one of the world's centers, a monument not only to the close and permanent links of traditional monasticism with the world, but of the long stretches of time over which these links have been formed. There is hardly any more powerful reminder of the

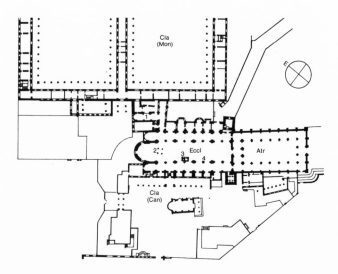

Plan of Sant'Ambrogio, Milan. The present church and atrium are mainly eleventh to twelfth century, incorporating elements from almost every century since the foundation of the basilica by St. Ambrose in the fourth. It lies between two great cloisters of the fifteenth century: the monks' to the north, the canons' to the south. It was severely damaged in 1943 and had to be extensively restored and partly rebuilt. 1. Chapel of S.Vittore (St.Victor) in Ciel d'Oro, with fifth-century mosaics. 2. Golden Altar and ciborium. 3. Pulpit. 4. Serpent.

force of tradition in the history of the church than the Basilica of St. Ambrose, Sant'Ambrogio, of Milan.

At first sight, the monasteries that have been formed and the religious life that has flourished in Sant'Ambrogio seem incidental to the Basilica's true significance, and there is a sense in which that is precisely the point of our visit. Here lie the relics of one of the greatest of the church fathers, surrounded by the Milanese martyrs in whose honor Ambrose himself first built the church. He began to build it in 379, and the young African rhetorician Augustine was one of those who witnessed its early progress. In 386 Ambrose consecrated his basilica and solemnly laid in a group of oratories around it: Sts. Nabor and

Felix, Valeria, Victor and Vitalis; in the basilica itself Sts. Gervasius and Protasius; and beside these martyrs Ambrose himself has lain since he was buried there in 397. It has always been the center of the cult, or group of cults, that made the Ambrosian Church in a measure rival Rome as the center of the church in Italy. Of all the great churches of Italy Milan sat the most lightly in the early Middle Ages in its allegiance to the papacy, and the papacy in return looked with a suspicious eye on the successor of St. Ambrose seated on the ancient throne in Sant'Ambrogio and the less ancient throne in the cathedral. As the centuries passed a separate rite distinguished the province of Milan from the rest of Italy, and in the end from the rest of western Christendom; Roman in origin, but yet sufficiently independent to symbolize the relations of the Ambrosian to the Petrine Church.

Sant'Ambrogio is a palimpsest on which many different epochs have scored their mark. Only fragments of the original basilica survive, though its general shape has been preserved through all the later rebuildings. So deep was the mark of tradition on its later builders that many different estimates have been made of the age of the basilica as we know it.[14] It seems now fairly clear that the crypt represents the first major reconstruction, that of the eighth century, dating from the years following 789, when Archbishop Peter was attempting to convert the church into a monastery. The monastic community was founded in that year and rapidly became one of the notable monastic centers of the empire of Charlemagne. There are few more splendid monuments of Carolingian art and wealth than the golden altar, presented to the basilica by Archbishop Angilbert about 835. On it are inscribed scenes from the life of Christ and of St. Ambrose; archbishop, abbot and monks celebrated mass in the presence of Christ and the archbishop's eminent predecessor, the saint who presided over abbey, basilica, city and province, whose alter ego the archbishop claimed to be. Although it sat outside the original limits of the city, surrounded by the ancient cemeteries and the other cemetery churches, the medieval city lapped round it, and it became a busy center of civic and monastic exchange.

It had become the home of monks, but not of monks only. This was true in a peculiar sense, for the canons, who had lived in Sant'Ambrogio and its precinct before 789 and were expected to fade away as the monks became established, obstinately refused to disappear. The result was that instead of replacing one presence by another, the archbishops had unintentionally established two quite different groups of clergy in one church. In the eleventh century the canons adopted a regular way of life and became—whatever they had been before—canons regular (see chapter 8); so that there were in effect two communities following different monastic or quasi-monastic Rules in the basilica. Hence the great cloisters on either side—that to the north, the cloister of the canons, the two to the south (now the Università Cattolica del Sacro Cuore), of the monks. Their present form is the result of a new design by Bramante (c. 1492) and of much later work, but they still reflect this extraordinary passage of history. The presence of two towers reflects these divisions even more vividly. An important part of the income of any monastic community in the early Middle Ages was likely to consist of the offerings of the faithful (see pp. 116–17). From the ninth century on, in the monks' tower, bells rang to summon the faithful to the monks' solemn mass. The canons also celebrated mass, but they had no tower yet and were not allowed to ring bells.

In the eleventh and twelfth centuries Milan grew in size, population, wealth and political power. The city had long been one of the major hubs and the undisputed ecclesiastical center of Lombardy. It now came to play a dominant political role in its region, originally under the aegis of St. Ambrose and his successors as archbishops, later under the city fathers, as they came, like those of other Italian cities, to be increasingly independent of the authority of the archbishop. Milan in the eleventh century was the scene of some of the most dramatic incidents in the investiture contest. The emperor Henry IV (1056–1106) strove to preserve his power in northern Italy by investing and supporting archbishops of the traditional, easygoing clerical dynasties. In response, Pope Gregory VII (1073–85: see pp. 89, 114) lent his support to a movement among the citizens that strove to oust the old aristocracy, to give rein to the fervent, ascetic, celibate clergy of the movement for ecclesiastical reform. The vicissitudes of the political scene, the political and ecclesiastical complexion of the archbishops, changed many times.

So too changed the fortunes of the monks and canons of Sant'Ambrogio, who found their own domestic controversy entangled with the affairs of archbishop, emperor, pope and commune. The canons were able to use the political vicissitudes to win a larger share of the offerings, but in 1098 they accused the monks of breaking into the basilica and taking their offerings by force. Early in the twelfth century the canons mounted a larger counterattack and began to build a bell tower loftier than the monks.' In the end, a series of uneasy compromises was enforced, which lasted until both communities disappeared in the age of the French Revolution. The culminating moment had come in 1144, when an archbishop at loggerheads with the city commune but at peace with both pope and emperor solemnly announced that the splendid new campanile of the canons, which the monks and the commune had sought to destroy, could remain. It has remained to this day, a symbol of the generations in the eleventh and twelfth centuries, when the affairs of pope and emperor and the future of Milan were closer than ever before or since to the altars of Sant'Ambrogio.

The great atrium, though itself of the eleventh and twelfth centuries, is in form a link between the world of St. Ambrose and St. Benedict and the epoch of this book. In form it resembles both the courtyard of a large house and the cloister of a monastery, like the cloisters for the houses of monks and canons raised by Bramante in the same complex of buildings. This kind of atrium, set before the western portal, was commonly attached to great basilicas in the fourth and fifth centuries.[15] It was not in early days monastic; it was essentially the meeting place of the laity, assembled to worship in the church, and it was commonly attached to a cemetery church, where martyrs were buried or commemorated, as at Sant'Ambrogio itself and its neighbor San Lorenzo, where substantial remains of an ancient atrium may still be seen. In due course a number of such churches came to have monasteries associated with them—as did both the Milanese cemetery basilicas, the Santi Quattro Coronati at Rome and a number more; they are found as parts of monastic complexes in northern Europe in Carolingian times, at Saint-Riquier and Essen.[16] By c. 1080, when the present atrium at Sant'Ambrogio was begun, it was old-fashioned but not wholly outmoded, since it retained a liturgical use, especially for great processions outside the church and through the western door on Palm Sunday. These and other festivities explain the common appearance, in many different forms, of western chapels and courtyards, often called paradises or galilees.

These were not confined to monastic churches, nor were cloisters set beside the church, for in Italy especially a cloister is commonly found attached to churches that were never monastic or conventual, and even in England the secular cathedrals acquired fine cloister walks in the later Middle Ages. Yet the cloister in its usual sense, a secluded garth between the church and the domestic buildings of a community, was in a special sense a vital feature of the monastic plan, in contrast to the atrium, a garth open to the laity, between the church and the world. The origin of the cloister is obscure (see pp. 6–8). Although it is unlikely that there was any sort of uniformity in the monastic plan before the central Middle Ages—for the imposition of a common plan in the eleventh and twelfth centuries gives the impression of a uniformity that may well be, for earlier times, deceptive—traces of a cloister or evidence of buildings grouped round a square courtyard of some kind have been found much earlier than this. It is possible that the cloister was modeled on the ancient atrium or that both grew out of the courtyards common in ancient Roman houses and villas. It is hard not to feel that it was a strange imposition in climates less kind than those of the Mediterranean lands where courtyards and atria were born. It is a nice question when its use became established, but it is essentially a product of the tenth and eleventh centuries. It is an even nicer question when in the cold north it became the practice to fix glass in the open arches of the cloister walk[17]: not perhaps before the thirteenth century. For three or four centuries, that is, the northern monk lived out his day almost in the open. The manner of life of the early Middle Ages makes this less surprising than it seems to us, but only a little. It is striking testimony to the force of tradition and the power of the customs that became associated with the Rule.

The cloister became the heart of the fortress within which monastic life was led, the symbol of separation from the world, of dedication to the life of the spirit, of stability in religion. In the fourth chapter of his Rule, St. Benedict listed the qualities and attitudes and virtues of a monk "the instruments of the craft of the spirit," he calls them. "And the workshop where we assiduously deploy all these skills are the *claustra* [the enclosure, the "cloister"] of the monastery, and stability in the communal life." It is a very characteristic passage in the Rule, since Benedict loved to mingle metaphor and concrete image in a way designed to baffle a translator. In suggesting the rendering of *claustra* as cloister we have cheated a little, since he meant simply the enclosure, the complex of buildings of the monastery; what we know as the cloister was devised some centuries later. But every monk of Benedict's obedience in the central and late Middle Ages was expected to know this passage—and the whole Rule—by heart; by the eleventh century the word *claustra* carried the overtone "cloister" in their minds. Originally it meant the locks that bolted and barred a fortress; Benedict enjoyed the word because it gave that sense of assurance and security which he wished above all to impart to those who dwelt within. Then it also meant a fortress, *ein' feste Burg*, God's fortress against the devil, man's fortress against the barbarous, lay, sinful world of the early Middle Ages. As time passed, a particular form was established for the buildings of this fortress. Just as the fortified towns of the ninth, tenth and eleventh centuries were receiving a pattern in which the wall round the periphery and the marketplace in the center were the essential features, so in the same epoch the monastic plan was formed and fixed. Its heart lay in a great church in which God's work, the *opus Dei*, was performed. Next to the church lay the more modest court-yard where man's work was performed, the cloister. It provided the central living and circulating space of a group of commu-nal buildings, and so was reckoned convenient; it was inward-looking and so symbolized the monastic ideal and stability; it came to be called the cloister, and so was associated for all time with the *claustra* of Benedict's Rule.

14.

1300: The Monastic Map
of Europe

Histories of monasticism tend to be of two kinds: those that
sketch the glories, the creative epochs, and those that plumb
the depths and chronicle the follies and aberrations of the
cloister. The humdrum and the ordinary leaves little memorial,
and often seems to belong only to what Pope called "the dull-
ness of the past," and yet most of us live in the humdrum of the
present, however we dramatize it, and there should therefore be
a natural sympathy and interest in the long life and mere survival of very numerous religious houses in many corners of
Europe.

The year 1300 marks a middle point between creation and
decay. In every part of Europe the pace of new foundation had
slackened, and the rise in population that had fed so many
houses had begun to ease. It is thus an ideal moment to unfurl
the map and take stock of the monastic geography of western
Christendom.

Such a map is bound to be a palimpsest. We shall readily see
a variety of patterns scored one over the other by the traditional monastic movements of the tenth and eleventh centuries, and the new orders of the eleventh and twelfth; in many

areas too we shall find a swarm of knights and friars. But another feature of the map is equally conspicuous: the distinction between the old homelands of western monastic observance and the frontier lands, newly colonized. Western Christendom was surrounded on the west by the Atlantic, on the south by Islam, on the east by Byzantium and the vast, menacing empire of the Mongols. By 1300 the frontiers were tolerably clear, and the threats that Islam might again engulf the Spanish peninsula, as it had nearly done in the eighth and ninth centuries, or that the Mongols would add the whole of Christendom to their empire, had subsided. The ancient core of western Christendom lay in Italy and France, western Germany and England, to which one may add the extreme north of Spain, and Scandinavia, Christian since the eleventh century though never very fertile territory for the monastic orders. The rest of Spain was frontier territory with Islam, a fact reflected in very obvious ways in its monastic geography; so in a lesser measure was Sicily; so too the islands of the Mediterranean still held by Christian powers, especially Rhodes and Malta and Cyprus, at various times centers of the orders of knights. The brief rule of the kings of Jerusalem had come to an end, and the small posse of monasteries in Palestine had all been withdrawn before 1300 (see p. 199). The Byzantine Empire had been ruled for a space after the Fourth Crusade of 1204 by western princes, and a certain influx of western religious had taken place. By 1300 this was over, and St. Benedict's disciples had withdrawn to the traditional areas of papal obedience, leaving St. Basil and his successors in command of the field in most of what would now be Greece, the Balkans and Russia. But in Poland, Bohemia and in parts of Hungary a certain number of monastic houses flourished; in Poland and Silesia especially, as in Ireland, many of these represented the meeting of two peoples and two cultures. Castile and Portugal were the frontier kingdoms par excellence; in Poland, eastern Germany and Ireland colonial governors and governed met in the monastic communities as they also met in the castles and the towns.

The interest of the religious history in Spain and Portugal is out of all proportion to the number of foundations that can be counted there. Before the mid–eleventh century only about one quarter of the peninsula was in Christian hands; and although in the early generations of the reconquest (c. 1050– c. 1100) Christians and Muslims coexisted in much of Spain without serious religious acrimony between them and there were substantial Christian communities in many of the Muslim emirates, monastic houses were confined to the north. In the eleventh century a certain number of Benedictine and Cluniac houses were revived or founded. In Catalonia they were in the world of the western Mediterranean with central and northern Italy and Provence; the chief influences for reform came from Saint-Victor at Marseille, a house under Cluniac influence, not directly from Cluny (see p. 67). In Aragon and Old Castile, on the roads that led to Santiago de Compostela, Cluny's influence was greater; especially at the turn of the eleventh and twelfth centuries. Although its direct impact has been somewhat exaggerated, the pilgrims on these roads passed several houses that were either subject to Cluny or independent centers of Cluniac observance. Thus in the east, the old house of Ripoll was reformed from Cuxa and Saint-Victor; farther west, Cluniac centers of reform appeared in Silos and Sahagún. By 1300 these were independent Benedictine abbeys, but about twenty-five priories dependent on Cluny still remained within the Cluniac province of Spain.

In the twelfth century several other orders penetrated into Spain and Portugal, but the most powerful influence was Cistercian. In the regions securely Christian there appeared in the mid–twelfth century a scatter of Cistercian houses from Poblet and Santes Creus (1150–51) in Catalonia to the north of Portugal, and they spread as far south as Alcobaça (c. 1153) and the outskirts of Lisbon, after the area had been conquered from Islam by a company that detached itself from the Second

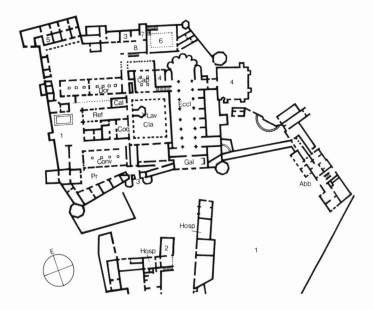

Plan of Poblet. The buildings range widely in date, from the church, cloister, calefactory, cloister and chapel of St. Stephen (twelfth century), lavabo, refectory, kitchen, chapter house (c. 1200), to the large sacristy, buildings for older monks, etc. of the eighteenth century. 1. Gardens. 2. Chapel of St. Catherine. 3. Royal Apartments. 4. Sacristies (the larger is of the eighteenth century). 5. Eighteenth-century buildings for the older monks. 6, 7. Twelfth-century cloister and chapel of St. Stephen. 8. Twelfth-century infirmary.

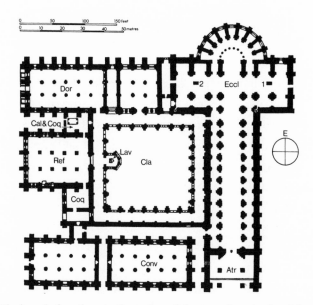

Plan of Alcobaça before the transformation of the west front in the eighteenth century. 1. Don Pedro's tomb. 2. Doña Inês's tomb.

Crusade in 1147. Poblet was a descendant of Clairvaux, and a proportion of the Castilian and most of the Portuguese houses likewise; Alcobaça was one of the last foundations direct from Clairvaux before St. Bernard's death. In due course some of these houses felt the presence of the Muslim, and Alcobaça itself had to be restored and largely rebuilt after a serious raid in the thirteenth century. In the north and northeast, a rival to the Catholic religious life appeared in the dualist Cathar or Albigensian heresy in the second half of the twelfth century. From Poblet the formidable Abbot Arnaud Amaury went on to be archbishop of Narbonne and ecclesiastical director of the Albigensian Crusade (1209). This was one of the first signs of a growing intolerance of differences of race and religion that was to clear the Muslims and the Jews out of Spain in the fifteenth century. The later stages of the reconquest showed a more

fanatical spirit than the earlier, and by 1300 most of the peninsula was in Christian hands. Thus it is easy to understand why
over much of the peninsula, and especially in the south, the
religious orders were most characteristically represented at this
time by the orders of knights. As well as fostering Templars and
Hospitallers, the Iberian peninsula gave birth to a whole family of new orders, some relatively local and short-lived,[1] and
others large enough to survive suppression and amalgamation,
like the Order of Santiago and the Order of Calatrava.[2] The
Orden de Cristo and the Order of Calatrava were among a
group founded under Cistercian auspices, and some of their
houses were indeed Cistercian in origin, but converted from
abbeys to castles in the wars and rumors of war of the thirteenth century. Thus by 1300 the religious houses, be they
havens of peace or war, often had embattled exteriors. The
influence of Cîteaux was very powerful, affecting not only the
knights but the ladies, as the great house of Las Huelgas particularly shows; nor were the canons regular negligible in their
influence, for the most important Spanish order of the Middle
Ages, that of the Friars Preacher, the Dominicans, was founded
by St. Dominic of Caleruega—an Augustinian canon of Osma.

To the islands and especially to Sicily the Cistercians also
spread in the twelfth century. Although Sicily had important
Benedictine foundations, it had lain too long outside the
Christian fold—it was only after two centuries of Muslim rule
that it was invaded in the 1060s, like England, by a Norman
army bearing a papal banner—for the influence of traditional
monachism to be deep. From the time of Gregory VII
(1073–85), and still more of Urban II, the Cluniac pope who
preached the First Crusade (1088–99), papal patronage and
intervention, combined with the generosity of the Norman

conquerors in the distribution of their own and other people's goods, had fostered the growth of houses formed or reformed from Monte Cassino and La Cava to replace the old Greek houses of the extreme south and of Sicily. At its height the subjects of La Cava included San Paolo fuori le Mura at Rome and the great abbey of Monreale in Sicily; and with the houses of La Cava came at first a sprinkling, then a stream of canons regular.

On the eastern frontiers of Europe another pattern of settlement and conquest was reflected in a monastic map quite different in some of its lineaments, though also closely dependent on its own story of conquest and settlement. The early stages are obscure, but in Poland and Bohemia, whose monastic history has been most thoroughly investigated, three distinct phases can be distinguished.[3] The conversion of Bohemia had been due to collaboration between the Roman monk of Bohemian origin, St. Adalbert or Vojtech, and the native dynasty; and the first two foundations were the work of the Princess Mlada-Maria, first abbess of the house at Hradcany in Prague, and of Adalbert himself in founding Brevnov abbey. In Poland another Italian influence, of hermits inspired by St. Romuald, played a part in the first formation of Christianity. In both countries, as had been for many centuries traditional, there were monks among the missionaries, and the early cathedral chapters—like that at Toledo in the late eleventh century—seem to have contained both monks and canons. Already in the mid–eleventh century Brevnov and its offshoots formed an important element in the secular as well as the spiritual life of Bohemia, much on the pattern of the German imperial monasteries. In Poland meanwhile, there was a generation of civil war and confusion in which the monastic life disappeared, followed by new foundations, of which Tyniec near Krakow was the most permanent and powerful. The third epoch in Poland came in the mid– and late twelfth century, with the arrival of the Cistercians. By this date Bohemia and eastern Germany had come more generally under western influence. The Cistercians and Premonstratensians formed major settlements in the frontier lands, as the boundaries of Germany advanced, and more and more German towns and villages were founded in lands traditionally Slav. In these areas monasteries were never so numerous as farther west, and ancient houses were exceedingly few. But the Cistercians, the canons regular and the friars flourished in every country in the papal allegiance. The nature of the Cistercian imprint can be gauged from rough figures: in Germany east of the Elbe, by 1300, about fifteen; in Poland, including Silesia, twenty-three; in Bohemia fourteen; in Hungary nine; in Romania and what used to be Jugoslavia seven.[4] The most remote were at Falkenau near Dorpat in Esthonia and at Dünamünde in Latvia, where a community gathered in 1208 and was massacred twenty years later. For the most part the Cistercian settlements were more peaceful than this, though not infrequently involved in local politics. The majority of these houses were descendants of Morimond, whose daughter and granddaughter houses had moved across the Rhine, through such centers as Altenberg, and formed huge numbers of communities in Germany— Maulbronn is a characteristic sample of a house in this family of the second generation—and central and eastern Europe. Poland was first colonized in the 1140s. The main effort there and elsewhere in Eastern Europe was c. 1175–1250.[5] In these regions, in general, the thirteenth century witnessed the monastic flowering characteristic of the twelfth century farther west. Already by 1250 there was strong competition from the friars, and the late entry of the monastic order is doubtless one of the reasons why the monastic houses were in the end so many fewer than the mendicant.

In the Slav lands, as in Ireland, there sometimes appeared within Cistercian communities a barrier in language and culture; in Ireland between Saxon and Celt, in Poland between German and Slav. The Irish case is much the better documented, and it has in the past been too readily assumed that racial conflict was commonly reflected in Cistercian communities east of the Elbe. It is in fact clear that in some cases they formed centers of reconciliation rather than citadels of colonialism, and also that the division between German- and Slav-speaking folk did not always correspond—perhaps rarely corresponded—with any precision to the division between choir monks and lay brothers in Cistercian cloisters.

If the family of Morimond reigned throughout the land mass of central and eastern Europe, along the Baltic littoral we meet the direct influence of St. Bernard and the family of Clairvaux. This family, by 1300, counted five houses near the southern Baltic coast (three of them now in Poland), five in Sweden—and one more on the island of Gotland—five in Denmark and three in Norway. This is not quite the whole count of the order in Scandinavia, but very nearly.[6] The writ of Cluny and Gorze never ran in these lands, which were only converted in the tenth and eleventh centuries. Thus traditional monasticism had very slight influence here. A daughter of the English house of Evesham was established at Odensee in Denmark shortly before 1100,[7] and elsewhere a small number of houses of English and German origin grew up. The crucial step, however, came with the sending of monks from Clairvaux to Alvastra in 1143, in a part of Sweden only recently and superficially converted. "I have left my father's house—put behind me everything desirable in this world…and come to you, father, hoping to enjoy your sweet presence," cried one of the monks of Clairvaux when enjoined by Bernard to set off for Sweden. "…I hoped to await the judgement day among the holy corpses of the brothers in this cemetery. And today you cast me out.…"[8] Bernard promised that he would die at Clairvaux, and the party set off to brave the northern climate, to found both Alvastra and Nydala, from which the order spread to other parts of Sweden. A few years later another party from Clairvaux started the first Danish community at Esrom, and Clairvaux's English daughters, Fountains and Kirkstead, had meanwhile sent colonies to Lyse and Hovedö in Norway in 1146–47.

In no part of western Europe was the monastic life more ancient or more deeply entrenched than in Ireland; yet the pattern of religious houses there was of the twelfth and thirteenth centuries, and not earlier. A new era had dawned c. 1124 when St. Malachy became abbot of Bangor, the first ancient house to be reformed; he was later to be bishop of three different sees and to spend much time in travel. After his death in 1148 his life was written by St. Bernard in person, a sign of the impression Malachy himself was able to make at the heart of the monastic world of the day. Malachy was deeply affected by the Cistercian way of life, and also by the practical utility of the canons regular, which he found for himself in the notable French abbey of Arrouaise,[9] whose customs had been influenced by Bernard. In the end some thirty to forty Cistercian houses were founded in Ireland between 1142 and c. 1230, and over a hundred Augustinian. Malachy had laid the foundations for a new Irish church in which native traditions and the new cosmopolitan fashions of the twelfth century mingled, but a tragic misfortune—the English invasion of the 1170s—was to make it in a measure a center of colonialism. From 1216 to 1228 the monks of the large house of Mellifont were in rebellion against a discipline that had become associated with foreign rule. In 1228 a brave English monk, Stephen of Lexington, then abbot of Stanley, later abbot of Clairvaux itself, was sent by the general chapter on visitation. He ended the rebellion, but in the process started a policy of appointing foreign abbots and settling foreign monks in the Irish Cistercian houses. This was not in its origin intended to mean English rule, but it rapidly became associated in Irish eyes with the more general policy of English dominion in their church; and as the hold of the general chapter weakened, the Cistercian overlords became ever more evidently English. The rebellion at Mellifont was the first of a long series of clashes. But it would be superficial to reckon colonial rule the only legacy of twelfth century monasticism in Ireland; for in later times, when the English dissolved their own monasteries, a small number of Irish communities enjoyed a revival, and final dissolution was delayed till the eighteenth century; no great space of time divides the old monasticism in Ireland from the new foundations of the nineteenth and twentieth centuries.

What Malachy inspired in Ireland on the grand scale—and (one would think) far beyond the economic resources of a poor country—King David (1124–53) attempted more modestly in Scotland. He was the youngest and most civilized of the sons of St. Margaret, and thus brother to Matilda, Henry I's queen, as well as earl of Huntingdon and Northampton and a leading English baron. His notable achievement was to spread a network of Norman Scottish baronies in the lowlands of Scotland, with a scatter of religious houses among them. Their nucleus lay near the border, where an anthology of religious orders owed him patronage—the Benedictines of Tiron at Kelso, the Cistercians at Melrose, the Augustinian canons at Jedburgh, the Premonstratensians at Dryburgh: a notable group whose fine remains are the monument to one of the most lavish and imaginative monastic patrons of the age.[10] Wales had no Malachy and no David, but in a country originally as poor as Ireland, there came to be a small group of Benedictine houses, mostly outposts of Norman settlement, a small group of Augustinian houses and a scatter of Cistercian, where Welsh and English met as genuinely as in the most successful of the houses in the borders of Germany and in the Slav countries.

None of these lands on the borders of western Christendom had any concentration of monastic houses and population to compare with those in England, France, Germany and Italy. In the current state of research, only for England can figures of any precision be given.[11] Between 1066 and the mid–twelfth century the number of houses increased about tenfold, from 60 to nearly 600 (of monks alone, from 48 to about 500); and this probably reflects a growth in monastic population from a little over 1,000 to 7 or 8,000. The grand total by 1300 was 1,000 houses and between 17 and 18,000 religious; but this included the friars, and a considerable part of the expansion consisted in small houses, especially of canons, and dependencies, some of them tiny. Nonetheless, it is clear that the increase was dramatic and that it was no peculiarity of the English scene. In all these countries the monastic map of 1300 is most obviously a palimpsest, on which the traditional monasticism of Cluny, Gorze, Glastonbury, Fruttuaria, La Cava, Hirsau and so on scored its mark widely and deeply, and the new movements of the late eleventh, twelfth and thirteenth

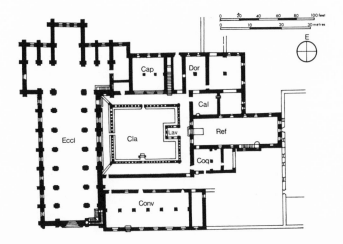

Plan of Fossanova showing the original layout, twelfth to fourteenth centuries.

centuries have scored theirs everywhere too. A traveler in 1300 would have been hard put to it to find a place in these lands more than twenty miles from the nearest religious house; and in the richest areas, in the Low Countries, the Rhineland, in Burgundy, Normandy, Poitou, Provence, Lombardy and Tuscany, more than fifteen—and to this day in many parts of western Europe one can walk from one surviving fragment of a medieval abbey to the next for weeks on end.

Such a traveler in 1300 would have found the friars and the Cistercians everywhere as ubiquitous as the traditional houses. But he would have found some notable changes in the pattern as he moved from region to region. In southern Italy, in the kingdom of Naples or of the Two Sicilies, he would enter the world of La Cava and Monte Cassino, where old movements still flourished and the Cistercians had a modest but visible foothold. Almost every order had its house in or near Rome; here the houses under Cassino's influence met those reformed from Fruttuaria in Lombardy; here too were Cistercians at

Fossanova, Casamari, Tre Fontane and elsewhere. In Umbria and the Marches, in the homeland of St. Francis, friars and her-mits lived side by side; here and in Tuscany lay most of the houses sprung from Camaldoli and Vallombrosa, on the peaks and in the cities. Further north again, we find traditional cen-ters in Fruttuaria and Sant'Ambrogio in Milan, and Cistercian at Chiaravalle; presently we pass from the world of Camaldoli to that of the Chartreuse, thinly spread all over the Alpine regions and the north of Europe, but with its center in the regions of Rhône and Rhine. In Burgundy we are in the homeland of Cluny and Cîteaux, the capitals of the largest of all monastic congregations. Even in its decline, in the late four-teenth and fifteenth centuries, Cluny reckoned it had about seven hundred dependencies, and the number was probably higher in the twelfth and thirteenth centuries.[12] Cîteaux had about the same number of daughters, no doubt still housing in 1300 a far larger number of monks than Cluny could count—for many Cluniac houses were diminutive and the lay brothers still swelled the Cistercian population. Cluny, Cîteaux and Prémontré are not far apart, and their daughters lay all over France and England. In Dijon, the center of Burgundy, lies Saint-Bénigne, home of St. William, who had inspired the observance of eleventh-century Normandy and early Norman England. In Germany and Provence we meet numerous houses influenced by Cluny, especially through Saint-Victor of Marseille and Hirsau; and Hirsau's influence had spread right through Germany in the late eleventh and twelfth centuries.

But in Germany itself we meet striking differences in the monastic map. First of all, there is the large area where Gorze and its offshoots had reigned, and not Cluny—though the houses of traditional monasticism must have looked much alike to casual visitors from both sides of the frontier of France and the Empire. Second, the Elbe formed the old frontier of German Christendom, and the pattern was quite different to its east, where Premonstratensian canons and Cistercian monks played a leading part in the settlement of some areas hardly inhabited before, and where the Cistercians in particular were pioneers in the study of forestry and the techniques of reclamation. Third, the female element was much stronger in Germany and the Low Countries than elsewhere. This is particularly noticeable among the Cistercian nuns. In England and Wales there were about thirty houses of nuns that claimed at one time or another to be Cistercian; most of them were relatively small and poor, and all but a handful were founded before 1200. In France the number is said to have been about 160, and a higher proportion were of the thirteenth century. In Germany the figure is over 250, most of them founded after 1200. Although these houses were often quite modest in size, the total number exceeded those of the men. The final total for the whole order throughout Europe was not so disparate: about 740 for men and about 650 for women.[13]

If we ask what quality of life the traveler would have found within the cloisters in 1300, we can gather many answers, and of a bewildering variety, from the comments of the day. In the end, however, we can only say one of two things: that we cannot now enter the lives of a hundred thousand or more religious in several thousand houses, or that what we know shows us that we would have found a cross section of humankind, in glory and in squalor: much that was humdrum and routine, much that was vicious, much that was devoted and something that was heroic. One such traveler (admittedly, a sharp critic of the monks) must speak for all. It was to the year 1300 that

Dante assigned his own pilgrimage to hell and purgatory and heaven—and not long after that in truth he composed his *Commedia*. In the seventh heaven, and canto 22 of the *Paradiso*,[14] he encountered St. Benedict himself, who thus addressed him:

> "In old days,
> That mountain, at whose side Cassino rests,
> Was, on its height, frequented by a race
> Deceived and ill-disposed: and I it was,
> Who thither carried first the name of Him,
> Who brought the soul-subliming truth to man
> And such a speeding grace shone over me,
> That from their impious worship I reclaim'd
> The dwellers round about, who with the world
> Were in delusion lost. These other flames,
> The spirits of men contemplative, were all
> Enliven'd by that warmth, whose kindly force
> Gives birth to flowers and fruits of holiness.
> Here is Macarius; Romoaldo [Romuald] here;
> And here my brethren, who their steps refrain'd
> Within the cloisters, and held firm their heart."

Dante asks to see Benedict's face, but is put off; first, like any follower of the Rule, he must climb the ladder of humility (see Rule, chap. 7).

> "Brother!" he thus rejoin'd, "in the last sphere
> Expect completion of thy lofty aim:
> For there on each desire completion waits,
> And there on mine; where every aim is found
> Perfect, entire, and for fulfilment ripe.
> There all things are as they have ever been:

For space is none to bound; nor pole divides.
Our ladder reaches even to that clime;
And so, at giddy distance, mocks thy view.
Thither the patriarch Jacob saw it stretch
Its topmost round; when it appear'd to him
With angels laden. But to mount it now
None lifts his foot from earth: and hence my rule
Is left a profitless stain upon the leaves;
The walls, for abbey rear'd, turn'd into dens;
The cowls, to sacks choak'd up with musty meal.
Foul usury doth not more lift itself
Against God's pleasure, than that fruit, which makes
The hearts of monks so wanton: for whate'er
Is in the church's keeping, all pertains
To such, as sue for heaven's sweet sake; and not
To those, who in respect of kindred claim,
Or on more vile allowance. Mortal flesh
Is grown so dainty, good beginnings last not
From the oak's birth unto the acorn's setting.
His convent Peter founded without gold
Or silver; I, with prayers and fasting, mine;
And Francis, his in meek humility.
And if thou note the point, whence each proceeds,
Then look what it hath err'd to; thou shalt find
The white grown murky. Jordan was turned back:
And a less wonder, than the refluent sea,
May, at God's pleasure, work amendment here."

15.

Epilogue:
1300 to the Present

The monastic houses of Europe have passed through many vicissitudes. Some have survived, or been revived; life at the Chartreuse, at Camaldoli, at Vallombrosa is much the same as it was in the Middle Ages; there are still—or perhaps one should say there are again—thousands of monks and canons scattered over the face of Christendom. A few samples show the kind of changes time has brought. The small Cistercian houses in Provence either survived or faded away; in either event they never commanded the resources or the ambition for great changes; they were never converted into great country houses or made quarries for local towns.[1] In many parts of Germany and Switzerland the Reformation swept the monasteries away as in England. What the Reformation began, the French Revolution and Napoleon carried further, especially in France and Italy, and most of the communities which were left have suffered extinction, for a time at least, in more recent anticlerical movements. But not quite all—in Einsiedeln, Switzerland, for example, one can visit the center of one of the longest stretches of continuous history to be found in Europe: a Benedictine house of immense antiquity, still a flourishing monastery; also the hub of a great estate and even one of the chief places of the Canton Schwyz. A visit to Catholic Einsiedeln from nearby Zürich, Zwingli's Zürich, one of the most important of the Protestant cities, is like passing into another world, where the Reformation is no more. But the continuing prosperity of the abbey is above all revealed by the total absence of any medieval buildings: It is an immense and powerful monument to the Baroque.

1300–1500

These were mighty changes of a later date, but let us first glance at one of the subtlest expressions of the course of monastic history in the centuries after 1300. At Lacock we can see a group of medieval monastic buildings melting into the country house of the sixteenth and eighteenth centuries. For this reason, they are an excellent witness of the nature of late medieval domestic planning and of the approach and habit of mind of the dissolvers. At Much Wenlock the change was slighter still. In the fifteenth century the prior built one of the most charming late medieval manor houses that survives anywhere in western Europe for his lodgement; the monks, meanwhile, made substantial alterations in the older infirmary alongside. Between the two buildings, domestic quarters of solid comfort and moderate privacy—not luxurious by our standards, but in reasonable accord with the standards of country gentry of moderate means of the fifteenth century—could be found for the senior monks at least, and probably for the greater part of the community. No doubt the monks preserved the fabric, and some semblance of the services, in their tremendous church. No doubt they visited the cloister, and the younger ones may have slept in cubicles in the dormitory and fed in the refectory, after washing their hands ceremonially in

Plan of Much Wenlock showing existing medieval walls and those which can be traced with reasonable confidence, and the line of the apse (perhaps eleventh century) excavated in 1901. Lavabo, infirmary and chapter house are twelfth century; church and refectory, thirteenth; the prior's lodging was built and the infirmary remodelled in the fifteenth.

the lavabo, still adorned with charming sculptures of the twelfth century.[2] But there seems to have been a tendency and drift toward the more domestic buildings of the convent, to the infirmary, where meat might be eaten and the great silence somewhat relaxed, and to the prior's lodging, which looks as if it were designed to be the center of their life, and certainly of their hospitality. At the dissolution such buildings needed no conversion to suit the needs of a line of country gentlemen of moderate fortune and large families. We must not unduly diminish the impact of dissolution. The monks departed; St. Milburga, who had presided over the little town and the church through many vicissitudes since the seventh century, was violently removed from her shrine. Church and cloister fell into decay. But life was quickly resumed in the prior's lodging and infirmary: and to this day it is a modest country seat.

Behind this story we may detect a world in which priors and monks lived in comparative ease, the lives of country gentlemen of moderate means: a far cry from the spiritual adventure that had founded and refounded Much Wenlock in earlier centuries or created the Cistercian complex at neighboring Buildwas. I use the word *detect* because we know little of the inner life of most monasteries in this age of vegetation. From time to time in the late Middle Ages there were movements for reform: Among the friars in particular these enjoyed some spectacular successes, and one or two orders, like the Carthusian, stood in no need of such reforms. But for the most part, so far as we can tell, from 1300 on until the Reformation and Counter Reformation, the religious were not climbing Jacob's ladder, as St. Bernard (and Dante's St. Benedict) had insisted that they must (see p. 88). For this they fell under severe criticism in the fourteenth and fifteenth centuries, and they have often been condemned in recent times, especially by two kinds of critic: from without, by stem Protestant opponents of the medieval church, like G. G. Coulton, who for all his Protestantism wrote about medieval monks as if he were himself a medieval reformer trouncing contemporary vices; and from within, from historians like Dom David Knowles, who have measured them by the standards of Benedict and Bernard, and found them wanting. Undoubtedly there were many scandals and abuses, but these can be found in the documents of the eleventh and twelfth centuries as well as in the fourteenth and fifteenth. Sometimes an intimate chronicle or the record of a bishop's visitation will show that something had gone drastically wrong. This should cause no surprise. It must also have been common, then as now, for communities to be tolerably well run under a shrewd and sensible direction, and to enjoy a happy sense of community, even though not a powerhouse of spiritual life. But if such a director is removed or if a spirit of gossip and faction is abroad, a community may rapidly degenerate, even without the sins against chastity, poverty and obedience that broke out from time to time in every age. Sometimes a weak abbot or a bickering council of elder monks demoralized a community; sometimes mismanagement of its affairs and debt led to real hardship, even to the dispersal of the monks or nuns. But much more often, so far as we can tell, communities survived without impressing their neighbors with their special fervor, nor impressing themselves on the historical record by scandal or disgrace. In the long run, somewhere between the extremes of fervor and corruption, innumerable communities lived on through the late Middle Ages to the Reformation—and in many countries far beyond the Reformation—in the humdrum circumstances represented by the prior's lodging at Much Wenlock. For all the criticism to which they were subjected, on the whole they accepted themselves, and were widely accepted, as a normal part of the social scene. Yet this acceptance could be seriously challenged, and there was no age between the eleventh and the nineteenth centuries in which a zealous reformer or a rapacious secular ruler did not suppress a number of houses in the name of reform.

Every age since Dante voiced his hope for a renewal of the religious life has seen something of the decline St. Benedict lamented, and something of the renewal. All that lies beyond 1300 must be for us an epilogue, a coda; but it would be quite

false to see even the last centuries of the Middle Ages as mere
decline, still less to end without any word upon the major
revival of the sixteenth and seventeenth centuries, and its successors in the eighteenth, nineteenth and twentieth.

The Black Death of 1348–49 and the sharp decline in the
population that had supplied the monasteries helped to
sharpen a crisis: Many communities became a tiny shadow of
what they had been; many seemed little more than caretakers
for an old heritage whose original purpose was but slightly
remembered. Yet at the same time St. Bridget in Sweden was
founding a new double order, and in the fifteenth century San
Bernardino inspired the growth of a renewal among the friars
that not only provided numberless houses like the Carceri
above Assisi with new life, but stirred revival in the end in all
the orders of friars.

Since 1500

Thus the stage was prepared for the drama of the sixteenth
century, and with the Reformation came the first major
onslaught: It started in Germany with Luther and his associates
in the 1520s, then passed on to England in the 1530s, when
Henry VIII was in search of marriage and money. When Henry
and Thomas Cromwell destroyed the whole monastic fabric in
England in the late 1530s innumerable communities were pensioned off with scarcely a murmur. Here and there voices were
raised very loudly indeed against so cynical an act of destruction and spoliation; and in a few houses—most notably among
the Carthusians of London—there were martyrs for the religious life. In the other parts of Europe in which the Protestant
cause succeeded, the religious were taken out of their monasteries and their lands confiscated. There was rarely so sudden

and complete a breach as in England—in Scotland, for example there were two generations of slow decay and secularization, so that lay lords gradually acquired the titles and properties of the abbots and the last monk might die in his abbey still in possession of some of his ancient rights. But nothing like the monastic life survived in the Protestant communions of the sixteenth century.

Thus by 1600 the monastic life had virtually disappeared from the British Isles, save in parts of Ireland, save also for Jesuits and others in hiding and under proscription. The abbeys of the Low Countries, of Protestant Germany and Scandinavia had gone, and many of those in France had suffered from Huguenot attacks. Elsewhere the sixteenth century was a new golden age of religious observance, when the Jesuits and the Discalced (barefoot) Carmelites—the orders of St. Ignatius Loyola, St. Teresa and St. John of the Cross, and many others—spread ideas of religion undreamed of in earlier ages. Both the contemplative and the active wings received new life and inspiration, and in the seventeenth century many an old abbey or congregation submitted to reform. These included the humane, scholarly, cultured congregation of Saint-Maur, the Benedictine reform unexpectedly founded under the patronage of Cardinal Richelieu. In due course its houses included Mont Saint-Michel and many other great centers, and its monks some of the most eminent theologians and church historians of the seventeenth and eighteenth centuries, above all Dom Jean Mabillon, a pious and humble monk who yet played a notable part in the scientific revolution of the seventeenth century by laying the foundations for the scientific study of medieval history.

Mabillon was a man of peace; but he was from time to time drawn into controversy, and among his most dramatic encounters was his pamphlet war with the most celebrated and puritanical of the reformers of the day, *l'abbé tempête*, Armand de Rancé, founder of the reformed Cistercian Order that we call Trappist, after his own abbey of La Trappe. The essence of de Rancé's position was that monks should not engage in intellectual pursuits: Mabillon's answer showed how wide and deep a share in the Benedictine tradition learning had enjoyed. De Rancé was in some respects a caricature of St. Bernard; yet he gave a genuine impulse to the contemplative life that helped the monastic ideal to survive the French Revolution, and he allowed his battle with Mabillon to end in one of those dramatic personal reconciliations such as Bernard himself greatly loved. But the Trappist was only one way of reform for the Cistercians, and Bernard's ideals, and the contemplative life itself, have followed many apart from those of the tempestuous abbot.

In certain respects the eighteenth century was like the fifteenth in monastic history: The orders survived; the storm was near but hardly heard within the cloister—and yet, there were many centers of new life and growth besides. But between 1780 and 1810 the large majority of the surviving religious communities in Europe were suppressed, their inmates pensioned off, turned away or forced into secular life. First, the "enlightened" despots showed their despotism in characteristic fashion, and Joseph II suppressed a handsome proportion of the religious houses in the Austrian Empire. Next, the French Revolution abolished all those in France: Many were understandably viewed as the symbols of privilege and caste and, as in Henry VIII's England, such feelings were exploited to excuse total destruction. As the armies of the Revolution and Napoleon marched about Europe, the abbeys fell in every land that was conquered—throughout Germany, much of Austria and Italy. A few survived, especially in Austria and the Catholic cantons of Switzerland, but a reasonable observer in the early or mid–nineteenth century might well have supposed that the religious life would soon be persecuted out of existence altogether. True, there were major revivals even in France; but in the nineteenth century such revivals tended to be comparatively short-lived, and anticlericalism became powerful once again under the Third Republic. Between 1880 and 1903 the monks of Solesmes were expelled four times, only finally to return in 1922.[3] There are a few abbeys, especially in the remoter parts of Switzerland and Austria, whose life has continued almost unhindered, but there is no country that has not witnessed some measure of repression, suppression, control or persecution—in the nineteenth century the religious suffered persecution above all under the banner of "liberalism." Paradoxically, it is in Protestant England that European monasticism has had its least troubled history in the last two centuries.

Under these conditions one might reasonably have supposed that today the religious life would be an antiquarian memory, that a few fragments of religious communities might live on here and there, forgotten or tolerated by complacent authority. It comes as a surprise, therefore, to learn that there are over a million Roman Catholic religious in the world today, not counting numerous monks in the Orthodox communions and that phenomenon of the modern world, the Protestant religious.[4] This is at first a staggering figure. Most educated people today, not closely in touch with the religious orders, are inclined to think of the Middle Ages as the epoch when monks and nuns were most numerous. No doubt there is a sense in which this is true. For if we guessed that there were in 1300 about 150 to 200,000 religious in western

Christendom, they doubtless included far more than the Benedictine, Cistercian and Carthusian monks who still follow the rule of St. Benedict today. Even if there may be more friars now than in 1300, it is only by a relatively small margin, whereas the population of the Catholic world has increased many times.

A study of late twentieth century statistics shows three outstanding differences: First, the orders are now worldwide, and even if persecution has effectively abolished them in some parts of Asia and Eastern Europe, America has been in recent times the home of many of the most flourishing houses of every complexion. Secondly, the greater number of religious belong to orders scarcely or never mentioned in this book. In 1972 there were about 20,000 monks following ancient rules, and over 50,000 friars; but there were also about 36,000 Jesuits and numerous members of the new orders that grew in the nineteenth and early twentieth centuries. Many were small, but they included some, like the Christian Brothers (nearly 18,000) and the Marist Brothers (about 10,000), of substantial size. The third characteristic of the modern orders is that the nuns outnumber the male religious by about three to one—in 1972 one million to about 300,000; in 1981, 950,000 to 225,000. Here is a dramatic change indeed, for in parts of western Europe in the twelfth and thirteenth centuries the men may have outnumbered the women by an even larger multiple, and even in Germany and the Low Countries it is unlikely that they commanded anything approaching equality.

It would be fascinating to pursue the comparison beyond this point and inquire below the superficial tale of figures into the inwardness of the religious life today. It is, however, essential to dwell on the contrasts between the Middle Ages and the present for a moment longer, for the differences stir us to question assumptions we might too readily accept as to the relation of society and monasticism in the Middle Ages, and also because the figures serve to remind us that our subject is alive and actual, not a story from a lost world.

Do these figures mean that the religious life is now flourishing and, in an atmosphere more tolerant than that of the nineteenth century, can look forward to a future as long and as prosperous as its past? No one can tell. The orders are trying to assimilate a wealth of new ideas and inspirations; they are under attack from without and within; not for the most part under persecution, but under a growing fervor of critical inquiry. This in itself is nothing new. Critical inquiry was especially characteristic of the *"crise du monachisme"* of the eleventh and twelfth centuries, which accompanied the golden age of monastic expansion in the west. The same could be said of the revivals of the nineteenth and twentieth centuries, when a remarkable resurgence of the religious orders accompanied the spread of agnostic thought, the denial of the roots of Christian belief on a scale without precedent since the early Middle Ages. It is evident that the growth of agnostic humanism has continued unabated, and in Europe, in numbers at least, the churches have in recent generations suffered an obvious decline—though not in America or the developing world. More than that, the religious life has in a fair measure depended on deep traditional attitudes within the Roman Catholic Church. While it is undoubtedly true that this way of life has often been grafted on new stock in the last two centuries and has come to flourish abundantly in ecumenical centers such as Taizé, in Burgundy, the ascetic, celibate ideal has been questioned even among Roman Catholics to a degree unprecedented. In former centuries it was widely accepted that the life of the religious was in some sense, often in a very obvious sense, higher and better than the married. To hint such a thought in the presence of many religious in the 1970s was already to invite an instant denial. Since the 1970s, within the Roman Catholic communion and in the ecumenical church at large, there has been a questioning of traditional positions so deep and wide that the notion of the monastic life as a privileged version of the Christian ideal has rapidly declined.

In the ten or twenty years following the Second World War, traditional monasticism enjoyed a rapid increase in recruits, in the contemplative as well as the more active orders. In the 1960s, this was sharply reversed, and the more enclosed orders seem to have suffered relatively the most. In part, this reflects the pattern in all the churches: Recruitment of clergy and ministers declined sharply in the 1960s; all began to face a crisis of identity; traditional attitudes to the clerical profession at large were subjected to criticism. Some traditionalists blame the new crisis, and the movement that they interpret as decline, on the flow of new ideas. One cannot but sympathize with their protest against the urge in some quarters to press every type of religious practice into a single mold. Yet the ferment seems to a sympathetic outsider to show, as could no era of peace or quiet, that there is vivid life in the religious orders. Such a comment would raise a smile on the faces of many monks and nuns of ancient orders, for a continuous, vivid and effective life is evidently carried on in numerous houses little affected by the hum of the world outside—and the spiritual life is not subject to statistics or quantitative measurement at all.

In the ferment of the eleventh and twelfth centuries controversy accompanied growth, not only in numbers, but in

variety and depth of experience. Similarly, when the call to a
more active life helped the orders of friars into flourishing life
in the thirteenth century, there was clearly a sense in which
new life in some orders was balanced by decline in others. The
malaise of the 1960s was in part a call for a more active life, for
an end to the barriers between the cloister and the world, and
for a new appraisal of the religious life in terms more active
even than those of St. Francis and St. Dominic. It was a tight-
ening of the ancient tension between the inward and the outward view. If this were the whole case, one might feel that it
was a tide ebbing and flowing that we are witnessing, not a
fundamental questioning of a traditional mode of life. In one
respect this seems an inadequate statement of the current
dilemma. In the past, Roman Catholic religious have been able
to see their vocation against a doctrine of marriage, which
rarely set the ideal of obedience between husband and wife in
the sacrament on a level with celibate obedience in religion.
This is no longer the case. For all the dangers that social custom,
fashion and law have laid in the way of Christian marriage, it
remains obvious enough, even from the most superficial reading of the literature of recent decades, that an ideal of marriage
is laid before the modern Christian, of whatever denomina-
tion, with a novel profundity; it sets a standard of partnership
and common action that strives to make genuine sense of the
likening of marriage to the union of Christ and the Church.
Theological tides are one cause of this; the social customs of
our day are another—for it would be absurd to pretend that it
is only among Christians that such ideals now flourish, and
contend with their very visible enemies in modern society.
One source of these changing customs has been the demand of
women for a freer and more equal place in the world; it is no

doubt also one of the reasons why the number of nuns grew so rapidly in the last century and is declining now. Modern custom, and the ideals of the new generations of the 1960s and the 2000s, seem to face the religious life with a challenge that is genuinely new.

An intelligent observer of the age of Napoleon might well have thought that the regular life was really defunct. He or she would look very foolish now. Equally, it would be ridiculous to argue that because there is novelty in the current challenges, the orders will succumb. On the contrary, they have shown themselves in the past remarkably resilient in the face of controversy and shifting fashion. There are still parts of the world where the monasteries are associated with all that is most repellent in social and economic privilege, as they were over much of western Europe before 1789. This is now rare; equally often they are seen to be in sympathy with the varied and genuine aspirations of our day. The ideal of marriage alone is unlikely to destroy them, for man is infinitely various, and there are many for whom total absorption in a single union is meaningless or inadequate. Hitherto it has been the keynote of our civilization that, whatever its ups and downs, the variety of occupation open to us has tended to increase rather than decline. If this continues, then the spiritual experience whose history has been traced in this book will surely continue to find adherents, and to inspire new generations of postulants—although St. Benedict may be even more astonished by the adventures of his children in the third millennium than he was when he met Dante in 1300.

Every monastery whose ruins are substantial carries on its face some stories of change and decay: rebuilding, alteration, destruction or mere neglect. Some carry the scars of war and revolutions; some of peaceful decay; some of long centuries of use; others of rapid and dramatic change. In every case we have to work back in imagination, through the centuries of epilogue to the building and to the community as it was in the eleventh, twelfth or thirteenth century. In this book I have tried to throw a pebble into the center of a pool of clear water. As the ripples spread we see the life of medieval monks and nuns spreading out into the whole history of an epoch. This book is selective and incomplete. But it has aimed to show how the history of a medieval monastery may reveal the history of life and thought, literature, society, economy and culture of the central Middle Ages.

Glossary

abbey   a monastery ruled by an abbot

anchorite or   a male or female hermit
anchoress

Augustinian canons   see chapter 8

Benedictine monks   see pp. 59–69 on
"traditional monasticism"

canons regular   canons living under a rule—Augustinians
and Premonstratensians, for example

canons secular   canons of a cathedral or large church
with individual incomes (prebends), liv-
ing in a separate house

chaplain   either the priest in charge of a chapel or
a cleric in the service of a bishop or king
or noble

Cistercian monks   see chapters 9 and 13

Cluniac monks   see pp. 62–69, 82–85

convent
: any community of religious—monks, canons, friars; nowadays most often, of nuns

deacon
: the higher orders of the church comprised bishop, priest, deacon and subdeacon. A deaconess was not strictly in orders, but a woman dedicated to pastoral care or similar service

friars
: members of the mendicant orders who lived mainly by begging and were usually engaged in pastoral work, less enclosed than monks: see especially Franciscans and Dominicans. These had three orders: the first was the friars, the second the nuns (Poor Clares, Dominicanesses), the third of laity connected with the order: see p. 227

Knights Hospitallers and Templars
: see chapter 10

lay brothers
: monks or friars who were not literate and not in orders: see pp. 13–14, 171–75

Mary and Martha
: the two sisters who gave Jesus hospitality, Mary sitting at his feet and Martha "cumbered about much serving" (Luke 10:38–42); thus they could be taken as models of the contemplative and active life (but see p. 308, chapter 8, note 2).

mendicant orders
: see friars

novitiate	the period of probation and training for a newly admitted monk, canon or friar—commonly one year
Premonstratensian canon	see pp. 217–19
priory	a monastery ruled by a prior (usually, but not always, a smaller house than an abbey)
scriptorium	the writing-office: the chamber or space in the cloister where monks wrote books and documents
secular church	as distinct from the religious orders: clergy and laity living in the world, not under specific religious rules

Notes

Abbreviations

Atlas Cist.
F. Van der Meer. *Atlas de l' Ordre Cistercien.* Amsterdam-Brussels, 1965.

Backmund
N. Backmund. *Monasticon Praemonstratense.* 3 vols. Straubing, 1949–56.

Brooke, *Churches and Churchmen*
C. N. L. Brooke. *Churches and Churchmen in Medieval Europe.* London, 1999.

Chadwick, *Asceticism*
Owen Chadwick. *Western Asceticism, Selected Translations.* London, 1958.

Chadwick, *Cassian*
O. Chadwick. *John Cassian.* 2nd ed. Cambridge, 1968.

Constable *Reformation*
G. Constable. *The Reformation of the Twelfth Century.* Cambridge, 1996.

Cottineau
L. H. Cottineau. *Répertoire topo-bibliographique des abbayes et prieurés.* 2 vols. Macon, 1939–70.

DHGE
Dictionnaire d'histoire et de géographie ecclésiastiques. Paris, 1912–.

Dickinson
J. C. Dickinson. *The Origins of the Austin Canons and Their Introduction into England.* London, 1950.

Dimier (1971)
L'art cistercien hors de France. Ed. M.-A. Dimier. Zodiaque, 1971.

GB
Germania Benedictina, Ottobeuren, etc., 1970–.

GP
Germania Pontificia. Ed. A. Brackmann, I–III. Berlin, 1911–35.

Hauck
A. Hauck. *Kirchengeschichte Deutschlands,* I–III, 3rd and 4th ed. Leipzig, 1904–6; IV–V, 1st and 2nd ed., Leipzig, 1903–20.

Hunt (1967)
Noreen Hunt. *Cluny under St. Hugh, 1049–1109.* London, 1967.

Hunt (1971)
Cluniac Monasticism in the Central Middle Ages (selected papers,

Eng. trans.). Ed. N. Hunt. London, 1971.

IP

Italia Pontificia, ed. P. Kehr *(et alii)*, I–IX, Berlin, 1906–62.

KH

D. Knowles and R. N. Hadcock. *Medieval Religious Houses, England and Wales*. 2nd ed. London, 1971.

Knowles, *GHE*

D. Knowles. *Great Historical Enterprises: Problems in Monastic History*. London, 1963.

Knowles, *MO*

D. Knowles, *The Monastic Order in England, 940–1216*. Cambridge, 1940; 2nd ed., pagination unaltered, but with additional notes etc., 1963.

Knowles, *RO*

D. Knowles. *The Religious Orders in England*. 3 vols. Cambridge, 1948–59.

Krautheimer

R. Krautheimer. *Studies in Early Christian, Medieval and Renaissance Art*. New York-London, 1969.

Map

Walter Map. *De nugis curialium: Courtiers' Trifles*. Ed. and trans. M. R. James, C. N. L. Brooke and R. A. B. Mynors. Oxford Medieval Texts, 1983.

La Mendola

Miscellanea del Centro di Studi Medievali, I–VI, Settimane...alla Mendola, Milan, 1956–71.

MRHS

I. B. Cowan and D. E. Easson.

Medieval Religious Houses: Scotland. 2nd ed. London, 1976.

MSA

D. Knowles and J. K. S. St. Joseph. *Monastic Sites from the Air*. Cambridge, 1952.

Norton and Park 1986

Cistercian Art and Architecture in the British Isles. Ed. C. Norton and D. Park. Cambridge, 1986.

PL

Patrologiae cursus completus, series latina. Ed. J. P. Migne. Paris, 1844–64.

Schmitz

P. Schmitz, *Histoire de l'Ordre de S. Benoit,* 7 vols., Maredsous, 1942–56 (quoted from French ed., vols. I, II, 2nd ed., 1949).

VCH

Victoria History of the Counties of England.

Introduction, pp. 5–22

1. See pp. 44–45, 49. On the history of the controversy, see D. Knowles, *Great Historical Enterprises: Problems in Monastic History* (London, 1963), pp. 139–95. Since 1963 supporters of the priority of the Master have grown in numbers and confidence: see *La Règle de Saint Benoît*, ed. A. de Vogüé and J. Neufville, 2 vols., Sources Chrétiennes 181–82 (Paris, 1972), I, 245–314.

2. See p. 45; M. Dunne in *English Historical Review* 105 (1990): 567–94; A. de Vogüé, ibid. 107

(1992): 95–103; and Dunne's reply, ibid. 107 (1992): 104–11.

3. "The Cloister Symposium," *Gesta* 12 (1973), esp. W. Horn, "On the Origin of the Medieval Cloister," pp. 13–52; P. Meyvaert, "The Medieval Monastic *Claustrum,*" pp. 53–59.

4. C. Brooke, "Reflections on the Monastic Cloister," in *Romanesque and Gothic: Essays for George Zarnecki,* 2 vols. (Woodbridge, 1987), I, pp. 19–25, partly resumed in what follows.

5. See *Medieval Archaeology* 13 (1969): 21–36, and other refs. in her article in *Blackwell Encyclopaedia of Anglo-Saxon England,* ed. M. Lapidge et al. (Oxford, 1999), pp. 325–26.

6. W. Horn in *Gesta* 12 (1973): 13–52; W. Horn and E. Born, *The Plan of St. Gall,* 3 vols, (Berkeley, 1979), esp. I, pp. 241–309 and II, pp. 315–59 (C. M. Malone and W. Horn), esp. I, pp. 243–46; B. Bischoff in *Studien zum St. Galler Klosterplan,* ed. J. Duft (St. Gallen, 1962), pp. 67–78. For an account of the state of discussion in the 1980s, see W. Sanderson in *Speculum* 60 (1985): 615–32.

7. *La Règle de Saint Benoît* (n. 1), cc. 4, 67 (I, 464; II, 662).

8. P. Meyvaert in *Gesta* 12 (1973): 53–59.

9. See *The Monastic Constitutions of Lanfranc,* 2nd ed., ed. and trans. D. Knowles and C. N. L. Brooke (OMT, 2001).

10. See C. Brooke, R. Highfield and W. Swaan, *Oxford and Cambridge* (Cambridge, 1988), esp. pp. 78–79 and pl. 47.

11. See pp. 172–75, and the qualification by C. Holdsworth noted in Brooke, *Churches and Churchmen,* p. 204, n. 33.

12. See p. 169; Knowles, *MO,* 1st ed., pp. 208–16. For what follows, see ibid., 1963 ed., pp. 752–53; D. Knowles, *Great Historical Enterprises: Problems in Monastic History* (London, 1963), pp. 197–222; above all, C. Holdsworth in *Cistercian Art and Architecture in the British Isles,* eds. C. Norton and D. Park (Cambridge, 1986), pp. 40–55 —still the most reliable guide to the literature of the controversies surrounding Cistercian origins. For the latest views, see C. Berman, *The Cistercian Evolution* (Ithaca, 2000). Constance Berman, in a remarkable book based largely on close study of a group of southern French Cistercian houses, proposes that the order in origin was not strictly an order, nor did it have a general chapter till the mid-twelfth century or later—but was rather an umbrella under which many communities and groups of communities (like Savigny's) came to shelter. That the order owed much to preexisting communities—that it absorbed many like-minded groups and individuals—is doubtless true.

But for reasons given in the text, I am convinced that it had a general chapter from early days and was more integrated than Berman supposes—whatever the true history of its constitutional documents.

13. C. Waddell, "The Early Cistercian Experience of Liturgy" in *Rule and Life, an Interdisciplinary Study*, ed. M. B. Pennington (Shannon, 1971), pp. 77–116, and other studies listed in *Cistercian Art and Architecture* (n. 12), pp. 427–28. For what follows, see refs. in Holdsworth (n. 12), p. 46 and n. 32, and his sceptical comment on the use of legislation.

14. See Holdsworth (n. 12), p. 53 and n. 61 for earlier perceptions of this obvious truth. The figures that follow are based on L. Janauschek, *Originum Cisterciensium tomus* I (Vienna, 1877), esp. the summary on pp. 294–95 (see also below, p. 316 ch. 14, n. 4).

15. Brooke, *Churches and Churchmen*, pp. 171–72, 216–17.

16. Holdsworth (n. 12), p. 43, citing L. J. Lekai, "Ideals and reality in early Cistercian life and legislation," in *Cistercian Ideals and Reality*, ed. J. R. Sommerfeldt (Kalamazoo, 1978), pp. 4–29, esp. pp. 19–24.

17. Holdsworth (n. 12), p. 53; *The Letters and Charters of Gilbert Foliot*, ed. A. Morey and C. N. L. Brooke (Cambridge, 1967), pp. 510–13.

18. See esp. Orderic, IV, 324–25.

19. Janauschek (n. 14), pp. xvi–xxiv.

20. This is based on the detailed evidence in KH for England and Wales, and a selective trawl of similar material for some other countries.

21. Such as the backdating of the entry of Savigny into the order in 1147 (see p. 337) to a variable and arbitrary date in the 1110s (Janauschek [n. 14], p. 96). For evidence that the general chapter met in 1119, perhaps in 1116, see Holdsworth (n. 12), p. 44.

22. *Scriptores ordinis Grandimontensis*, ed. J. Becquet (Turnhout, 1968); cf. Brooke, *Churches and Churchmen*, p. 248 and nn. 56–57; the articles of Dom Becquet listed in Constable, *Reformation*, p. 331, esp. in *Revue Mabillon* 46 (1956): 15–32; C. Hutchison, *The Hermit Monks of Grandmont* (Kalamazoo, 1989). What follows resumes and expands Brooke, *Europe in the Central Middle Ages*, 3rd ed. (Harlow, 2000), p. 370.

23. For the lay brothers' rebellions, see *The Book of St. Gilbert*, ed. R. Foreville and G. Keir (OMT, 1987), pp. 76–85, 134–67; cf. ibid., pp. lv–lxii, corrected by B. Golding, *Gilbert of Sempringham and the Gilbertine Order* (Oxford, 1995), pp. 40–51, 458–62; Brooke, *Churches and Churchmen*, p. 248 (and for the meaning of "lay" in

this context, ibid., pp. 247–48 and nn.).

24. Brooke, *Churches and Churchmen*, pp. 249–51; R. B. Brooke, *Early Franciscan Government* (Cambridge, 1959), pp. 243–45, cf. pp. 197–98.

25. See pp. 85, 87–88, 206.

26. See R. and C. Brooke, *Popular Religion in the Middle Ages* (London, 1984), p. 64 and pl. 8.

27. Cambridge, 1996: henceforth Constable, *Reformation*. Cf. my comments in Brooke, *Europe in the Central Middle Ages*, 3rd ed. (Harlow, 2000), pp. 368–71.

28. Constable, *Reformation*, pp. 42–43; cf. Brooke, *Europe in the Central Middle Ages*, p. 369.

29. Constable, *Reformation*, p. 65. The references for what follows are in ibid., pp. 65–74, esp. 65, 69.

30. Constable, *Reformation*, p. 65 and refs. in n. 88.

31. Ibid.

32. Constable, *Reformation*, p. 69.

33. Brooke, *Europe in the Central Middle Ages*, pp. 132–34 and refs., esp. to P. Dronke, *Women Writers of the Middle Ages* (Cambridge, 1984), ch. 6.

34. KH, p. 493—modified in detail by S. Thompson, *Women Religious: The Founding of English Nunneries after the Norman Conquest* (Oxford, 1991).

35. S. Foot, *Veiled Women*, 2 vols. (Aldershot, 2000), esp., II, 158; Thompson, *Women Religious*, chs. 2, 4, esp. pp. 23, 56–61, on St. Albans, including what fol-

lows. On women religious there is now a very extensive literature, much of it cited in the notes to Constable, *Reformation*, pp. 65–74; on English women religious, see esp. Thompson, and S. K. Elkins, *Holy Women of Twelfth-Century England* (Chapel Hill, 1988); B. M. Kerr, *Religious Life for Women c. 1100–c. 1350: Fontevraud in England* (Oxford, 1999)— which is also useful for recent views on Robert of Arbrissel and the early history of Fontevraud.

36. *The Life of Christina of Markyate*, ed. and trans. C. H. Talbot, 2nd ed. (OMT, 1987). For the problem of its veracity, see C. Brooke, *The Medieval Idea of Marriage* (Oxford, 1989), pp. 144–45.

37. *The Book of St. Gilbert* (n. 23), esp. pp. 36–37, 44–47; B. Golding, *Gilbert of Sempringham* (n. 23), ch. 2, esp. pp. 133–37.

38. A. Blamires, *The Case for Women in Medieval Culture* (Oxford, 1997); *Woman Defamed and Women Defended: An Anthology of Medieval Texts*, ed. A. Blamires, K. Pratt and C. W. Marx (Oxford, 1992).

39. For what follows, see R. and C. Brooke, "St. Clare" in Brooke, *Churches and Churchmen*, ch. 15, esp. pp. 280–82.

40. See references in Constable, *Reformation*, p. 65 n. 87.

41. For the Dutch mystics, see S. Murk Jansen, *The Measure of*

Mystical Thought (Göppingen, 1991); Hadewijch, *The Complete Works*, trans. C. Hart (New York, 1980). For *The Life of Mary of Oignies* see *Acta Sanctorum Ordinis S. Benedicti*, ed. L. D'Achery and J. Mabillon (Paris, 1668–1701), V, 542–72. For the whole movement, see H. Grundmann, *Religious Movements in the Middle Ages* (English trans. S. Rowan, Notre Dame, 1995). B. Bolton, "Mulieres sanctae," *Studies in Church History* 10 (1973): 77–95, is an admirable summary and discussion of the movement. The more recent literature is copious: see n. 35.

Chapter 1
Prelude, pp. 25–43

1. Matthew 19:5–29 (cf. Luke 18, esp. 29). The opening sentence is quoted from the Authorized Version, the rest from the New English Bible.
2. Many critics doubt whether the epistle was written by St. Paul; yet it seems reasonable to accept that even if he was not the author it was evidently the work of a disciple who believed himself wholly faithful to the apostle's teaching.
3. Acts 4:32.
4. Matthew 10:9ff.; Mark 6:8ff.; Luke 9:3ff.; 10:4ff. See p. 226.
5. See pp. 141, 153–54, 221–23, 226.
6. Cf. D. J. Chitty, *The Desert a City* (Oxford, 1966), pp. 1ff. The

movement owed much, needless to say, to non-Christian as well as Christian thinkers. It has in the past been much disputed whether Christian monasticism was grafted on pagan stock or essentially original. The answer must in large measure depend on how precisely the question is framed; for it is evident that a large movement of this time was likely to draw on a range of experience both wider and more ancient than the Christian Church; equally, that many of its special features, and its essential inspiration, are unintelligible except in the context of the early church. Nothing of this is said in the text, since the aim is to introduce the monasticism of the Middle Ages; but it is a topic of great interest.

7. *Collations,* 18, esp. cc. 5ff., quoted from Chadwick, *Asceticism,* pp. 266–67.
8. Chadwick, *Cassian* (1968 ed.), pp. 25–26, 86ff., esp. 89, where Jerome's attack on Evagrius's conception of *apatheia* is explained and refuted.
9. *Collations,* 18, c. 4; Chadwick, *Asceticism,* p. 266. See below, pp. 45–46.
10. Since the theme of this book is the Western monastic tradition, no more can be said of the Eastern, Basilian, Orthodox tradition of monastic life. See next note, and A. J. Festugière, *Les moines d'orient,* 4 vols. in 3

(Paris, 1961–65 [lives of Eastern monks with introduction]).

11. W. K. Lowther Clarke, *The Ascetic Works of St. Basil* (London, 1925), pp. 163–66 (Longer Rules, c. 7).

12. See pp. 155–56.

13. Matthew 6:26.

14. See R. A. Markus in *Work: An Enquiry into Christian Thought and Practice,* (London, 1960), pp. 13–26.

15. *Confessions,* bk. viii, cc. 14–15.

16. *Institutes,* bk. iv, *ad fin.,* quoted in Chadwick, *Cassian,* p. 93.

17. The use of Cassian in later monastic history has never been fully studied. Manuscripts of the *Collations* are very numerous and catalogues of great monastic libraries from the ninth century on rarely omit all reference to it. Yet in some of the major monastic thinkers of the eleventh and twelfth centuries (such as St. Anselm and St. Bernard) his direct influence seems slight. His indirect influence, through St. Benedict and Gregory the Great, was constant and immense.

18. *Collations,* 9, c. 6; 1, c. 6; trans. Chadwick, *Asceticism,* pp. 198, 217.

19. *Collations,* 1, cc. 5, 7, trans. Chadwick, *Asceticism,* pp. 197–98.

20. *Collations,* 1, c. 8, trans. Chadwick, *Asceticism,* p. 200.

21. *Collations,* 9, cc. 9–15, trans. Chadwick, *Asceticism,* pp.

219–20; based on 1 Timothy 2:1.

22. *Collations,* 9, c. 31, trans. Chadwick, *Asceticism,* p. 229; and see pp. 178–81. "Abba" was a term of respect used for senior monks in Cassian and other early writers, etymologically the equivalent of "abbot" but not necessarily implying authority over a community (cf. Chadwick, *Asceticism,* p. 31).

23. Matthew 5:48—echoed in many passages of the *Collations* and the Rule; specifically the theme of *Collations,* 11, "On Perfection."

Chapter 2
The Rule of St. Benedict, pp. 44–51

1. The view here stated is that of A. de Vogüé in the introduction to his edition. See n. 3—and above, pp. 5–6, for a different view.

2. R. W. Southern, *Western Society and the Church in the Middle Ages,* Pelican History of the Church, II, 1970, p. 222.

3. Knowles, *GHE,* p. 146, from his admirable survey of the controversy down to 1962, ibid., pp. 139–95.

4. The quotations are my own translation from *Regula Magistri* (hereafter referred to in the notes as *Reg. Magistri*), ed. A. de Vogüé, prol., 45, I, 326; and from P. Schmitz's edition of the Rule (see p. 320), prol., pp. 5–6.

5. C. 1, p. 7; what follows is from c. 73, pp. 99–100. The analysis of

the four types is based on the *Reg. Magistri, c.* 1; both are derived from Cassian, *Collations,* 18, esp. cc. 4ff. (trans. Chadwick, *Asceticism,* pp. 265ff.).

6. See pp. 38–43. On the version of Basil's Rule that was known to Benedict, see Chadwick, *Cassian,* pp. 62–63.

7. The audience of the Rule has been much discussed: see, e.g., Knowles, *GHE,* p. 144, indicating the general rejection of Abbot Chapman's thesis that it was officially commissioned by the pope. It seems clear that Benedict had no idea of compiling a manual for general use, or one to be followed by any great number of communities; but that he was writing with the idea in mind that the Rule might be studied and pondered elsewhere than at his own houses (i.e., Subiaco and its neighbors, or Monte Cassino).

8. Cf. Rule, c. 2, with *Reg. Magistri,* c. 2.

9. Ecclesiasticus 32:24 (v. 19 AV).

Chapter 3
The Formation of the Monastic Tradition, pp. 52–69

1. Gregory the Great, *Dialog.,* ii, 36 (ed. U. Moricca, Fonti per la storia d'Italia, Rome, 1924, p. 131). Echoes and quotations from the Rule are strikingly absent from Gregory's monastic writings, and this has never been satisfactorily explained—save by those writers who maintain the paradoxical view that Gregory did not know it (K. Hallinger in *Studia Anselmiana* XLII (Rome, 1957), pp. 231–319; *contra,* Knowles, *MO,* 1963 ed., pp. 750–52; P. Meyvaert, *Bede and Gregory the Great* (Jarrow Lecture, 1964, p. 26 n.). I say "paradoxical" since most commentators are impressed by the appropriateness of Gregory's reference to the Rule, cited in the text, and assume that the reference, and Gregory's whole attitude to Benedict, presuppose knowledge of the Rule. The question is open.

2. On the earliest MS of the Rule, Oxford, Bodleian Lib., Hatton MS 48, see *Early English MSS in Facsimile,* XV, ed. D. H. Farmer (Copenhagen, 1968), esp. p. 25.

3. What follows is based on K. Hughes, *The Church in Early Irish Society* (London, 1966; 2nd ed. 1980), esp. chaps. 6–9, 13; *q.v.* for some of the rich modern literature on Celtic monasticism.

4. Bede, *Hist. Eccl.,* iii, 5, 14–17, etc. (ed. B. Colgrave and R. A. B. Mynors [Oxford Medieval Texts, 1969], pp. 226–29, 258–67).

5. See introd. by A. de Vogüé and F. Neuville to the Rule; this MS was edited by P. Schmitz (Maredsons, 1946).

6. Wolfram von Eschenbach's *Willehalm* was written c. 1210–20. The story was derived from earlier

French *chansons de geste*. See p. 146.

7. E. Bishop, *Liturgica Historica* (Oxford, 1918), p. 213. For recent controversies on Benedict of Aniane, see Constable 1996, p. 200 and refs.

8. See Bishop, pp. 349ff.; and on the history of Reichenau and St. Gall below, pp. 135.

Chapter 4
Life, Work and Prayer,
pp. 70–85

1. To save confusion, I call the first two offices Matins and Lauds; the earlier names, still used in the eleventh century customaries, were Nocturns and Matins. For the literature of Cluny and its customaries, see pp. 320–21.

2. These hours have, of course, a spurious air of precision; I quote them to make the approximate length of the day clear. They are given in Knowles, *MO*, p. 449, on the basis of a wide study of medieval customs.

3. See the historical chapters in the Downside Symposium entitled *Work* (p. 302, chap. 1, n. 14) (London, 1960).

4. On the library of Cluny, see L. Delisle, *Le Cabinet des manuscrits de la Bibl. Nationale,* II (Paris, 1874), 458ff.; Delisle, *Inventaire des mss. de la Bibliothèque Nationale: Fonds de Cluni* (Paris, 1884); A. Wilmart in *Revue Mabillon* XI (1921), 89ff.—it is

in the last that the booklist of the 1040s is dated and analyzed.

5. On this and on Cluny's economy see G. Duby in *Petrus Venerabilis* (p. 320), pp. 128–40. The monks of Cluny wore the familiar black habit. The practice arose in the eleventh century for monks in some humbler monastic houses, such as Bec in Normandy, to wear undyed cloth, and this practice was consecrated as part of their constitution by the Cistercian monks. There is some doubt as to what this meant in practice in early days, for Cistercian MSS of the early twelfth century show the monks sometimes in a brown, sometimes a greyish-white habit; in the end, the latter became the norm, hence they were called the "white monks."

6. Ulrich, c. 17, col. 760. For a fuller account of monastic baths, see *The Monastic Constitutions of Lanfranc,* 2nd ed., eds. D. Knowles and C. N. L. Brooke (Oxford Medieval Texts, 2002), pp. 14–17.

7. On poor-relief in the Middle Ages, see B. Tierney, *Medieval Poor Law* (Berkeley and Los Angeles, 1959); M. Rubin, *Charity and Community in Medieval Cambridge* (Cambridge, 1987).

8. See Duby, art. cit. (n. 5).

9. For the interpretation of the *Apologia*, see now C. Rudolph, *The Things of Greater Importance* (Philadelphia, 1993), partly cor-

recting Knowles, *Historian and Character and Other Essays* (Cambridge, 1963), chap. 4, esp. pp. 62–63, which provides a brilliant summary of the *Apologia*. On pp. 70–71 he summarizes Peter's *Statuta* (now edited by G. Constable in *Corpus Consuetudinum Monasticarum*, VI [1975], 19–106), which confess to many abuses; but one cannot help feeling that some of these, such as public use of the cloister and abuse of trust by some of the servants, were a natural concomitant of the traditional monasticism in its heyday and that both Professor Knowles and Abbot Peter are a little curt with some of their monks, since they cannot forget that Cistercian eyes have been reading the Rule of St. Benedict: for what this meant, see pp. 169–71.

10. Constable 1996, p. 27 and refs.

11. Peter the Venerable, *Letters*, ed. G. Constable (Cambridge, Mass., 1967), no. 20, esp. I. 37–38.

Chapter 5
The Hermits, pp. 86–99

1. For revisions of this chapter, see above, p. 14. On the work of Adalbert in Bohemia and Poland, see *La Mendola*, IV, 336ff. (J. Kloczowski); J. Kloczowski, *A History of Polish Christianity* (Cambridge, 2000), chap. 1. Contemporaries sometimes distinguished the more stable hermit from the wandering anchorite, and the word *hermitage* was used of isolated communities as well as of cells for individuals (cf. J. Leclercq in *Cluniac Monasticism,* ed. N. Hunt [London, 1971], p. 217 n.). Outstanding examples of itinerant founders, after St. Romuald, were St. Robert of Molesme and St. Bruno (see pp. 166, 91, respectively).

2. Bernard, *Epistola* 91, in *Opera S. Bernardi,* ed. J. Leclercq et al. (Rome, 1957–77), VII, 240 (trans. B. S. James [London, 1953], no. 94).

3. *PL,* CXLV, 246ff.

4. What follows are extracts from *Magna Vita,* i, 7, 13 (ed. Douie and Farmer, 1, 23–24, 38ff.).

5. On Peter of Tarentaise, see M.-A. Dimier in *Bibliotheca Sanctorum,* 23 (Rome, 1968), 772–74 and references.

6. Called Gerard in the *Magna Vita*; but see Map, pp. 80–81 n. 2.

7. *Magna Vita,* i, 10, iv, 12 (I, 32–33; II, 55–56).

8. Evidence on the furnishing of dormitories is scanty in early days. But the Rule of St. Benedict and many of the customaries clearly presuppose a dormitory without partitions and with the sparsest furniture; and this is consistent with surviving examples down to the period (approximately the late thirteenth and fourteenth centuries) when paneling, wainscoting and partitioning

became regular features both of domestic and of ecclesiastical architecture.

9. *Magna Vita,* ii, 11 (I, 81); cf. the similar story of the monk of Rievaulx told by Walter Daniel, *Life of Ailred,* pp. 30–31, etc.

10. See D. Knowles and W. F. Grimes, *Charterhouse* (London, 1954); *MSA,* pp. 234–35.

Chapter 6
The Cloister and the World, pp. 100–25

1. See C. Brooke, *Medieval Church and Society* (London, 1971), p. 153 and n.

2. For what follows, see H. E. J. Cowdrey, *The Cluniacs and the Gregorian Reform* (Oxford, 1970), pp. 3ff. and passim.

3. On churches and monasteries as property, see the discussion in C. Brooke, *Europe in the Central Middle Ages,* 3rd ed. (Harlow, 2000), pp. 97–99. The title "vicar of Christ" was occasionally applied to kings and emperors in the tenth and eleventh centuries; it only became a specifically papal title in the twelfth and thirteenth.

4. *The Liber Vitae of the New Minster and Hyde Abbey, Winchester,* ed. S. Keynes, Early English Manuscripts in Facsimile (Copenhagen, 1996).

5. G. Constable, *Monastic Tithes* (Cambridge, 1964), p. 145; Schmitz, 1, 264–65; cf. also J. Leclercq in *Studia Monastica* III

(1961): 137ff. On the development of daily mass, see S. J. P. Van Dijk and J. H. Walker, *The Origins of the Modern Roman Liturgy* (London, 1960), pp. 51ff.: it was widely assumed to be a normal practice as early as the eleventh century, but was by no means universal even in the thirteenth.

6. For the various meanings of "convert," see *The Monastic Constitutions of Lanfranc,* 2nd ed., ed. and trans. D. Knowles and C. N. L. Brooke (Oxford Medieval Texts, 2002), p. 7 n.19.

7. From *Epistola* 8 (7) (ed. T. P. McLaughlin, *Mediaeval Studies* XVIII (1956): 275, trans. C. K. Scott Moncrieff [London, 1925], p. 188).

8. See E. A. Wrigley and R. S. Schofield, *The Population History of England, 1541–1871* (London, 1981)—but the debate continues.

9. On the urban "renaissance" of the eleventh through the thirteenth centuries, see C. Brooke and G. Keir, *London 800–1216* (London, 1975), chap. 3.

10. KH, passim, esp. pp. 488ff.

11. For a recent study, see E. Cownie, *Religious Patronage in Anglo-Norman England* (Woodbridge, 1998).

12. He had certainly been a monk, almost certainly not at Cluny: see references in C. Brooke, *Europe in the Central Middle Ages,* 3rd ed. (Harlow, 2000), p. 323 n.15.

13. On pastoral work performed by monks see U. Berlière in *Revue Bénédictine* XXXIX (1927): 227–50, 340–64; G. Constable, *Monastic Tithes,* esp. pp. 145ff.; D. J. A. Matthew, *The Norman Monasteries and their English Possessions* (Oxford, 1962), esp. pp. 51–65; M. Chibnall, in *Journal of Eccl. History* XVIII (1967): 165–72 (cf. Brooke, *Churches and Churchmen in Medieval Europe* [London, 1999], p. 88 n. 66). On tithes, see Constable, esp. pt. ii, chaps. 3–6.

14. *Vita Gauzlini* (p. 322), ii, 57ff., pp. 104ff.; *Les Miracles de S. Benoit,* ed. E. de Certain (Paris, 1958), viii, 25–27, 30, pp. 317–28. The second fire and the beginning of the new scheme seem to have belonged to the time of Abbot William, c. 1069–80 (cf. *DHGE,* XVII, 449, 470).

15. For what follows, see esp. G. Duby in *Annales* VII (1952): 155–71.

16. *Letters,* ed. G. Constable (p. 320), no. 89, 1, 229; cf. Brooke, *Churches and Churchmen* (n.13), pp. 150–52.

17. See Brooke, *Medieval Church and Society,* chap. 8. On San Zeno, see p. 338.

Chapter 7
The Monastic Contribution to the Twelfth-Century Renaissance, pp. 126–49

1. See J. Harvey, in *Antiquaries Journal* XLVIII (1968): 87–99; cf. Brooke, *Twelfth Century Renaissance* (London, 1969/70), pp. 101ff.

2. On Suger, see esp. E. Panofsky, *Abbot Suger on the Abbey Church of Saint-Denis* (Princeton, 1946)—the quotation on p. 131 is from pp. 62–63; E. Male, *L'art religieux du xiie siècle en France,* 4th ed. (Paris, 1940), chap. 5; L. Grant, *Abbot Suger of Saint-Denis: Church and State in Early Twelfth-Century France* (London, 1998).

3. See C. R. Dodwell, *Painting in Europe 800–1200* (Harmondsworth, 1971), pp. 89ff.; C. Oursel, *Miniature du xiie siècle à l'abbaye de Cîteaux* and *Miniatures cisterciennes (1109–1134)* (Dijon, 1926, 1960).

4. For a protest against too dogmatic a statement of this view, see D. L. d'Avray, *Medieval Marriage Sermons* (Oxford, 2001), pp. 26–30, showing how active many friars were in thirteenth-century book production. Among the Benedictines, the case of Matthew Paris (died 1259), who wrote and illustrated his own lavish books, has long been well known.

5. For a corpus of material, see Joan Evans, *Romanesque Architecture of the Order of Cluny* (Cambridge, 1938); and on the Hirsau congregation, W. Hoffmann, *Hirsau und die "Hirsauer Bauschule"* (Munich, 1950), concluding that Hirsau was not the center of a specific school of architecture.

6. Theophilus, *De diuersis artibus*, ed. and trans. C. R. Dodwell (Nelson's Medieval Texts, 1961), i, prol., pp. 1–4; on the MS tradition, see ibid., pp. xxxivff., lviiff.; B. Bischoff, *Mittelalterliche Studien,* 11 (Stuttgart, 1967), pp. 175–82.

7. See R. W. Southern, *St. Anselm and His Biographer* (Cambridge, 1963), pp. 209–17, and literature cited.

8. Eadmer, *Vita Anselmi,* ed. and trans. R. W. Southern (Nelson's Medieval Texts, 1962; repr. Oxford Med. Texts, 1972), pp. 37–38.

9. My own version in *Europe in the Central Middle Ages,* 3rd ed. (Harlow, 2000), pp. 21–22, (slightly adapted); cf. Orderic Vitalis, *Ecclesiastical History,* ed. and trans. M. Chibnall (Oxford Medieval Texts, 1968–80), VI, 550–57.

Chapter 8
The Augustinian
Canons, pp. 153–65

1. See pp. 115–16 and Constable, *Monastic Tithes* (Cambridge, 1964), pp. 165ff.

2. For the very various interpretations of Mary and Martha, see G. Constable, *Three Studies in Medieval Religion and Social Thought* (Cambridge, 1995), chap. 1.

3. Essentially because, although both rules were interpreted freely, both could be studied literally, and this lay at the root of many of the distinctively monastic movements, notably those like the Cistercian (see chap. 9), which depended on the literal interpretation of the Rule of St. Benedict. For reflections on the relationship, see Brooke, *Churches and Churchmen* (1999), chap. 12.

4. Cf. J. F. Rivera in La Mendola, III, 1, 220–37. Toledo and (apparently) Osma later became secular. The list of Spanish cathedrals at one time or another Augustinian on p. 236 omits these and adds Siguenza (cf. pp. 233–35) and the collegiate church of Soria.

5. The canons of Saint-Trophime at Arles were subjected to a rule *c.* 1060 (J. C. Dickinson, *Origins of the Austin Canons* (London, 1950), p. 43; *Gallia Christiana Novissima,* III (Valence, 1901), pp. 168–69, 176; *Gallia Christ.* (Paris ed., 1715–1865), 1, Instruments, p. 96); whether they were then, and remained, strictly Augustinian, is not clear. But Arles is not far from Avignon, and it is reasonable to presume a link with the cathedral there and with Saint-Ruf (cf. A. Borg, *Architectural Sculpture in Romanesque Provence* (Oxford, 1972), p. 67 and n. 22). Surviving communal buildings and inscriptions in the cloister show them to have been subject to a rule in the mid– and

late twelfth century; they were
presumably Augustinian then.

6. Dickinson, pp. 108ff., 125–26,
etc.; Brooke, *Churches and
Churchmen*, pp. 150–57, esp. pp.
154–55.
7. *Libellus de diuersis ordinibus,* ed.
G. Constable and B. Smith
(Oxford Medieval Texts, 1972),
with a full commentary.
8. See Brooke, *Churches and
Churchmen*, chap. 12.
9. On the various kinds of monastic "order," see esp. Constable,
Reformation, pp. 174–76.
10. *Canterbury Tales,* Prologue,
slightly modernized. "Austin"
and "Benet" are the traditional
vernacular forms of Augustine
and Benedict. "Maure" was St.
Maurus, Benedict's companion;
he was not in fact the author of
a separate Rule. This is more
fully discussed in Brooke,
Churches and Churchmen, pp.
213–18.
11. Knowles, *RO,* II, appendix 1, pp.
365–66; but see Brooke,
Churches and Churchmen, p. 215.

Chapter 9
The Cistercians,
pp. 166–94

1. For the problems and controversies surrounding the foundation of Cîteaux, see above, pp.
8–12 and below, n. 4.
2. The most famous case is his
reconciliation with Abelard,
arranged by Peter the Venerable
partly, at least, at Bernard's

request. Bernard also tried to
arrange a reconciliation with
Gilbert de la Porrée, the other
theologian whom he attacked;
but the reconciliation, like the
attack, was unsuccessful (John
of Salisbury, *Historia Pontificalis,*
ed. and trans. M. Chibnall
[Nelson's Medieval Texts,
1956], pp. 26–27).
3. Stephen Harding's letter was
edited by C. H. Talbot in
Collectanea Ord. Cist. Reformat.,
III (1936), 66–69; D. L. Bethell,
Downside Rev., LXXIX (1961):
349–50.
4. Printed in *Statuta Capitulorum
Generalium Ordinis Cisterciensis,*
ed. J.-M. Canivez, I (Louvain,
1933), with other early Cistercian statutes; but it has been
shown in recent years that some
of the clauses, especially those
describing the general chapter
and system of visitation, belong
to the mid–twelfth century, not
to the time of Stephen Harding.
For the surviving early versions
see J. de la Croix Bouton and J.
B. Van Damme, *Les Plus Anciens
Textes de Cîteaux* (Ache1, 1974);
and for the story of its discovery
and recent controversies on
Cistercian origins, Knowles,
GHE, pp. 197ff., corrected by C.
Holdsworth in *Cistercian Art and
Architecture in the British Isles,* ed.
C. Norton and D. Park
(Cambridge, 1986), pp. 40–55—
see above, p. 9.
5. Mystical knowledge and expe-
rience have been thus defined in

D. Knowles, *The English Mystical Tradition* (London, 1961), pp. 2–3. "This knowledge, this experience, which is never entirely separable from an equally immediate and experimental union with God by love, has three main characteristics. It is recognized by the person concerned as something utterly different from and more real and adequate than all his previous knowledge and love of God. It is experienced as something at once immanent and received, something moving and filling the powers of the mind and soul. It is felt as taking place at a deeper level of the personality and soul than that on which the normal processes of thought and will take place, and the mystic is aware, both in himself and in others, of the soul, its qualities and of the divine presence and action within it, as something wholly distinct from the reasoning mind with its powers. Finally, this experience is wholly incommunicable, save as a bare statement, and in this respect all the utterances of the mystics are entirely inadequate as representations of the mystical experience, but it brings absolute certainty to the mind of the recipient. This is the traditional mystical theology, the mystical knowledge of God, in its purest form." For a sympathetic, but critical, account of Dom David Knowles's view of mysticism, see A. Sillem in *David Knowles Remembered*, ed. C. Brooke (Cambridge, 1991), chap. 2.

6. In several churches, especially Rievaulx, Fountains and Tintern, traces can still be seen of partitions in the nave aisles, doubtless to increase the number of altars; those at Rievaulx are of the twelfth century.

7. *Vita prima S. Bernardi*, ii, 5 (PL, CLXXXV, 285; quoted in Brooke, *Europe in the Central Middle Ages*, 3rd ed. [Harlow, 2000], p. 76).

8. Because King John mulcted, or taxed, the English Cistercians in the early stages of his dispute with the pope, he was later induced to found the Cistercian abbey of Beaulieu in Hampshire, partly to compensate for what he had taken from the Cistercians.

9. See Brooke, *Medieval Church and Society*, p. 166 and n.; M. Aubert, *L'architecture cistercienne en France* (p. 325), I, 317, etc. On Bernard's attitude to art and architecture, see Brooke, *Churches and Churchmen*, chap. 11.

10. As was emphasized by Dom Jean Leclercq, in *S. Bernard et l'esprit cistercien* (p. 324), p. 20.

11. For the plan, see the works of Dimier, Aubert, Esser and Hahn, cited below, p. 325 (and below, n.12). For the constitution, above, n. 4—and esp. pp. 9–12.

12. "Über den Kirchenbau des Hl. Bernhard von Clairvaux," *Archiv*

für mittelrheinische Kirchengeschichte V (1953): 195–222; cf. F. Bucher, "Cistercian architectural purism," *Comparative Studies in Society and History*, III (1960–61), 89–105, at pp. 97–98, 105. Esser's chart was based on M.-A. Dimier, *Recueil des plans des églises cisterciennes* (Grignan/ Paris, 1949; Supplement, 1967), which rarely reveals its sources of information. The history of the square east end, its significance and proportions, are considerably sophisticated in H. Hahn's *Frühe Kirchenbaukunst der Zisterzienser* (Berlin, 1957), and the uncertainties surrounding some of the plans in Dimier's *Recueil* must diminish the value of Dr. Esser's dramatic presentation of the basic evidence. Hahn's study of proportions etc. has shown, e.g., that at Eberbach there was a change of plan while the church was being built. For more recent studies of Cistercian architecture, see below, p. 325.

13. I am informed that extensive tree felling over the centuries has substantially reduced the water supply in the valley.

14. The design of the Sénanque chapter house was evidently altered in course of construction, and the heavy ribs seem to be an afterthought. But the basic layout is characteristic of Cistercian cloisters and must be as originally intended.

15. For what follows, see Walter Daniel's *Life of Ailred of Rievaulx,*

ed. F. M. Powicke (Nelson's Medieval Texts, 1950), pp. 12–13.

16. Ibid., pp. 10–12.

17. But see Powicke's note, p. 38. The chapter house at Rievaulx was originally of more normal form; it was rebuilt, very likely in Ailred's time, and the new shape is strikingly similar to the twelfth-century chapter house at Durham, Ailred's original home. Cf. Richard Halsey in Norton and Park, 1986 (n.4 above), pp. 84–85, who suggests on stylistic grounds a date in the late 1140s: Ailred became abbot in 1147.

18. *Life of Ailred,* pp. 36–38.

19. E.g., those quoted in Brooke, *Europe in the Central Middle Ages* (2000), pp. 381–84; *Letters,* trans. B. S. James (London, 1953), nos. 95, 146, 204.

20. *Sermones in Canticum,* no. 26 (*Opera*, I, ed. J. Leclercq, C. H. Talbot, H. M. Rochais [Rome, 1957], p. 172).

Chapter 10
The Knights, pp. 195–200

1. See D. W. Lomax, *La Orden de Santiago (1170–1275),* Madrid, 1965.

2. The fullest study is V. Gervers-Molnár, *A Középkori Magyarország Rotundái* (Budapest, 1972, in Hungarian, with English summary), pp. 84–90.

3. See M. Gervers, "Rotundae Anglicanae," *Actes du xxiie*

Congrès Internationale de l'Histoire de l'Art (1969; Budapest, 1972), pp. 359–76. On the order of the Holy Sepulchre, see J. C. Dickinson in *Trans. Royal Hist. Soc.*, 5th Series, I (1951): 71ff., esp. p. 73.

Chapter 11
On Abbesses and
Prioresses, pp. 201–16

1. Edited by Dom Germain Morin (Bonn, 1933).
2. For England. See KH, esp. p. 494 (strictly 48 to 13 c. 1066, but the disproportion rapidly increased for a time after the Norman Conquest); for France no comparable statistics have been made: The statement in the text is based on a survey kindly undertaken for me by Dr. E. Hallam Smith.
3. See pp. 61, 155.
4. A. Schulte, *Der Adel und die deutsche Kirche im Mittelalter,* Kirchenrechtliche Abhandlungen, ed. U. Stutz, 63–64 (Stuttgart, 1910), pp. 401ff. On Matilda of Essen, see E. van Houts, "Women and the Writing of History in the Early Middle Ages," *Early Medieval Europe*, I (1992): 53–68; E. van Houts, *Memory and Gender in Medieval Europe* (Basingstoke, 1999), pp. 69–70.
5. N. Hunt, *Cluny under St. Hugh* (London, 1967), pp. 186ff.
6. As has been shown by S. Thompson, *Women Religious*

(Oxford, 1991), esp. chap. 4; and S. Foot, *Veiled Women*, esp. vol. II (Basingstoke, 2000).
7. A father who placed a daughter in a nunnery was expected to present the convent with a "dowry," though the exaction of dowries was forbidden by reforming councils. A good example of a house of very modest origins that rose to tolerable prosperity by enjoying the neighborhood of rich citizens whose daughters and legacies greatly benefited its endowments was Haliwell, the earliest to be founded of the London convents of nuns (see C. Brooke and G. Keir, *London 800–1216* [London, 1975], chap. 11, esp. pp. 329–31).
8. See KH, p. 251—a theme much developed by S. Thompson, *Women Religious* (Oxford, 1991).
9. E.g., by R. R. Bezzola, *Les origines et la formation de la littérature courtoise en occident* (Paris, 1958–60), esp. II, ii, 275–92. The theory of a direct connection has found little support, but Bezzola's interesting discussion has drawn attention to certain parallels that cannot be due solely to chance. On Robert of Arbrissel, see J. Dalarun, *L'impossible sainteté: La vie retrouvée de Robert d'Arbrissel* (Paris, 1985); and on the early history of Fontevrault, M. Parisse in *Doppelklöster und andere Formen*

der Symbiose... (Paris, 1992), pp. 135–48.

10. I follow G. Zarnecki (see *The Monastic Achievement* [London, 1972], pp. 93–94) in dating the effigies of the kings to c. 1200–4, and the other two to c. 1220 or soon after.

11. Among the many notable exceptions are Hildegard and Heloise (see Brooke, *Europe in the Central Middle Ages*, pp. 132–41; P. Dronke, *Women Writers of the Middle Ages* (Cambridge, 1984), chaps. 5–6).

12. On which see esp. *Temptations from Ancrene Wisse*, I, ed. and trans. Y. Wada, (Osaka, 1994).

13. The correspondence is edited by J. T. Muckle and T. P. McLaughlin in *Mediaeval Studies,* XII, XV, XVII, XVIII (1950–56); translated B. Radice (Harmondsworth, 1974). The quotations below are from *Mediaeval Studies,* XVII, 243, 247 (my translation). In what follows I accept the authenticity of the correspondence: see C. Brooke, *The Medieval Idea of Marriage* (Oxford, 1989), chaps. 4–5, esp. pp. 116–18).

14. See p. 300 n. 36.

Chapter 12
St. Norbert and
St. Francis, pp. 217–32

1. See esp. "Un débat sur le sacerdoce des moines au xie siècle," ed. R. Foreville and J. Leclercq, *Studia Anselmiana,* XLI: 8–118.

But Giles Constable gives a much needed warning against taking twelfth-century polemic too seriously: Constable *Reformation,* esp. p. 26.

2. See Brooke, *Medieval Church and Society* (London, 1971), chap. 7, esp. pp. 147ff., and books cited, esp. H. Grundmann, *Religiöse Bewegungen im Mittelalter* (2nd ed., Hildesheim, 1961)—English translation by S. Rowan, *Religious Movements in the Middle Ages* (Notre Dame, 1995).

3. St. Gilbert formed his first convent at Sempringham in Lincs in the 1130s, and in 1147 traveled to Cîteaux with the idea of placing the house under Cistercian jurisdiction. The Cistercians refused to accept his plan in the form in which he wished it; but he took much advice from Bernard and the Cistercian pope, Eugenius III (1145–53), in forming his Rule. The Gilbertines never spread outside England. See *The Book of St. Gilbert,* ed. and trans. R. Foreville and G. Keir (Oxford Medieval Texts, 1987); B. Golding, *Gilbert of Sempringham and the Gilbertine Order* (Oxford, 1995).

4. On this and all that follows, see R. B. Brooke, *The Coming of the Friars* (London, 1975), esp. chap. 2.

5. Though many scholars doubt if Francis influenced Dominic in any crucial way, and some have

doubted if they ever met. I have discussed this problem in *Medieval Church and Society*, pp. 222–29.

6. *Die Opuscula des hl. Franziskus von Assisi*, ed. K. Esser (Grottaferrata, 1976), p. 232.

7. *Epistola ad ministrum* (*Die Opuscula*, p. 232); for the reading *non*, "not," in the text above, see R. B. Brooke, *Early Franciscan Government* (Cambridge, 1959), p. 173 n.

8. *Scripta Leonis, Rufini et Angeli*, ed. R. B. Brooke (Oxford Medieval Texts, 1970), no. 98, pp. 260–63.

9. The Franciscan renunciation of property was absolute both in theory and practice, though the relation between possession and ownership led to many difficulties, and they were compelled in the long run to accept that the Holy See could hold property for their use, which in effect meant (contrary to the founder's intention) for their exclusive use. The Dominican renunciation was not so fundamental nor quite so complete; but in practice both orders lived on alms. On the Franciscan idea and practice, see M. D. Lambert, *Franciscan Poverty*, 2nd ed. (London, 1991). Nothing is said in this book about the other orders of friars, which proliferated in the thirteenth century. Of these the most important—and the only ones to survive in the long

run—were the Orders of Carmelite and Austin Friars. See Knowles, *RO*, I, chap. xvii; KH, pp. 232ff.

Chapter 13
Three Visits, pp. 235–60

1. Studley Park was laid out by John Aislabie (chancellor of the exchequer, 1718–21; died 1742) and rounded off by his son, William Aislabie, who bought the Fountains estate. Their successors by degrees converted the abbey from a romantic folly into a well-preserved ruin, and it is now in the custody of the National Trust and English Heritage.

2. Walter Map, *De nugis curialium*, i. 25, ed. and trans. M. R. James, C.N.L. Brooke and R.A.B. Mynors (Oxford Medieval Texts, 1983), pp. 92–3. Map's quotation is from Ovid, *Heroides*, i.53.

3. See R. A. Donkin, in *Bulletin of the Inst. of Hist. Research* XXXIII (1960): 141–65; M. W. Barley, in *Nottingham Mediaeval Studies* I (1957): 75–89. In practice, even the Cistercians had to accept deviations from their basic rules, and these increased as time went on (see Knowles, *MO*, 2nd ed., pp. 746–47, for articles by R. A. Donkin and C. V. Graves on settlement and economic activities of the Cistercians in England). See above, p. 10.

4. St. Bernard, *Epistola* 106, quoted in *MO*, p. 221, slightly adapted; Brooke, *Europe in the Central Middle Ages*, 3rd ed. (Harlow, 2000), p. 374.

5. Cf. Brooke, *Twelfth-Century Renaissance* (London, 1969), pl. 23.

6. See refs. in *Heads of Religious Houses, England and Wales*, I, ed. D. Knowles, C. N. L. Brooke and V. C. M. London, 2nd ed. (Cambridge, 2001), p. 132 n.1, esp. to L. G. D. Baker in *Northern History*, IV (1969): 29–43 and *Analecta Cisterciensia* XXV (1969): 14–41.

7. L. G. D. Baker, in *Northern History*, IV (1969): 38ff.

8. *Millénaire monastique du Mont St-Michel* (p. 327), II, chap. II (M. Lelegard); in chapter I (J. Hourlier) evidence is adduced for an earlier foundation, c. 550–75, as an annex of a monastery at Asteriac. But the effective history of Mont St-Michel begins with St. Aubert in 708. For literature on the abbey, see p. 327. On the cult of St. Michael, see *Millénaire* III; O. Chadwick in H. M. Chadwick et al., *Studies in Early British History* (Cambridge, 1954), pp. 182–84; cf. W. Levison, *England and the Continent in the Eighth Century* (Oxford, 1946), p. 263.

9. Monastic life was revived for a time in more recent days.

10. This does not mean, as has sometimes been supposed, that the abbey became a naval power; see M. Mollat in *Millénaire*, II, 73ff.

11. In L. Delisle's edition of the *Chronicle of Robert of Torigny* (2 vols., Rouen, 1872–73); omitted in the edition by R. Howlett, *Chronicles of the Reigns of Stephen*, etc., IV (Rolls Series, 1889).

12. W. Swaan, *The Gothic Cathedral* (London, 1969), pp. 151–54, 200–7.

13. I.e., cathedrals served by chapters or communities of secular canons (see p. 293) or monks; Durham itself, and Winchester, were monastic cathedrals.

14. For the building I follow the conclusions of F. Reggiori, *La Basilica di Sant'Ambrogio* (1966); a useful and well illustrated brief account is that by A. M. Romanini (Tesori d'Arte Cristiana, 8, 1966). On the history of the two communities, especially in the eleventh and twelfth centuries, I am much indebted to the advice of Mgr. Prof. P. Zerbi, and to his articles in *Studi Medievali*, 3 ser., IV (1963): 136–216; *Vescovi e diocesi in Italia nel Medioevo* (Padua, 1964), pp. 245–313; and in *Miscellanea Gilles Gerard Meersseman* (Padua, 1970), I, 107–32.

15. As at the neighboring Basilica of San Lorenzo, where a fragment of the atrium may still be seen. At Cassian's St. Victor, Marseille (if correctly identi-

fied), the traces of the original atrium can also be seen.

16. Now destroyed (see pp. 202–3). For Saint-Riquier, see A. W. Clapham, *English Romanesque Architecture before the Conquest* (Oxford, 1930), pp. 78ff.

17. Modern restoration has no doubt often obscured the vestiges of medieval glazing in cloister arcades. Such vestiges are clear, however, in the double arcade at Eberbach.

Chapter 14
1300: The Monastic Map of Europe, pp. 261–77

1. D. W. Lomax, *La Orden de Santiago (1170–1275)* (Madrid, 1965), p. 50.

2. Lomax, passim, esp. pp. 41–50.

3. J. Kloczowski in *La Mendola*,VI, 153–72; J. Kloczowski, *A History of Polish Christianity* (Cambridge, 1999), chap. 1.

4. These details are based on *Atlas Cist.*; for corrections, see E. Krausen and P. Zakar in *Analecta Cisterciensia* XXII (1966): 279–90; F. Vongrey and F. Hervay in *Analecta Cisterciensia* XXIII (1967): 115–27. I have followed frontiers of the mid–twentieth century in the rough figures quoted.

5. See *Atlas Cist.* On Poland, there are rich details on history as well as architecture in *Sztuka Polska przedromanska i romanska do schylku XIII wieku,* ed. M.

Walicki, 2 vols., (Warsaw, 1968), with Cistercian family tree on I, 167, by J. Kloczowski; for lists of Polish religious houses in the eighteenth century, with copious maps, see L. Bienkowski, J. Kloczowski, Z. Sulowski, *Zakony Meskie w Polsce w 1772 Roku* (Lublin, 1972). See now Kloczowski, *A History of Polish Christianity.*

6. See *Atlas Cist.*, esp. map VIII: there were two other houses in Denmark, one in Sweden. Surviving remains are illustrated in A. Tuulse, *Scandinavia Romanica* (German trans., Vienna-Munich, 1968).

7. Knowles, *MO*, p. 164 and n.; the date there suggested, 1095–96, depends on Robert, abbot of Evesham, corrected in *Heads of Religious Houses, England and Wales, 940–1216,* ed. D. Knowles, C. N. L. Brooke and V. C. M. London, I, (Cambridge, 2001), p. 47. But the foundation seems to have occurred before the death of William II in 1100.

8. *Vita Bernardi,* vii, 27, 55 (PL, CLXXXV, 445) cited E. Vacandard, *Vie de S. Bernard,* 4th ed. (Paris, 1910), II, 416–17.

9. See L. Milis, *L'ordre des Chanoines réguliers d'Arrouaise* (Bruges, 1969). On Malachy and the Irish church, see J. A. Watt, *The Church and the Two Nations in Medieval Ireland* (Cambridge, 1970), chap. 1; and ibid. passim for what follows.

The figures are based on A. Gwynn and R. N. Hadcock, *Medieval Religious Houses, Ireland* (London, 1970).

10. See Brooke, *Churches and Churchmen*, chap. 9.

11. In KH, upon which what follows is based.

12. See the fourteenth-fifteenth-century lists printed in M. Marrier, *Bibliotheca Cluniacensis* (Paris, 1614; rep. Mâcon, 1915), cols. 1705–52; and by J. Evans, *Romanesque Architecture of the Order of Cluny* (Cambridge, 1938), pp. 153–76. This has not been subjected to critical scrutiny nor have comprehensive and reliable lists been compiled for earlier periods—for the difficulties, see N. Hunt, *Cluny under St. Hugh* (London, 1967), pp. 5ff.

13. See Vongrey and Hervay, art. cit. (n. 4), XXIII, 137–38, who give 742 and 654.

14. H. F. Cary's translation of lines 35–50, 61–93. Benedict names, among his fellow monks, Macarius and Romuald: two of the best-known early monks in Egypt were called Macarius; for Romuald, see pp. 87–88.

Chapter 15
Epilogue: 1300 to the Present, pp. 278–92

1. In some cases monastic buildings dismantled at or after the French Revolution quickly fell into the hands of owners who were personally interested in preserving and restoring them; this helps to explain, e.g., the fine state of preservation of Sénanque.

2. The fundamental study of late medieval monastic life, Barbara Harvey's *Living and Dying in England, 1100–1540: The Monastic Experience* (Oxford, 1993) is based on Westminster Abbey, where a significant portion of the community (but not the whole) remained in the cloister.

3. G. Moorhouse, *Against All Reason* (Harmondsworth, 1972), p. 54.

4. The figures for 1972 are quoted from Moorhouse, pp. 275–77; but cf. his cautions on pp. 82ff. on the reliability of the figures; the figures for 1981 are from his 2nd edition (1986), p. 289. I have not seen any later figures. On non-Roman Catholic religious, see ibid., esp. chapter 1, on Taizé.

Bibliographical Notes

The purpose of these notes is to guide further reading and to provide an explanation of the literature on which the text is based. Part I contains general studies covering a wide area of the field; II gives the literature chapter by chapter (some more specific points are dealt with in the footnotes); III gives brief notes of some of the literature on individual monasteries that figure in text and illustrations.

I

Some major studies of the late twentieth century are discussed in the introduction, especially Giles Constable, *The Reformation of the Twelfth Century* (Cambridge, 1996). Some of my own studies are gathered in C. N. L. Brooke, *Churches and Churchmen in the Middle Ages* (London, 1999—henceforward Brooke, *Churches and Churchmen*).

For reference, two valuable encyclopedias of the subject are *Encyclopedia of Monasticism*, ed. W. M. Johnston, 2 vols. (Chicago, 2000), and the more elaborate *Dizionario degli Istituti di Perfezione*, ed. G. Pelliccia and G. Rocca, 9 vols. (Rome, 1974–97—henceforward *Dizionario*). There are also many useful articles, with bibliographies, in *DHGE*, *New Catholic Encyclopedia*, *Dict. de Spiritualité*, *Dict. de Théologie Catholique*, *Enciclopedia dell'Arte Medievale*.

On earlier studies: three scholars who made an exceptionally rich contribution in the mid–twentieth century to the historical literature on medieval monasticism were Professor Dom David Knowles, Dom Ursmer Berlière and Dom Jean Leclercq.

D. Knowles, *Monastic Order in England, 940–1216* (Cambridge, 1940; 2nd ed., 1963, cited as *MO*); *Religious Orders in England*, I–III (Cambridge, 1948–59, cited as *RO*): both these great books have much to say on the continental background. Knowles gave a brief general survey in *Christian Monasticism* (London, 1969). A number of his essays are reprinted in *The Historian and Character and Other Essays* (Cambridge, 1963). For lists of English houses, Knowles and R. N. Hadcock, *Medieval Religious Houses, England and Wales,* 2nd ed. (London, 1971: KH). For other countries, see p. 327. Knowles and J. K. S. St. Joseph, *Monastic Sites from the Air* (Cambridge, 1952: *MSA)* opened a new era in the study of monastic sites.

U. Berlière, *L'ordre monastique* (Maredsous, 1923), *L'ascèse bénédictine* (Paris, 1927) are clear introductions by an eminent scholar. Dom Jean Leclercq, *L'amour de lettres et le désir de Dieu* (Paris, 1957; English trans., New York, 1962); *Études sur le vocabulaire monastique du moyen âge* and *Otia monastica* (Rome, 1961–63; Studia Anselmiana, fasc. 48, 51).

A rich store of learning, often ill organized and polemical in tone, but on St. Benedict and St. Bernard (e.g.) sympathetic and penetrating, is to be found in G. G. Coulton's *Five Centuries of Religion*, 4 vols. (Cambridge, 1923–50), the chief of his many works on the subject.

Collected papers of great scholars on monastic and liturgical history are to be found in E. Bishop, *Liturgica Historica* (Oxford, 1918); A. Wilmart, *Auteurs spirituels et textes dévots du moyen âge latin* (Paris, 1932).

Studies covering many aspects of this book are collected in the publications of the La Mendola confer-

ences *(Miscellanea del Centro di Studi Medioevali,* of the Università Cattolica del Sacro Cuore, I–X, Milan, 1956–80: see below).

Other useful general books are: G. Zarnecki, *The Monastic Achievement* (London, 1972); P. Cousin, *Précis d'histoire monastique* (Paris-Tournai, 1959); P. Schmitz, *Histoire de l'Ordre de S. Benoit,* 7 vols. (Maredsous, 1942–56). Of many periodicals, the *Revue Bénédictine* and the *Revue Mabillon* are especially useful (and see below); W. Braunfels, *Monasteries of Western Europe: The Architecture of the Orders* (London, 1972) is an interesting, if not altogether successful, attempt to relate the history and architecture of the religious orders. A model local study is Janet Burton, *The Monastic Order in Yorkshire* (Cambridge, 1999).

There are bibliographies in most of the general works listed; and running bibliographies published yearly in *Revue d'histoire ecclésiastique.*

II
Chapter 1

On early monasticism, see especially D. J. Chitty, *The Desert a City* (Oxford, 1966); O. Chadwick, *Western Asceticism* (London, 1958); G. Gould, *The Desert Fathers on Monastic Community* (Oxford, 1993). On St. Basil, W. K. L. Clarke, *The Ascetic Works of St. Basil,* London, 1925. On Cassian, O. Chadwick, *John Cassian* (Cambridge, 1950, 2nd ed., 1968), *Conferences,* ed. and French trans. E.

Pichery, Sources Chrétiennes, 3 vols. (Paris, 1955–59), *Institutions Cénobitiques,* ed. and French trans. J.-C. Guy, ibid., 1965.

Chapter 2

On the problem of the *Regula magistri* and the Rule of St. Benedict, Knowles, *GHE*, pp. 135–95; A. de Vogüé's introductions to his editions of both, Sources Chrétiennes, (Paris, 1964–73); M. Dunne, in *English Historical Review,* CV (1990), 567–94—and see pp. 297–98 n. 2. His is the best edition of the Rule; on other editions, see P. Meyvaert in *Scriptorium,* XVII (1963), 83ff. and D. H. Farmer in *Early English MSS in Facsimile,* XV (1968), pp. 28–9. English translations in Chadwick, *Asceticism,* and by J. McCann (1952). The quotations are my own translation from P. Schmitz's edition of the Sangallensis (Maredsous, 1946). Our knowledge of Benedict apart from the Rule comes almost exclusively from the *Dialogues* of Gregory the Great (ed. U. Moricca, Rome, 1924), bk. II; there is a convenient summary in J. McCann, *St. Benedict* (London, 1939). On the history of Rules and obedience, Knowles, *From Pachomius to Ignatius* (Oxford, 1966).

Chapter 3

On Cassiodorus, *DHGE,* XI, 1349–1408 (D. M. Cappuyns); on Celtic and Anglo-Saxon monasticism, K. Hughes, *The Church in*

Early Irish Society, 2nd ed. (London, 1980); J. Ryan, *Irish Monasticism* (London, 1931); H. Mayr-Harting, *The Coming* of *Christianity to Anglo-Saxon England* (London, 1972). On eighth–ninth centuries, W. Levison, *England and the Continent in the Eighth Century* (Oxford, 1946); D. A. Bullough, *The Age* of *Charlemagne* (London, 1965). On St. Benedict of Aniane, *DHGE,* VIII, 177–88 (P. Schmitz); Knowles in *MO*, pp. 25ff.; *Vita* in *PL,* CIII, 353–84 (the decrees are in *Corpus Consuetudinum Monasticarum*—see below—I, 423ff.). In general, and for the tenth-century movements, see Schmitz I, and below; for Gorze, see below; for England, Knowles, *MO.*

Chapters 4 and 6

On Cluny, see Hunt (1967), and Hunt (1971)—a useful collection of essays—with references to the rich continental literature; J. Evans, *Monastic Life at Cluny, 910–1157* (Oxford, 1931); K. J. Conant, *Cluny* (Macon, 1968); *Spiritualità Cluniacense* (Todi, 1960); J. Leclercq, *Pierre le Vénérable* (St.-Wandrille, 1946); *Petrus Venerabilis,* ed. G. Constable and J. Kritzeck, Studia Anselmiana 40 (Rome, 1956), including G. Duby on Cluny's economy, pp. 128–40; J. Wollasch, *Cluny—Licht der Welt* (Düsseldorf, 1996); on her budget, Duby in *Annales,* VII (1952), 155–71; *Letters of Peter the Venerable,* ed. G. Constable, 2 vols. (Cambridge, Mass., 1967). On William of Hirsau and his movement, H. Jakobs, *Die Hirsauer* (Köln-Graz, 1961).

On Gorze, see now J. Nightingale, *Monasteries and Patrons in the Gorze Reform* (Oxford, 2001). For general historical background, R. W. Southern, *Making of the Middle Ages* (London, 1953) and *Western Society and the Church in the Middle Ages* (Harmondsworth, 1970); books listed in C. Brooke, *Europe in the Central Middle Ages*, 3rd ed. (Harlow, 2000), esp., on papal reform and monasticism, pp. 434–35; to these should be added La Mendola VI (1971).

For social background and relations with patrons, La Mendola VI; essays in *Millénaire monastique du Mont St.-Michel*, ed. J. Laporte et al. (Paris, 1966–71); D. J. A. Matthew, *The Norman Monasteries and Their English Possessions* (Oxford, 1962). On economic background, G. Duby, *L'économie rurale et la vie des campagnes dans l'occident médiéval*, 2 vols. (Paris, 1962; Eng. trans. by C. Postan, London, 1968); G. Constable, *Monastic Tithes from Their Origins to the Twelfth Century* (Cambridge, 1964); L. Musset in *L'abbaye bénédictine de Fécamp*, I (Fécamp, 1959), pp. 67–79.

The documents on which these chapters are mainly based are:

1. MONASTIC CUSTOMS. Cluny's early customaries are printed (ed. K. Hallinger et al.), in *Corpus Consuetudinum Monasticarum*, esp. VII, ii (Siegburg, 1983); M. Herrgott, *Vetus Disciplina Monastica* (Paris, 1726; repr. Siegburg, 1999), pp. 133–364 (Bernard of Cluny, c. 1067; cf. *Monastic Constitutions of Lanfranc* [below], pp. xl–xlii), PL, CXLIX, 635–778 (Ulrich, c. 1075). The *Corpus Consuetudinum Monasticarum*, ed. K. Hallinger and P. Engelbert is drawing the whole body of literature together. See also the vols. of the Henry Bradshaw Society; and the major English customaries of the tenth–eleventh centuries, the *Regularis Concordia* (c. 970), ed. and trans. T. Symons (Nelson's Medieval Texts, 1953) and *The Monastic Constitutions of Lanfranc*, ed. and trans. D. Knowles and C. N. L. Brooke (3rd ed., Oxford Medieval Texts, 2002).

2. LIBRI VITAE, NECROLOGIES ETC. Cf. Wollasch in Hunt (1971), chap. 9; the *Liber Vitae* of New Minster, Winchester, is British Library, Stowe MS 944; ed. S. Keynes, *Early English Manuscripts in Facsimile*, XXVI (Copenhagen, 1996). For prosopography, the material is extremely scattered: for lists of abbots etc. see Hauck; *Germania Sacra* (Berlin etc, 1929–); GB; *Gallia Christiana* (Paris ed., 1739–1877); *Heads of Religious Houses, England and Wales*, I, *940–1216*, ed. D. Knowles, C. N. L. Brooke and V. C. M. London, 2nd ed. (Cambridge, 2001); II, *1216–1377*, ed. D. M. Smith and V. C. M. London (Cambridge, 2001).

3. BIOGRAPHIES. See esp. Eadmer's *Life of St. Anselm*, ed. and trans. R. W. Southern (Nelson's Medieval Texts, 1962–63; rep. Oxford Med. Texts, 1972; cf. R. W.

Southern, *St. Anselm and His Biographer* (Cambridge, 1963), Southern, *St. Anselm: A Portrait in a Landscape* (Cambridge, 1990), and Eadmer's *Historia novorum* (ed. M. Rule, Rolls Series, 1884; Eng. trans. G. Bosanquet, London, 1964); "Vita Herluini" (founder of Bec) in J. A. Robinson, *Gilbert Crispin* (Cambridge, 1911); and in Gilbert Crispin, *Works*, ed. A. S. Abulafia and G. R. Evans (Oxford, 1986); the Autobiography of Guibert, abbot of Nogent-sous-Coucy (*PL,* CLVI, 837–962; Eng. trans. C. C. Swinton Bland, London, 1925; also in *Self and Society...,* by J. F. Benton, Harper Torchbook, 1970); André de Fleury, *Vie de Gauzlin, abbé de Fleury,* ed. and French trans. R.-H. Bautier and G. Labory, Sources d'Histoire Médiévale (Paris, 1969); *Vita S. Godehardi* (*PL,* CXLI: see pp. 68–69, citing col. 1174); *Vita* of William of Hirsau, *Monumenta Germaniae Hist., Scriptores,* XII, 209–25.

4. THE MORE REFLECTIVE, OR EXPANSIVE, MONASTIC CHRONICLES. Esp. Orderic Vitalis (quoted on pp. 148–49; ed. and trans. by M. Chibnall, 6 vols. (Oxford Medieval Texts, 1968–80); Rodulfus Glaber, *Opera,* ed. and trans. J. France, N. Bulst et al. (Oxford Medieval Texts, 1989); Hugh Candidus, *Chronicle* (of Peterborough abbey), ed. W. T. Mellows (Oxford 1949; also trans. C. and W. T. Mellows, Peterborough, 1941).

5. PRAYERS, SERMONS ETC. OF LEADING SPIRITUAL DIRECTORS. Crucial guides are

A. Wilmart, *Auteurs spirituels,* and the writings of J. Leclercq (pp. 319, 324), esp. Leclercq and J. P. Bonnes, *Un maître de la vie spirituelle du xie siècle, Jean de Fécamp* (Paris, 1946).

Chapter 5

On the "crisis of monasticism" in the eleventh-twelfth centuries, see esp. C. Dereine in *Revue du moyen âge latin,* IV (1948), 137–54; *Revue d'hist. ecclésiastique,* LIV (1959), 41–65; Leclercq in Hunt (1971), chap. 11 (the phrase, in the form "crise du cénobitisme," seems to have been coined by Dom G. Morin, in *Revue Bénédictine,* XL [1928], 99).

On the hermits, see H. Leyser, *Hermits and the New Monasticism* (London, 1984); *La Mendola IV: L'eremitismo* (1965). On the Carthusians, Knowles, *MO,* chap. 22; *PL,* CLII, CLIII: E. M. Thompson, *The Carthusian Order in England* (London, 1930); Guigo or Guy II (prior of the Chartreuse), *The Scale of the Cloister,* trans. B. S. James (London, 1937); on St. Hugh, *Magna vita S. Hugonis,* ed. and trans. D. L. Douie and H. Farmer, 2 vols. (Nelson's Medieval Texts, 1961–62, repr. Oxford Medieval Texts, 1985). On the background of movements in Rome, G. Ferrari, *Early Roman Monasteries* (Rome, 1957); B. Hamilton in *Studia monastica,* IV (1962), 35–68. On Camaldoli and Vallombrosa, pp. 329, 338. On Grandmont, *Corpus Christianorum, Cont. Med.,* VIII, ed. J. Becquet

(Turnholti, 1968), and C. Hutchison, *The Hermit Monks of Grandmont* (Kalamazoo, 1989). On St. Peter Damian, see J. Leclercq, S. *Pierre Damien* (Rome, 1960); St. Peter Damian, *Selected Writings on the Spiritual Life,* trans. with introd. by Patricia McNulty (London, 1959).

Chapter 7

On the general themes of this chapter, C. Brooke, *Twelfth-Century Renaissance* (London, 1969), with bibliog. on pp. 203ff.; *Renaissance and Renewal in the Twelfth Century,* ed. R. I. Benson, G. Constable and C. D. Lanham (Cambridge, Mass., 1982). On Anselm, Eadmer and Orderic, above, note to chaps. 4, 6.

On art and architecture, G. Zarnecki, *Romanesque Art* (London, 1971; first publ. in German trans., *Romanik,* Stuttgart, 1970); R. Oursel, *Invention de l'architecture romane* (Zodiaque, 1970); *Propyläen Kunstgeschichte,* V, Das Mittelalter, ed. K. Fillitz, 1969, esp. the chapter by G. Zarnecki on Romanesque sculpture; O. Demus, *Romanische Wandmalerei* (Munich, 1968; Eng. trans., London, 1970); C. R. Dodwell, *Painting in Europe, 800–1200* (Harmondsworth, 1971), W. Swaan, *The Gothic Cathedral* (London, 1969); O. von Simson, *The Gothic Cathedral* (New York, 1956); P. Frankl, *Gothic Architecture* (Harmondsworth, 1962); *Age of Chivalry: Art in Plantagenet England 1200–1400,* ed. J. Alexander and P.

Binski (London, 1987); and the classic studies of E. Mâle, *L'art religieux du XIIe siècle en France,* 6th ed. (Paris, 1953) and *L'art religieux du XIIIe siècle…*6th ed. (Paris, 1925; Eng. trans. D. Nussey, *The Gothic Image,* new ed., London, 1961).

On the monastic contribution, G. Zarnecki, *The Monastic Achievement* (London, 1972); C. R. Dodwell, *The Canterbury School of Illumination* (Cambridge, 1954); E. Panofsky, *Abbot Suger on the Abbey Church of Saint-Denis* (Princeton, 1946); O. Pächt, C. R. Dodwell and F. Wormald, *The St. Albans Psalter* (London, 1960).

On Cistercian art and architecture, see refs. in notes to chap. 8, esp. to *Cistercian Art and Architecture in the British Isles,* ed. C. Norton and D. Park (Cambridge, 1986); C. Oursel, *La miniature du xiie siècle à l'abbaye de Cîteaux* and *Miniatures cisterciennes (1109–1134)* (Dijon, 1926, 1960); cf. Brooke, *Churches and Churchmen,* p. 203 and refs. in n. 23. On the Cluniacs, J. Evans, *Romanesque Architecture of the Order of Cluny* and *Cluniac Art of the Romanesque Period* (Cambridge, 1938, 1949).

On Theophilus, see *De diuersis artibus,* ed. and Eng. trans. C. R. Dodwell (Nelson's Medieval Texts, 1961; cf. chap. 7, n. 6). On professional artists and craftsmen, V. W. Egbert, *The Mediaeval Artist at Work* (Princeton, 1967); A. Martindale, *The Rise of the Artist* (London, 1972).

On William of Malmesbury, see now his *Gesta Regum Anglorum,* ed. and trans. R. A. B. Mynors, R. M.

Thomson and M. Winterbottom, 2 vols. (Oxford Medieval Texts, 1998–99) and *Gesta Pontificum*, ed. and trans. R. M. Thomson and M. Winterbottom (Oxford Medieval Texts, forthcoming).

Chapter 8

J. C. Dickinson, *The Origins of the Austin Canons;* C. Dereine, esp. "Chanoines" in *DHGE*, XII, 353–405; also in *Revue d'histoire ecclésiastique*, XLI (1946), 365–406, XLIII (1948), 411–42; *Les chanoines réguliers au diocése de Liège...* (Brussels, 1952); and *La Mendola*, III. The most thorough study of the Rule of St. Augustine is L.Verheijen, *La règle de S. Augustin*, 2 vols. (Paris, 1967). On the *conversi* see C. D. Fonseca in La Mendota, V, 262–305.

Chapter 9

On the Cistercians and St. Bernard, Knowles, *MO*, chaps. XII–XIV, XXXVII and *Historian and Character and Other Essays* (Cambridge, 1963), chap. III (on Bernard); J. Leclercq, *St. Bernard et l'esprit cistercien* (Paris, 1966)—a brief, penetrating survey with ample quotations and useful short bibliography; the standard life is still E. Vacandard, *Vie de S. Bernard*, 2 vols., 4th ed. (Paris, 1910); we await the life by Christopher Holdsworth (Harlow, forthcoming). Bernard's works have been edited by J. Leclercq, C. H. Talbot and H. M. Rochais, 8 vols. (Rome, 1957–77).

Of many translations in various languages, the most useful are *The Works of St. Bernard* (Cistercian Fathers Series, Shannon etc., 1970–); *Letters*, Eng. trans. by B. S. James (London, 1953). An interesting general account is L. J. Lekai, *The White Monks* (Okauchee, 1953). For reference, R. A. Donkin, *Cistercian Bibliography* (Rochefort, 1969), followed by *Bibliographie Générale de l'Ordre Cistercien*, La Documentation Cistercienne (Rochefort, 1977–).

On St. Ailred of Rievaulx, Walter Daniel's *Life*, ed. and trans. F. M. Powicke (Nelson's Medieval Texts, 1950); A. Squire, *Aelred of Rievaulx* (London, 1969); *Opera Omnia*, in progress, *Corpus Christianorum, Cont. Med.*, I, ed. A. Hoste and C. H.Talbot (Turnhout, 1971–).

The controversies on Cistercian origins are clarified in Knowles, *GHE*, pp. 197–222, with references to the literature and texts; corrected and updated by C. Holdsworth in *Cistercian Art and Architecture in the British Isles*, ed. C. Norton and D. Park (Cambridge, 1986), pp. 40–55. On the Cistercian economy, Knowles, *RO*, I, chap. VII; Constable, *Monastic Tithes* (p. 306); Donkin, art. cit. (p. 314–15, chap. 13, n. 3; cf. list in *MO*, 2nd ed., p. 746); H. Dubled in *Revue d'histoire ecclésiastique*, LIV (1959), 765–82; C. Platt, *The Monastic Grange in Medieval England* (London, 1969). On work, C. J. Holdsworth in *Studies in Church History*, X (1973), 59–76.

For the spread of the order, and for excellent maps, charts of affiliation, plates, notes on individual houses, etc., *Atlas Cist.;* for England, KH, pp. 110ff.; for the Low Countries, J.-M. Canivez, *L'ordre de Cîteaux en Belgique...* (Forges-lez-Chimay, 1926); and other books, below. For detailed studies, the chief periodicals are *Analecta Cisterciensia* (formerly *Anal. S. Ordinis Cist.)* and *Cîteaux* (formerly *Cîteaux in de Nederlanden)*. On Cistercian architecture, see above, under chap. 7; *Cistercian Art and Architecture* (as above); P. Fergusson, *Architecture of Solitude* (Princeton, 1984); M. Aubert, *L'architecture cistercienne en France,* 2nd ed., 2 vols. (Paris, 1947); H. P. Eydoux, *L'architecture des églises cisterciennes d'Allemagne* (Paris, 1952); M.-A. Dimier, *Recueil des plans des églises cisterciennes* (Grignan-Paris, 1949; supplement, 1967); supplemented by the series of volumes published by Zodiaque, ed. by Pére Dimier and others, on *L'art cistercien,* esp. *L'art cist. hors de France* (1971). There is an interesting survey of "Cistercian architectural purism" by F. Bucher in *Comparative Studies in Society and History,* III (1960–61), 89–105; the special contribution of St. Bernard is discussed by K. H. Esser in *Archiv für mittelrheinische Kirchengeschichte,* V (1953), 195–222; Brooke, *Churches and Churchmen,* chap. 11; the fullest study of church plans and proportions, and of the relations of Cistercian and local styles, is H.

Hahn, *Die frühe Kirchenbaukunst der Zisterzienser* (Berlin, 1957), based on Eberbach. The article "Cistercensi" by V. Ascani in *Enciclopedia dell'Arte Medievale,* IV (Rome, 1993), pp. 816–35, has a useful bibliography.

Chapter 10

On the knights, see esp. J. Riley-Smith, *The Knights of St. John in Jerusalem and Cyprus, c. 1050–1310* (London, 1967); idem, *Hospitallers: The History of the Order of St. John* (Hambledon, 1999); *New Catholic Encyclopedia,* arts. Knights of Malta, Templars; B. A. Lees, *Records of the Templars in England in the Twelfth Century* (London, 1935); D. W. Lomax, *La Orden de Santiago, 1170–1275* (Madrid, 1965).

Chapter 11

On women religious there is now a copious literature: see above, pp. 312–13; S. Thompson, *Women Religious* (Oxford, 1991); S. K. Elkins, *Holy Women of Twelfth-Century England* (Chapel Hill, 1988); M. Parisse, *Les nonnes au moyen âge* (Paris, 1983); J. Burton, *The Yorkshire Nunneries in the Twelfth and Thirteenth Centuries* (York, 1979). Eileen Power's *Medieval English Nunneries* (Cambridge, 1922) retains its value. On Heloise, see P. Dronke, *Women Writers of the Middle Ages* (Cambridge, 1984), chap. 5; C. Brooke, *The Medieval Idea of Marriage* (Oxford, 1989), pp. 89–118; on Hildegarde, Dronke, chap. 6 and below, p. 335 (Rupertsberg); on the thirteenth-century movements, see p. 338 under Villers, H. Grundmann, *Religious Movements in the Middle Ages* (English trans. S. Rowan, Notre Dame, 1995), and B. Bolton in *Studies in Church History,* X (1973), pp. 77–95.

Chapter 12

On the Premonstratensians, see H. M. Colvin, *The White Canons in England* (Oxford, 1951, with good bibliography); Backmund; C. Dereine, "Les Origines de Prémontré', in *Revue d'histoire ecclésiastique,* XLII (1947), 352–78. The two early lives of St. Norbert are in *Monumenta Germaniae Hist., Scriptores,* XII (1856), 663ff., and *PL,* CLXX, 1253–1344.

On the friars, see R. B. Brooke, *The Coming of the Friars* (London, 1975); *RO,* I; P. Gratien, *Histoire de la Fondation et de l'Évolution de l'Ordre des Frères Mineurs au XIIIe siècle* (Paris-Gembloux, 1928); J. R. H. Moorman, *A History of the Franciscan Order* (to 1517) (Oxford, 1968); R. B. Brooke, *Early Franciscan Government* (Cambridge, 1959); R. F. Bennett, *The Early Dominicans* (Cambridge, 1937). On St. Francis, the classic is P. Sabatier, S. *François d'Assise* (Paris, 1893–94; Eng. trans. by L. S. Houghton, 1922; on Sabatier's *Life,* see C. Brooke, *Medieval Church and Society,* chap. 10); M. Robson, *St. Francis of Assisi* (London, 1997). Francis's and Clare's writings are trans. R. J.

Armstrong and I. C. Brady (Ramsey, N.J., and London, 1982); texts in *Die Opuscula des hl. Franziskus von Assisi,* ed K. Esser (Grottaferrata, 1976), and Claire d'Assise, *Écrits,* ed. M.-F. Becker et al. (Paris, 1985); for contemporary lives etc., see R. B. Brooke, in *Latin Biography* (ed. T. A. Dorey, London, 1967), pp. 177–98, and her ed. of *Scripta Leonis...* (Oxford, 1970, revised repr. 1990). On St. Dominic, M.-H. Vicaire, *Histoire de S. Dominique* (2 vols., Paris, 1957; Eng. trans. K. Pond, London, 1964); for contemporary lives etc., see *Early Dominicans: Selected Writings,* ed. S. Tugwell (Ramsey, N.J., and London, 1982); C. Brooke, *Medieval Church and Society,* chap. 11. For both saints there are vivid introductions in L. von Matt's pictorial biographies *(St. Francis of Assisi,* with W. Hauser; *St. Dominic,* with M.-H. Vicaire; London 1956–57). For detailed studies, there are numerous periodicals, e.g., *Archivum Franciscanum historicum, Franciscan Studies, Collectanea Franciscana* (with annual bibliography), *Archivum Fratrum Praedicatorum.*

Chapter 13

On Fountains see *MSA,* pp. 93–7; W. H. St. John Hope in *Yorks Archaeological Journal,* XV (1900), 269–402; P. Gilyard-Beer, *Fountains Abbey* (London, HMSO, 1970); articles by L. G. D. Baker (chap. 13, n. 6). On the earliest buildings, see R. Halsey in *Cistercian Art and*

Architecture..., ed C. Norton and D. Park (Cambridge, 1986), pp. 65–85 esp. pp. 73–77.

On Mont Saint-Michel, *Millénaire monastique du Mont Saint-Michel,* ed. J. Laporte, R. Foreville, M. Baudot and M. Nortier (Paris, 1966–); P. Gout, *Le Mont Saint-Michel,* 2 vols. (Paris, 1910); G. Bazin, *Le Mont Saint-Michel* (Paris, 1933); J. J. G. Alexander, *Norman Illumination at Mont Saint-Michel 966–1100* (Oxford, 1970), esp. p. 4 and n. 3 for bibliog. on early buildings.

On Sant'Ambrogio, F. Reggiori, *La Basilica di Sant' Ambrogio* (see pp. 315–16, chap. 13, n. 14; shorter introduction in A. M. Romanini, *Milano: S. Ambrogio);* see also articles by P. Zerbi (ibid.), and for Milanese society, C. Violante, *La pataria milanese e la riforma ecclesiastica,* I (Rome, 1955).

Chapter 14

Especially helpful for this chapter are *Atlas Cist.,* Cottineau, and for individual countries KH and its companion volume by I. B. Cowan and D. E. Easson for Scotland, 2nd ed. (1976) and A. Gwynn and R. N. Hadcock for Ireland (1970); J. A. Watt, *The Church and the Two Nations in Medieval Ireland* (Cambridge, 1970); Hauck; *Gallia Christiana* (see p. 308); *GB;* and for Poland and Bohemia, J. Kloczowski in *La Mendola,* III, IV and VI, and his *History of Polish Christianity* (Cambridge, 2000).

Chapter 15

For the late Middle Ages, see esp. Knowles, *RO,* III. For Much Wenlock, *MSA,* pp. 53–55. The chief sources for the internal life of monasteries from the late twelfth to the fifteenth centuries are the comparatively few chroniclers who tell us the gossip of a community, of whom Jocelin of Brakelond (ed. and trans. H. E. Butler, Nelson's Medieval Texts, 1949; trans. D. Greenway and J. Sayers [Oxford, 1989]) is the most celebrated, and visitation records. On these, see esp. Knowles, *RO,* II, chap. XV; the most substantial early records of visitations are in the fascinating mid-thirteenth century diary, alias *Register of Eudes of Rouen,* trans. S. M. Brown, ed. J. F. O'Sullivan (Columbia Records of Civilisation, 1964). Barbara Harvey, *Living and Dying in England, 1100–1540: The Monastic Experience* (Oxford, 1993) has transformed our view of late medieval monastic life.

It is impossible to summarize briefly the books on recent monastic history. A readable general survey, from without but based on extensive inquiry, is G. Moorhouse, *Against All Reason* (London, 1969; 2nd ed. 1986). Helpful examples of modern literature are *The Cistercian Spirit: A Symposium,* ed. M. B. Pennington (Shannon, 1970) and H. van Zeller, *The Benedictine Idea* (London, 1959). A laywoman's encounter with the monastic world is the theme of Kathleen Norris, *The Cloister Walk* (New York, 1996).

A new perspective on the monastic revivals—and the disasters—of the eighteenth and nineteenth century will be provided by Derek Beales, *Prosperity and Plunder: European Catholic Monasteries in the Age of Revolution, 1650–1815* (Cambridge, 2003).

III

This section comprises a list of monasteries used as examples in this book, and shown on the map, pp. viii–ix; it is intended to give very brief details—country, order, date of foundation—and basic references for each. The selection is aimed to support the text and plates and indicate further reading; it is sometimes slanted toward the history of a house, sometimes toward its physical remains, or some special feature, according to the use of the house as an example in the book.

Abbreviations

Aug.   Augustinian Order
           (canons regular)
f.   founded
O.Cart.   Carthusian Order
O.Cist.   Cistercian Order
O.F.M.   Order of Friars Minor
           (Franciscan friars)
O.P.   Order of Preachers
           (Dominican friars)
O.Praem.   Premonstratensian Order
O.S.B.   Order of St. Benedict
           (Benedictine monks)

For other abbreviations, see pp. 296–97.

Abingdon (England), O.S.B., f. 7th cent., ref. c. 954. KH, pp. 52, 58.

Alcobaça (Portugal), O.Cist., f. c. 1153. Dimier (1971), pp. 254–98; *Dizionario*, I 478–79 (J. Gibert).

Altenberg (Dhüntal, Germany), O.Cist., f. 1133. *Germania Sacra*, neue Folge 11, Berlin, 1965 (H. Mosier).

Alvastra (Sweden), O.Cist., f. 1143. *Atlas Cist.*, p. 270; see p. 296.

Apt (France), early monastery, f. c. 420. Cf. O. Chadwick, *John Cassian,* 2nd ed. (Cambridge, 1968), pp. 37ff.

Arles (France), Saint-Trophime, Cathedral, Aug. (see pp. 308–9, chap. 8, n. 5). L. H. Labande, *L'église Saint-Trophime d'Arles,* Paris, 1930; A. Borg, *Architectural Sculpture in Romanesque Provence,* Oxford, 1972, chap. 5.

Arrouaise (France), Aug., f. c. 1090. L. Milis, *L'ordre de chanoines réguliers d'Arrouaise,* 2 vols., Bruges, 1969; *Constitutiones,* ed. L. Milis and J. Becquet, Turnhout, 1970.

Assisi (Italy), Basilica and Sacro Convento (f. 1228), Carceri, and San Damiano (f. 1213), O.F.M. L. von Matt and W. Hauser, *St. Francis of Assisi, a Pictorial Biography,* Eng. trans., London, 1956; B. Kleinschmidt, *Die Basilika San Francesco in Assisi,* 3 vols., Berlin, 1915–28; R. B. Brooke, *The Image of St. Francis in the Thirteenth Century* (forthcoming).

Bangor (Ireland), early monastery, 6th cent.; Aug. A. Gwynn and R. N. Hadcock, *Medieval Religious Houses, Ireland,* London, 1970, pp. 30, 161.

Bec (France), O.S.B., f. c. 1039. A.A. Porée, *Histoire de l'abbaye du Bec*, 2 vols., Évreux, 1901; *Spicilegium Beccense*, I, Congrès international du IXe centénaire de l'arrivée d'Anselme au Bec, Le Bec-Paris, 1959.

Bernay (France), O.S.B., f.–1017. *Gallia Christiana*, XI (Paris ed., 1874), coll. 830ff.; A. W. Clapham, *English Romanesque Architecture after the Conquest* (Oxford, 1934), pp. 4ff.

Bingen, see Rupertsberg.

Blanchland (England), O.Praem., f. 1165. H. M. Colvin, *The White Canons in England* (Oxford, 1951), pp. 97–99, 371.

Bobbio (Italy), f. 613. Schmitz, 1, 68 f.; IP, VI, ii, 245ff.; *DHGE*, IX, 275–84 (F. Bonnard).

Bologna (Italy), San Domenico, formerly St. Nicholas, O.P., f. 1219. M.-H. Vicaire, *St. Dominic* (p. 326), pp. 270ff., 300ff., 371ff. (Eng. trans.).

Bologna, Santo Stefano, O.S.B., f. 973 (as monastery; the complex is ?5th cent. in origin). G. Aprato, *Bologna, Complesso di S. Stefano,* Tesori d'Arte Cristiana, II (Bologna, 1966); IP,V, 264ff.; Krautheimer, pp. 127ff.

Brevnov, see Prague.

Brogne (France), O.S.B., f. 914. Schmitz, 1, 160ff.; *DHGE*, X, 818–32 (F. Baix).

Buildwas (England), O.Cist., f. 1135 (Savigniac till 1147). *MSA*, pp. 106–7; Dimier (1971), pp. 137–80.

Bury St. Edmunds (England), O.S.B.,

f. 1020–2. KH, pp. 53, 61; *MSA*, pp. 14–15; *Bury St. Edmunds: Medieval Art, Architecture, Archaeology and Economy*, ed. A. Gransden (British Archaeological Association Conference Transactions, XX, 1998).

Caen (France), Saint-Etienne, O.S.B., and La Sainte-Trinité, O.S.B., nuns, f. c. 1066. L. Musset, *Les actes de Guillaume le Conquérant et de la reine Mathilde pour les abbayes caennaises* (Caen, 1967).

Camaldoli (Italy), f. ?c. 1000. *DHGE*, XI, 509–12 (on order), 512–36 (on monastery) (A. des Mazis); P. Ciampelli, *Guida storica illustrata di Camaldoli e sacro eremo…*(Udine, 1906 and later eds.).

Canterbury (England), Christ Church Cathedral Priory, O.S.B., f. 598, refounded 997. R. W. Southern, *St. Anselm and his Biographer* (Cambridge, 1963). chap. VII, and passim; Knowles, *MO, passim; A History of Canterbury Cathedral*, ed. P. Collinson, N. Ramsay and M. Sparks (Oxford, 1995).

Canterbury, St. Augustine's, O.S.B., f. 598–605. A. W. Clapham, *St. Augustine's Abbey, Canterbury* (London, H.M.S.O., 1955).

Carceri, see Assisi.

Carlisle (England) Cathedral Priory, Aug., f. 1133 (as Cathedral). Dickinson, pp. 245–51; J. Le Neve, *Fasti Ecclesiae Anglic., 1066–1300*, II, ed. D. E. Greenway (London, 1971), pp. 19, 21; H. Summerson, *Medieval Carlisle* (1993).

Casamari (Italy), O.S.B., f.–1030; O. Cist., f. 1140. *Atlas Cist.,* p. 275; Dimier (1971), pp. 199–207.

Cava dei Tirreni, La (Italy), O.S.B., f. 1011. Schmitz, I, 185ff., and bibliog. note, p. 185, n. 39; *DHGE,* XII, 21–5 (P. Schmitz); 1P,VIII, 309–30.

Cefalù (Sicily), Cathedral, Aug., f. 1131. O. Demus, *The Mosaics of Norman Sicily* (London, 1949 [1950]), chap. 1.

Chartreuse, La Grande (France), O.Cart., f. 1084. See p. 322.

Chiaravalle (Italy, near Milan), O.Cist., f. 1135–6. *Atlas Cist.,* p. 275.

Chiusa (Italy), *see* Sagra di S. Michele.

Cîteaux (France), O.Cist., f. 1097–8. *DHGE* XII, 852ff. (J.-M. Canivez); Knowles, *GHE,* pp. 197–222. See pp. 166ff., 324.

Clairvaux (France), O.Cist., f. 1115. E. Vacandard, *Vie de S. Bernard,* 2 vols., 4th ed. (Paris, 1910).

Cluny (France), O.S.B. (Cluniac), f. 910. See pp. 320–21.

Colchester (England), St. Botolph, Aug., f. c. 1093, completed by 1106. KH, pp. 139, 155; Dickinson, pp. 98ff.

Conques (France), O.S.B., refounded 8th cent. *Rouergue roman* (Zodiaque, 1963), pp. 27–184.

Cuxa, St.-Michel-de- (France), O.S.B., f. -841; revived 10th cent. *DHGE,* XIII, 1121–42 (C.-M. Baraut).

Dijon (France), St.-Bénigne, O.S.B., f. 6th cent., refounded 1001. R.

Oursel, Invention de l'architecture romane (Zodiaque, 1970), pp. 71ff.; *Bourgogne romane,* ed. R. Oursel (5th ed., Zodiaque, 1968), pp. 47ff.; Knowles, *MO,* pp. 84ff.; Hunt (1971), chap. 6, and refs. (the last two on the work and influence of St. William of Volpiano and Dijon).

Dryburgh (Scotland), O.Praem., f. 1150–2. J. Bulloch, *Adam of Dryburgh* (London, 1958), esp. chap. 5; J. S. Richardson and M. Wood, *Dryburgh Abbey* (Edinburgh, HMSO, 1948).

Dünamunde (U.S.S.R., formerly Latvia), O.Cist., f. before 1208. *Atlas Cist.,* p. 277.

Durham (England) Cathedral Priory, O.S.B., f. 1083. *MSA,* pp. 2–3; T. S. R. Boase, *English Art 1100–1216* (Oxford, 1953), chaps. I, VIII; *Anglo-Norman Durham 1093–1193,* ed. D. Rollason, M. Harvey and M. Prestwich (Woodbridge, 1994).

Durrow (Ireland), early monastery, f. ?c. 556; Aug., mid 12th cent. A. Gwynn and R. N. Hadcock, *Medieval Religious Houses, Ireland* (London, 1970), pp. 174–75.

Eberbach (Germany), O.Cist., f. c. 1135 (previously O.S.B.). Hahn (p. 311, chap. 9, n. 12); Dimier (1971).

Einsiedeln (Switzerland), O.S.B., f. 934. *DHGE,* XV, 95–7 (R. Henggeler); *GP,* II, ii, 65–72.

Esrom (Denmark), O.Cist., f. 1154. *Atlas Cist.,* p. 278.

Essen (Germany), O.S.B., nuns, f. c. 850. *DHGE,* XV, 1009–12 (A. Franzen); Dr. Sandforth, *Der Essener*

Münsterschatz (Essen, n.d.); H. Köhn, *Das Essener Münster* (Essen, 1953).

Essen-Werden (Germany), O.S.B., f. (by St. Liudger) 799–801. Hauck, II, 407,804; Zarnecki, *Romanik* (p. 323), p. 72 and pl. 102; W. Zimmermann et al., *Die Kirchen zu Essen-Werden*, Essen, 1959; R. Wesenberg, *Frühe mittelalterliche Bildwerke*, Düsseldorf, 1972, pp. 101–2.

Evesham (England), O.S.B., f. 8th cent., refounded c. 995. KH, pp. 54, 65; *The Evesham Chronicle of Thomas of Marlborough*, ed. and trans. J. Sayers and L. Watkiss (Oxford Medieval Texts, forthcoming).

Falkenau (nr Dorpat, Esthonia), O.Cist., f. 1233–4. *Atlas Cist.*, p. 278.

Farfa (Italy), early monastery, later O.S.B., f. 7th cent. *DHGE*, XVI, 547–53 (I. Tassi); IP, II, 55ff.

Finchale (England), O.S.B., cell of Durham, f. 1170. KH, pp. 65, 66; C. Peers, *Finchale Priory* (London, HMSO, 1933).

Fleury, St.-Benoît-sur-Loire (France), O.S.B., f. 672–4. Schmitz, I, 37–8 and n. 76; G. Chenesseau, *L'Abbaye de Fleury à Saint-Benoît-sur-Loire* (Paris, 1931); S. *Benoît-sur-Loire* (Zodiaque, 1962).

Florence (Italy), see references under Camaldoli.

Florence, San Miniato, O.S.B., f. ?before 783, refounded early 11th cent. *DHGE*, XVII, 546–8 (C. C. Calzolai).

Fonte Avellana (Italy), O.S.B., f. c. 990. *DHGE*, XVII, 888–91 (G. M. Cacciamani); *IP*, IV, 92ff.

Fontevrault (France), O. Fontevrault, f. 1099. *DHGE*, XVII, 961–71 (J. Daoust); M. Melot, (L'abbaye de) Fontevrault (Petites Monographies…, Paris, 1971); on the tombs see esp. G. Zarnecki, *The Monastic Achievement* (London, 1972), pp. 93–94. On the founder see above pp. 312–13, n.9.

Fossanova (Italy), O.S.B., f. 8th–9th cent., O.Cist., f. 1135. Dimier (1971), pp. 189–98; C. d'Onofrio e. C. Pietrangeli, *Le abbazie del Lazio* (Rome, 1971), pp. 229–44.

Fountains (England), O.Cist., f. 1132–3. See chap. 13.

Fruttuaria (Italy), O.S.B., f. c. 1003. Schmitz, I, 183; *DHGE*, XIX, 246–51 (G. Picasso); bibliog. in Cottineau, I, 1227–8.

Fulda (Germany), O.S.B., f. 744. Hauck, I, 580ff., II, passim; Krautheimer, pp. 209ff.

Gandersheim (Germany), nuns, f. 852–56. Hauck, II, 601ff., 799; A. Schulte, *Der Adel und die deutsche Kirche im Mittelalter* (Stuttgart, 1910), pp. 405ff.

Gernrode (Germany), nuns, f. 961. Hauck, III, 1017; Schulte, pp. 407ff.; *DHGE*, XX, 994–95 (N. Backmund).

Glastonbury (England), early monastery (? 6th cent.), then O.S.B., refounded c. 940. *MSA*, pp. 28–31; KH, pp. 54, 66; *The Archaeology and History of*

Glastonbury Abbey: Essays in Honour of the Ninetieth Birthday of C. A. Ralegh Radford, ed. L. Abrams and J. Carley (Woodbridge, 1991).

Gloucester, see Llanthony.

Gorze (France, formerly Germany), O.S.B., f. c. 933. K. Hallinger, *Gorze-Kluny*, 2 vols. (Rome, 1950–51); and see esp. John Nightingale, *Monasteries and Patrons in the Gorze Reform* (Oxford, 2001).

Grandmont (France), O. Grandmont, f. after 1076. C. Hutchison, *The Hermit Monks of Grandmont* (Kalamazoo, 1989)

Heidenheim (Germany), double monastery for monks and nuns, f. 751. Hauck, II, 798; *GP*, II, 10–15; *GB*, II, 114–17.

Heiligenkreuz (Austria), O.Cist., f. c. 1135. *Atlas Cist.*, p. 282; GP, I, pp. 253–6.

Helmarshausen (Germany), O.S.B., f. 997. Hauck, III, 1022; Theophilus, ed. Dodwell (p. 308), pp. xliff.

Hexham (England), early monastery, f. 674; later Aug., f. 1113. KH, pp. 140,159–60.

Hirsau (Germany), O.S.B., f. before 830, refounded by Abbot William in the years following 1069. H. Jakobs, *Die Hirsauer*, Köln-Graz, 1969; W. Hoffmann, *Hirsau und die "Hirsauer Bauschule"* (Munich, 1950).

Hovedö (Norway), O.Cist., f. 1147. *Atlas Cist.*, p. 283.

Las Huelgas (nr Burgos, Spain), O.Cist., nuns, f. 1187. *Atlas Cist., p.* 283; *DHGE*, XXV, 73–85.

Iona (Scotland), early monastery, f. late 6th century. A. Gwynn and R. N. Hadcock, *Medieval Religious Houses, Ireland* (London, 1970), p. 38; *Adomnan's Life of Columba*, ed. and trans. A. O. and M. O. Anderson (Edinburgh/London, 1961).

Jarrow (England), early monastery, then O.S.B., f. 681, refounded 1073–74. Early mon. joint with Monkwearmouth, and the home of Bede. KH, pp. 68, 71; *Medieval Archaeology*, X (1966), 169 f., XI (1967), 263 f.; XII (1968), 155–6; XVI (1972), 148–52 (reports of R. Cramp's excavations).

Jedburgh (Scotland), Aug., f. c. 1138. *MRHS*, pp. 92–3; *MSA*, pp. 188–9; *Royal Commission on Ancient Monts., Scotland, Roxburghshire* (1956), I, 194–207.

Jumièges (France), O.S.B., f. c. 654. *Jumièges, Congrès scientifique du xiiie centénaire*, 2 vols. (Rouen, 1955); R. Martin du Gard, *L'abbaye de Jumièges* (Montdidier, 1909); L. Jouen, *Jumièges, Histoire et légendes...* (Rouen ed., 1954); E. Remnant in *Journal of the Brit. Arch. Association*, 3rd Series, XX–XXI (1957–8), 107–38 and bibliog. on p. 138.

Kelso (Scotland), O.S.B. Tironian, f. (Selkirk) 1113, (Kelso, c. 1127). *MRHS*, pp. 68–70; *MSA*, pp. 60–61; *Roxburghshire* (see Jedburgh), I, 240–46.

Kingswood (England), O.Cist., f. 1139. KH, pp. 113, 121; *Letters and Charters of Gilbert Foliot*, ed. A. Morey and C. N. L. Brooke (Cambridge, 1967), pp. 510–13.

Kirkstead (England), O.Cist., f. 1139. KH, pp. 113, 121; *MSA*, pp. 126–27.

Lacock (England), Aug. nuns, f. 1230–32. *VCH Wiltshire*, III, 303–16 (H. M. Chew); H. Brakespear in *Archaeologia*, LVII (1901), 125–48; C. H. Talbot in *Journ. of the Brit. Archaeol. Assoc.,* New Series, XI (1905), 175–210; *MSA*, pp. 264–65.

Laon (France), Templars, f. before 1160 (later Hospitallers), now in the Musée municipal garden. *Guide Bleu, Flandre, Hainaut, Artois, Picardie* (1966 ed.), p. 531.

Leicester (England), Aug., f. 1143. *VCH Leics.*, II, 13–19 (R. A. McKinley).

Lézat (France), O.S.B., f. 940. Hunt (1971), pp. 100ff. (article by A. M. Mundó).

Llanthony (Gwent and England), two houses closely linked, O.S.A., I, f. 1103–8, II (in Gloucester), f. 1136. *MSA*, pp. 208–9, 210–11, and references.

London (England), Charterhouse, O.Cart., f. 1371. M. D. Knowles and W. F. Grimes, *Charterhouse* (London, 1954).

London, Holy Trinity Priory, Aldgate, Aug., f. 1107–8. Dickinson, pp. 109ff.; *Cartulary of Holy Trinity Aldgate*, ed. G. A. J. Hodgett (London Rec. Soc., 1971); C. Brooke and G. Keir, *London 800–1216* (London, 1975), pp. 314–25.

London, Clerkenwell, Hospital of St. John of Jerusalem, Hospitallers, f. c. 1144; *Royal Commission on Hist. Monuments, London*, II, 16ff.

London, Temple Church, Templars, f. c. 1128, moved to present site 1161; suppressed 1308–12. *Records of the Templars in England in the 12th Century*, ed. B. A. Lees (London, 1935).

Lucca (Italy), San Frediano, Aug., f. before 1046, but probably not Aug. till 12th cent. M. Giusti in *La Mendola*, III, i, 447–48, and references.

Luxeuil (France), early monastery, then O.S.B., f. c. 590. Schmitz, I, 59ff.

Lyse (Norway), O. Cist., f. 1146–7. *Atlas Cist.*, p. 286.

Marcigny (France), Cluniac, nuns, f. c. 1055. Hunt (1967), chap. 5; E. M. Wischerman, *Marcigny-sur-Loire* (Munich, 1986).

Maria Laach (Germany), O.S.B., f. 1093. A. Schippers, *Das Laacher Münster* (ed. T. Bogler, Köln, 1967); T. Bogler, *Maria Laach,* 6th ed. (Munich-Zürich, 1968).

Markyate (England), O.S.B., nuns, f. 1145. *The Life of Christina of Markyate*, ed. and trans. C. H. Talbot (Oxford Medieval Texts, 1987); O. Pächt, C. R. Dodwell and F. Wormald, *The St. Albans Psalter* (London, 1960).

Marseille (France), St. Victor, early monastery (John Cassian's), later O.S.B. On early history, Chadwick, *Cassian*, esp. pp. 32ff.

Maulbronn (Germany), O.Cist., f. 1138–47. *Atlas Cist.*, p. 287; *GP*, III, pp. 124–28.

Mazan (France), O.Cist., f. 1120. *Atlas Cist.*, p. 287.

Mellifont (Ireland), O.Cist., f. 1142. J. A. Watt, *The Church and the Two Nations in Medieval Ireland* (Cambridge, 1970), chap. 4.

Melrose (Scotland), O.Cist., f. 1136. *MSA*, pp. 64–65; J. S. Richardson and M. Wood, *Melrose Abbey,* 2nd ed. (Edinburgh, HMSO, 1949); *Roxburghshire* (see Jedburgh), II, 265–91.

Milan (Italy), Sant'Ambrogio, O.S.B., f. 789. See pp. 252–58, and pp. 315–16, chap. 13, n. 14.

Moissac (France), O.S.B. (for a time Cluniac), f. mid–7th cent. E. Rupin, *L'abbaye et les cloîtres de Moissac* (Paris, 1897); A. Anglès, *L'abbaye de Moissac* (Petites Monographies…, Paris, n.d.); *Quercy Roman,* ed. M. Vidal, J. Maury, J. Porcher, 2nd ed. (Zodiaque, 1969), pp. 33ff.; E. Mâle, *L'art religieux du xiie siècle…* (1940, ed.), pp. 4ff.

Molesme (France), O.S.B., f. c. 1075. Knowles, *MO*, pp. 198–99, 752–53 and references.

Monkwearmouth (England), early monastery, then O.S.B., f. 674, refounded c.1075. See Jarrow.

Monreale (Sicily), Cathedral, O.S.B., f. 1174. O. Demus (see Cefalù), chap. 4.

Mont Saint-Michel, Le (France), O.S.B., f. c. 708, refounded 966. See p. 245–52.

Monte Cassino (Italy), O.S.B., St. Benedict's abbey, f. c. 530. Schmitz, I, 20ff., 72 f., 179 f.; H.E.J. Cowdrey, *The Age of Abbot Desiderius* (Oxford, 1983).

Montserrat (Spain), O.S.B., f. 1022–23. Hunt (1971), pp. 106ff.; A. Albareda, *L'abat Oliva, fundador de Montserrat* (Montserrat, 1931).

Morimond (France), O. Cist., f. 1115. *Atlas Cist.,* p. 289.

Mount Grace (England), O. Cart., f. 1398. *MSA*, pp. 234–35; W. Brown and W. H. St. John Hope in *Yorks. Archaeol. Journ.,* XVIII (1905), 252–309; A. W. Clapham in *VCH North Riding of Yorks.,* II, *24–27.*

Much Wenlock, see Wenlock.

Niederaltaich (Germany), O.S.B., f. 8th cent., ?741. Hauck, I, 508, II, 809; *GP,* I, 178–82; *GB,* II, 188–97.

Nonnberg, see Salzburg.

Northampton (England), St. Andrew, Cluniac, f. 1093–1100. *VCH Northants.,* II, 102–9.

Norwich (England), Cathedral priory, O.S.B., f. 1096–1101. *Norwich Cathedral: Church, City and Diocese 1096–1996,* ed. I. Atherton, E. Fernie, C. Harper-Bill and H. Smith (London, 1996).

Nydala (Sweden), O.Cist., f. 1143. *Atlas Cist.,* p. 290.

Odensee (Denmark), O.S.B., f. c. 1095–1100. Knowles, *MO,* p. 164; see p. 316, chap. 14, n. 7.

Osma (Spain), Cathedral priory, Aug., f. (as Aug.) 1128–40. La Mendola, III, i, 233 (J. F. Rivera).

Ottobeuren (Germany), O.S.B., f. before 826, ?764. Hauck, II, 568, 798; *GP,* II, 78–81; *GB,* II, 209–20.

Paraclet(e) (France), O.S.B., nuns; the home of Heloise, f. 1129–31, see pp.

209–11, 313, chap. 11, n. 11; M. Clanchy, *Abelard, a Medieval Life* (Oxford, 1997); C. Mews, *The Lost Love Letters of Abelard and Heloise* (New York, 1999).

Paris, see St.-Denis.

Poblet (Spain), O.Cist., f. 1150–1. Dimier (1971), pp. 125–36; *Scriptorium Populeti* (Poblet, 1966–).

Pontefract (England), Cluniac, f. c. 1090. KH, pp. 97, 102.

Prague (Bohemia), Hradcany and Brevnov, O.S.B., nuns and monks, f. after 967 and c. 993. J. Kloczowski in La Mendola, VI, 159 f.

Prémontré (France), O.Praem., f. c. 1121. See chap. 12.

Quedlinburg (Germany), nuns, f. 936. Hauck, III, 1016; Schulte *(see* Gandersheim), pp. 401ff.

Ratzeburg (Germany), O.Praem. Cathedral, f. 1154. Backmund, I, 241–3, with bibliog.; A. Kamphausen, *Der Dom zu Ratzeburg,* 2nd ed., 1966.

Reading (England), O.S.B., f. 1121. Knowles, *MO,* pp. 281–82; Brooke, *Churches and Churchmen,* pp. 151–54; B. R. Kemp (ed.), *Reading Abbey Cartularies,* esp. I (London, 1986), pp. 13–19.

Reichenau (Germany), O.S.B., f. 724. *Die Kultur der Abtei Reichenau,* ed. K. Beyerle, 2 vols. (Munich, 1925); *GP,* II, i, 147–58; H. Mayr-Harting, *Ottonian Book Illumination,* 2 vols. (London, 1991), I, 203–9.

Reichersberg (Germany), Aug., f. 1080–84. P. Classen in La Mendola,

III, i, 304–41; Classen, *Gerhoch von Reichersberg* (Wiesbaden, 1960).

Rievaulx (England), O.Cist., f. 1131–32. *MSA,* pp. 82–5; P. Fergusson and S. Harrison, *Rievaulx Abbey* (New Haven, 1999); on Ailred, above pp. 186–91.

Ripoll (Spain), O.S.B., f. late 9th cent. Hunt (1971), chap. 7 (by A. M. Mundó); F. Rahlves, *Kathedralen und Klöster in Spanien* (Eng. trans., London, 1966, pp. 118–21); G. Sanoner in *Bulletin Monumental,* LXXXII (1923), 352–99 (on the portal).

Ripon (England), early monastery, f. c. 654–60, later secular minster. KH, pp. 417, 435.

Rome (Italy), Santi Quattro Coronati, early Basilica, O.S.B. from early 12th cent. (Camaldolensian 16th cent.; now nuns). A. Carletti, *Basilica dei SS. Quattro Coronati* (Rome, n.d.); *IP,* I, 40–42.

Rome, San Paolo fuori le Mura, early Basilica, O.S.B. from 8th cent., refounded mid–10th cent. *IP,* I, 164ff.; W. Oakeshott, *Mosaics of Rome* (London, 1967), pp. 295ff., 383.

Rupertsberg, nr. Bingen (Germany), O.S.B., nuns, home of St. Hildegard, f. 1147–48. H. Liebeschütz, *Das allegorische Weltbild der heiligen Hildegard von Bingen,* 2nd ed. (Darmstadt, 1964); P. Dronke, *Women Writers of the Middle Ages* (Cambridge, 1984), chap. 6, esp. pp. 150–53.

Sagra di San Michele (Chiusa), nr. Turin (Italy), O.S.B., f. 966 or

999–1002. *IP*, VI, ii, 120ff.; V. Moccagatta, *Torino: Sagra di S. Michele*, Tesori d'Arte Cristiana (Bologna, 1966); G. Gaddo, *La Sacra di S. Michele...* (Genoa, 1958); C. Verzár, *Die romanischen Skulpturen der Abtei Sagra di San Michele* (Bern, 1968).

Sahagún (Spain), O.S.B., f. before 1000, Cluniac from 1080. J. Perez and R. Escalona, *Historia del real monasterio de Sahagún* (Madrid, 1782); H. E. J. Cowdrey, *The Cluniacs and the Gregorian Reform* (Oxford, 1970), pp. 230–44.

St. Albans (England), O.S.B., f. c. 793, refounded c. 970. *MSA*, pp. 6–7.

St.-Denis, nr Paris (France), O.S.B., f. 7th cent. *Abbot Suger on the Abbey Church of St.-Denis* (Princeton, 1946); L. Grant, *Abbot Suger of St.-Denis: Church and State in early Twelfth-Century France* (London, 1998).

St.-Évroult (France), O.S.B., f. mid–7th cent., refounded shortly before 1050. *Ecclesiastical History of Orderic Vitalis*, ed. and trans. M. Chibnall, esp. III (Oxford, 1972), pp. xvff., and passim.

St. Gallen (St. Gall) (Switzerland), early monastery, later O.S.B., f. by St. Gall, disciple of St. Columbanus, c. 613. J. M. Clark, *The Abbey of St. Gall* (Cambridge, 1926); for the St. Gall plan, see pp. 67, 298 n. 6.

St.-Gilles (France), O.S.B., f. 8th cent. R. Hamann, *Die Abteikirche von St. Gilles and ihre künstlerische*

Nachfolge, 3 vols. (Berlin, 1955); E. Goiffon, *St.-Gilles* (Nîmes, 1882).

St.-Guilhem-le-Desert (France), O.S.B., f. early 9th cent. *Gallia Christiana*, VI (Paris, 1739), 580ff.

St.-Martin-du-Canigou (France), O.S.B., f. 1001. *Roussillon roman*, ed. M. Durliat, 2nd ed. (Zodiaque, 1964), pp. 115ff.; Hunt (1971), pp. 105ff.; M. Durliat in *Bulletin Monumental*, CXXX (1972), 353.

St.-Odile (France, formerly Germany), nuns, f. 7th cent. Home of Herrad(e), mid–late 12th cent. abbess and author of the *Hortus deliciarum*, ed. R. Green (London, 1979); cf. E. Mâle, *L'art religieux du xiie siècle*, 4th ed. (Paris, 1940), pp. 317–18.

St.-Riquier (France), O.S.B., f. mid–7th cent. Cottineau, II, 2868–69; *Gallia Christiana*, X, 1241–63; G. Durand, *L'église de S. Riquier* (Petites Monographies . . ., Paris, 1933); A. W. Clapham, *English Romanesque Architecture before the Conquest* (Oxford, 1930), pp. 78ff.

St.-Ruf (nr Avignon, France), Aug., f. c. 1039. Dickinson, p. 42; C. Dereine in *Revue Bénédictine*, LIX (1949), 161–82; A. H. Duparc in La Mendola, III, 114–28; C. Egger in *Adrian IV: The English Pope*, ed. B. Bolton and A. J. Duggan (Aldershot, forthcoming), chap. 2.

St.-Savin-sur-Gartempe (France), O.S.B., f. early 9th cent. R. Crozet in *Dict. des églises de France*, III, C, pp. 188–93; O. Demus, *Romanesque Mural Painting* (Eng. trans., London, 1970), pp. 420–23; *La Bible de S.*

Savin, ed. R. Oursel (Zodiaque, 1971).

Salzburg, Nonnberg (Austria), nuns c. 700. Hauck, I, 376, II 808.

San Juan de la Peña (Spain), O.S.B., f. early 11th cent. *Aragon roman,* ed. A. Canellas-Lopez and A. San Vicente (Zodiaque, 1971), pp. 69ff.

Santes Creus (Spain), O.Cist., f. 1150. Dimier (1971), pp. 245–53.

Santo Domingo, see Silos.

Savigny (France), O.S.B., f. 1112; from 1147, with its whole order, O.Cist. *Atlas Cist.,* p. 296; Cottineau, II, 2965–67; lives of early abbots and monks ed. E. P. Sauvage in *Analecta Bollandiana,* I (1882), 355–410, II (1883), 475–560 (and see Tiron).

Sées (France), Cathedral, Aug. from 1131. Dickinson, p. 29; *Letters of Arnutf of Lisieux,* ed. F. Barlow (London, 1939), pp. xvii f., 55ff.

Sempringham (England), Gilbertine Order, f. c. 1131. See pp. 313–14, chap. 12 n.3.

Sénanque (France), O.Cist., f. 1148. *Atlas Cist.,* p. 297; *Abbaye de Sénanque* (Lyon, n.d.).

Silos, Santo Domingo de (Spain), O.S.B., f. early 10th cent., home of S. Domingo, abbot 1041–73. *DHGE,* XIV, 623–27 (A. Ruiz on S. Domingo); M. Férotin, *Histoire de l'abbaye de Silos* (Paris, 1897); J. Perez de Urbel, El *Claustro de Silos* (Burgos, 1930); *Castille romane,* II, ed. L.-M. de Lojendio and A. Rodriguez (Zodiaque, 1966).

Silvacane (France), O.Cist., f. 1147.

Atlas Cist., p. 297; P. Pontus, *L'abbaye de Silvacane* (Caisse Nat. des Monuments Hist., Paris, 1966).

Solesmes (France), O.S.B., f. 1010; refounded 1664 (Maurist), 1833–37. Cottineau, II, 3055–57.

Subiaco (Italy), f. early 6th cent., home of St. Benedict (before Monte Cassino). *IP,* II, 83ff.

Sulejów (Poland), O.Cist., f. 1177. *Atlas Cist.,* p. 298; *Sztuka polska przeromanska i romanska…,* ed. M. Wahckiego (2 vols., Warsaw, 1971), I, 176, pls. 227, 230–32, 240, II, 826.

Tegernsee (Germany), O.S.B., 8th cent. Schmitz, II, 128ff.; *GP,* I, 360–70; *GB,* II, 297–304.

Le Thoronet (France), O.Cist., f. c. 1146. R. Berenguier, *L'abbaye du Thoronet* (Caisse Nat. des Monts. Historiques, Paris, 1971); P. Colas in *Monts. Historiques de la France,* nouv. sér., IV (1958), 32–41, XV (1969), 50–51.

Tiron (France), O.S.B. (Tironian), f. c. 1105. Knowles, *MO,* pp. 200–201; H. Grundmann, *Religious Movements in the Middle Ages* (trans. S. Rowan, Notre Dame, 1995), pp. 18–19, 210–11, 224–25, (on Bernard of Tiron, Vitalis of Savigny); R. B. Brooke, *The Coming of the Friars* (London, 1975), pp. 49–57 (on the same).

Toledo (Spain), Cathedral and S. Leocadia, Aug., f. early 12th cent., 1156–62. *La Mendola,* III, i, 221–8.

Tomar (Portugal), Templars, f. c. 1160, after suppression of Templars

Orden de Cristo, *Guia de Portugal,* II, (Lisbon, 1927), 456–83.

Toulouse (France), S. Sernin, early monastery O.S.B., from 9th cent.; Cottineau, II, 3183–85.

La Trappe (France), O.Cist., f. 1122 (Savigniac, 1140, Cist. 1147), refounded 1664. *Atlas Cist.,* p. 299; H. Brémond, *L'abbé tempête* (Paris, 1929, Eng. trans., London, 1930).

Tre Fontane (Italy), O.Cist., f. 7th cent., Cist. 1140. *Atlas Cist.,* p. 299.

Trier, S. Maximin (Germany), O.S.B., f. ? (cf. Hauck, I, 255), refounded 934. Hauck, III, 364ff., 372ff.; K. Hallinger, *Gorze-Kluny* (Rome, 1950–51), I, 59 f., 96ff.; J. Nightingale (*see* under Gorze).

Turin, see Sagra di S. Michele.

Tyniec (nr Krakow, Poland), O.S.B., f. c. 1060. J. Kloczowski in *La Mendola,* VI, 163.

Vallombrosa (Italy), f. c. 1039. Cottineau, II, 3286–87; *IP,* III, 834ff.; D. F. Tarani, *L'ordine Vallombrosano* (Florence, 1921).

Verona (Italy), San Zeno Maggiore, O.S.B., f. c. 800. *IP,*VII, i, 267–71; L. Puppi, *Chiesa di S. Zeno, Verona* (Tesori d'Arte Cristiana, Bologna, 1967); *Verona e il suo Territorio,* II (Verona, 1964), pp. 670–86, 693–744 etc.

Vézelay (France), O.S.B., f. c. 863–68 (Cluniac, 11th–12th cents.). F. Salet, *La Madeleine de Vézelay* (Melun, 1948); H. E. J. Cowdrey, *The Cluniacs and the Gregorian Reform* (Oxford, 1970), pp. 13–14, 85–87; *Monumenta Vizeliacensia,* ed. R. B. C. Huygens,

Corpus Christianorum, Cont. Mediaeualis 42 (Turnhout, 1976); Hugh of Poitiers, *The Vézelay Chronicle,* trans. J. Scott, R. Thomson and J. Ward (Sydney, 1988—Latin text in *Monumenta*).

Villers-la-Ville (Belgium), O.Cist., f. 1146. *Atlas Cist.,* pp. 301–2; E. de Moreau, *L'abbaye de Villers en Brabant aux xiie et xiiie siècles* (Brussels, 1909); S. Roisin, "L'efflorescence cistercienne et le courant féminin de piété au xiiie siècle', *Revue d'Histoire Ecclésiastique,* XXXIX (1943), 342–78.

Vivarium (Italy), early monastery, home of Cassiodorus, f. c. 555. *DHGE,* XI, 1357ff. (D. M. Cappuyns).

Vreden (Germany), nuns, f. c. 839. Hauck, II, 806; Schulte (see Gandersheim), pp. 55ff.

Wenlock, Much (England), nuns, f. 7th cent., refounded as Cluniac 1080–81. *MSA,* pp. 53–5; R. Graham, *The History of the Alien Priory of Wenlock* (London, HMSO, 1965); M. Chibnall in *VCH Shropshire,* II, 38–47.

Werden, see Essen-Werden.

Whitby (England), double house under St. Hilda, 7th cent. (c. 657), refounded O.S.B., before 1077. Bede, *Eccl. History,* esp. bk. iv, c. 23 (21); H. Mayr-Harting, *Coming of Christianity to Anglo-Saxon England* (London, 1972), pp. 149ff., 297–98; *MSA,* pp. 18–19.

Winchester (England), Cathedral Priory of St. Swithun, and New

Minster, later Hyde Abbey, O.S.B., f. 964. R. Willis, *Architectural Hist. of Winchester Cathedral* (London, Archaeol. Inst., 1845–46); M. Biddle, *The Old Minster...* (Winchester, 1970); M. Biddle and B. Kjølbe Biddle in *Winchester Studies*, IV (forthcoming).

Witham (England), O.Cart., f. 1178–9. *Magna Vita S. Hugonis,* ed. and trans. D. L. Douie and H. Farmer (2 vols., Nelson's Medieval Texts, 1961–62), esp. I, pp. xxiiff.

Worcester (England) Cathedral Priory, O.S.B., f. ?969. *MSA,* pp. 10–11; Knowles, *MO*, pp. 74ff.

Xanten (Germany) Cathedral, unsuccessful attempt at regular reform by St. Norbert, 1115 (H. M. Colvin, *White Canons in England,* Oxford, 1951, pp. 1–2).

York (England), St. Mary, O.S.B., f.–1086. *MSA,* pp. 20–21; *Heads of Religious Houses, England and Wales,* I, ed. D. Knowles, C. N. L. Brooke, V. C. M. London (2nd ed., Cambridge, 2001), p. 84; *The Noble City of York,* ed. A. Stacpoole (York, 1972).

Index

Aachen, 58, 200; council at, 61
abbesses and prioresses: Augustine
    and, St., 37, 201; Chaucer's por-
    trait of prioress, 214, 216; to
    eleventh century, 201–6; endow-
    ments and, 204–5; in England,
    57; in Essen, Germany, 203;
    Lacock and, 214–16; in twelfth
    and thirteenth centuries, 206–14.
    See also nuns; women's move-
    ment
Abelard, Peter, 84, 108, 144, 147,
    192, 209–10
Abingdon, England, O.S.B., 68
Abraham, 148
Acre, 199
"active life," 39, 41, 290. See also
    Martha and Mary
Acts, book of, 27, 141
Adalbert (archbishop of Milan), 87
Adalbert, St. (or Vojtech), 267
Adam and Eve, 36–37, 139
Adela (countess of Blois), 118,
    203
Adelaide (abbess of Quedlinburg,
    Gernrode, Vreden and Gander -
    sheim), 202
Adige (river in Italy), 122–23
Adrian IV, Pope (Nicholas Brake-
    speare), 158, 160
Æthelweard (chronicler), 203

Africa, North, 33, 86
Agnes of Bohemia, Blessed, 214
Aida, 122
Aidan, St., 55–56
Ailred, St. (abbot of Rievaulx),
    186–91, 243
Albigensian Crusade (1209), 146,
    265. See also Cathars
Alcobaça, Portugal, O.Cist., 186,
    264–65
Alcuin, 59
Aldgate, London, 159
Alexander (ex-monk of Witham,
    later Cluniac), 98
Alexander II, Pope (1061–73),
    157–58
Alexandria, Egypt, Christian
    Platonists of, 29, 31
Alfonso VI, King of León-Castile
    (1072–1109), 119–20
almoner, 79–80
Alps, 58, 90, 109, 122
altars and frontals, 75, 128, 180–81;
    Cîteaux, France, 171, 181; Golden
    Altar, 253–55
Altenberg, Germany, 268
Altmann, St. (bishop of Passau
    [1065–91]), 158–59
Alvastra, Sweden, O.Cist., 269–70
Amaury, Arnaud (abbot and arch-
    bishop of Narbonne), 265

Ambrose, St. (bishop of Milan), 253–54
America, monasteries in, 287
anchorites, 30. *See also* hermits
Ancren Riwle, 209
Ancrene Wisse, 209
Angilbert (archbishop of Milan), 254
Anglo-Saxon Chronicle, 203
Aniane. *See* Benedict of Aniane, St.
Anjou, France, 206
Anselm, St. (abbot of Bec and archbishop of Canterbury [c. 1033–1109]): biography of, 143; canons regular and, 155, 157–58, 163; humanism and, 143–49; theology of, 143–49
Antony, St. (c. 251–356), 28–32, 36–37, 42, 113, 238
apatheia, 31
Apocalypse, 131
Apostles (disciples). *See specific names*
Apostles, Acts of, 27, 141
Apostolic life, *vita apostolica,* 27–28, 140–42, 153–55, 226–27
apses, 180–81
Apt, France, early monastery, 38–39
Aquitaine, Duke of, 103. *See also* Eleanor of Aquitaine; William IX
Aragon (Spanish kingdom), 263
architecture. *See* monastic buildings; *specific types*
Arezzo, Italy, 88
Arles, France, 159, 199; Saint-Trophime Cathedral, 133
Arnaud Amaury (abbot of Poblet and Cîteaux, archbishop of Narbonne), 265
Arnold of Morimond, 12
Arrouaise, France, Aug., 270
Arthur, King, 143
Assisi, Italy, Carceri and, 14–15, 146, 227, 283. *See also* Francis of Assisi, St.
Atcham, England, 148
Athanasius, St. (bishop of Alexandria), 28
Athelstan, King of Wessex, 203

Aubert, St. (bishop of Avranches), 245
Augustine, St. (bishop of Hippo [354–430]): abbesses and prioresses and, 37, 201; Antony, St., and, 37; Chaucer and, 164–65; *Confessions* of, 36–37; Dominic of Caleruega, St., and, 158; friars of, 157, 162–63; monastic tradition and, 35–88; nuns and, 37; Premonstratensian Order and, 157; Rule of, 36, 154–57, 218, 225–26, 231; work and manual labor and, 36–37. *See also* Augustinian canons
Augustinian and Austin friars, 157, 162–63
Augustinian canons: apostolic life and, 153–55; architectural style, 136; in Austria, 158–62; Benedictine Order and, 156, 162–63; Chaucer and, 164–65; in England, 158–62; founders and, 161–62; in France, 157–58; in Germany, 158–62; in Ireland, 158–62; in Italy, 157–58; Knights Templars and, 200; monks and, 162–63; Rule of Augustus and, 155–59; in Scotland, 158–62; in Spain, 157–58; in Wales, 158–62
Austria, 122: abbeys in, 286; Augustinian canons in, 158–62
Autun, France, 131, 133
Avignon, France, 158
Avranches, France, Cathedral, 250

Balkans, monasteries in, 262
Balthild, St., 202
Bangor, Ireland, early monastery, 55
Bartholomew (bishop of Laon), 218
Basil of Caesarea, St. (d. 379): monastic tradition and, 34–35; Rule of, 34–35
Bavaria, 122–23
Beatus of Liebàna, 131
Becket, St. Thomas (archbishop of Canterbury [1162–70]), 136

Bede of Northumbria,Venerable (d.
735): *Ecclesiastical History,* 142;
Hilda and, St., 57; *History of
Recent Events,* 143; *Life of St.
Anselm,* 143; monasteries of,
57–58; monastic tradition and,
56–57; William of Malmesbury
and, 143
bees and beekeeping, 81
Beguines, 22, 214
Benedict Biscop, St. (founder of
Bede's monasteries), 54–55
Benedict of Aniane, St. (d. 821), 54,
58–62
Benedict of Nursia, St.: Cassian and,
39, 46, 48–49; *claustra* term used
by, 7; Dante's references to,
276–77, 281; Gregory I and, 54;
Heloise's references to, 210;
monastic tradition and, formation of, 52–62; monks and,
virtues of, 259; work and manual
labor and, 139. *See also* Benedictine Order; Rule of St.
Benedict
Benedictine Order: Augustinian
canons and, 156, 162–63; in
England, 60–61; founders and
independence, 60–61; historical
perspective, 60–61; in Sicily, 266;
in thirteenth century, 163; in
Wales, 272
Bernard de Rodez (abbot of Saint-
Victor, Marseille), 67
Bernard, Bernardus Grossus, St.
(founder of Tiron), 207
Bernard, St. (abbot of Clairvaux [c.
1090–1153]): Alvastra and, 270;
Apologia of, 82; birth of, 167;
Cassian and, 42; Cistercian Order
and, 163–69, 179; Cîteaux and,
10–11, 163–69; Cluny and,
82–83; death of, 10; England and,
11; Fountains Abbey and, 238–39;
humanism and, 146–47; influence
of, 220–22; Knights Templars and,
195–96; *Life,* 186; Norbert and,

St., 211, 218, 220; Peter the
Venerable and, 84; Rievaulx and,
186–87; writings of, 179
Bernardino of Siena, St., 227, 283
Bernay, France, 251
Bible: Cassiodorius and, 53; New
Testament, 26–27, 42, 141; Old
Testament in bronze and stone,
123. *See also* Apocalypse
biography, writing of, 142–43
Black Death (1340s), 108, 174, 283
Blanchland, England, O.Praem., 220
Blessed Virgin, 143–44, 204, 219
blood-letting, 80
Bobbio, Italy, 55
Bohemia. *See* Czechoslavakia
Bologna, Italy, 97, 122
Boniface, St., 56–57
books of Christian devotion and the-
ology, ancient: apostolic life and,
140–43; biography and, 142–43;
at Cluny, 75–76, 139–40; copy-
ing, 59, 140; history and, 142–43;
illumination of, 128, 132; survival
of, 58–59
Brakespeare, Nicholas. *See* Adrian IV
Bramante, cloisters by, 255, 257
Brenner Pass, 122–23
Brevnov abbey, 267
Bridget, St. of Sweden, 214, 216, 283
Bridgettine Order, 214
British Isles. *See* England; Ireland;
Scotland; Wales
Bruno, St. (teacher from Rheims),
91, 166
Buckfast, England, O.Cist., later
O.S.B., 134
building and buildings. *See* monastic
buildings
Buildwas, England, O.Cist., 175–78,
183–86, 207, 281
Burgos, Spain, Museo Arqueológico.
See Huelgas, Las
Burgundy: art and sculpture in, 131;
bishops of, 103; monasteries in,
274; vineyards, 120. *See also*
Cluny; Vézelay

Bury St. Edmunds, England, O.S.B., 144
Byzantine Empire, Byzantium, 262; art and architecture and, 127, 132

Caen, France, abbey, 129, 251
Calatrava, Order of, 266
Camaldoli, Italy, and Camaldolensian Order, 87–90, 97, 274, 278
candles, 80–81, 120
Canigou. *See* Saint Martin-du-Canigou
canon of Liège, 162–63
canons, regular, 219. *See also* Augustinian canons
Canterbury Cathedral, England, 122, 136–37. *See also* Anselm, St.
Capetian kings, 103. *See also* Louis VII, Louis XIV; Philip II, Philip IV
Cappadocia, 33–34
Carceri in Assisi, Italy, 14–15, 146, 227, 283
Carmelite friars, 284
Carolingian renaissance, 58–59, 62, 254
Carolingian scholars, 59
Carta caritatis ("Charter of Divine Love"), 9–10, 169
Carthusian Order, 90–95, 97, 99, 156, 281, 283
Casamari, Italy, O.Cist., 274
Cassian, John: Benedict and, St., 39, 46, 48–49; Bernard and, St., 42; biographical information, 38–43; Cistercian Order and, 170; *Collations* of, 29–30, 33, 39–41, 44, 46, 48; in Egypt, 38; heresy accusations against, 42–43; *Institutes* of, 38–39, 44, 46, 48; monastic tradition and, 32, 38–43; obedience and, 49; Rule of St. Benedict and, 39, 46, 48–49, 141
Cassino. *See* Monte Cassino, Italy
Cassiodorus (c. 485–c. 580), 52–53
Castile (Spanish kingdom), 263

Catalonia, 128, 183, 263–64
Cathars, 145, 225
Catherine, St., of Siena, 214, 216
Cava dei Tirreni, La, Italy, O.S.B., 66, 87, 267, 273
Cefalù, Sicily, Cathedral, Aug., 159
celibacy, 25–27. *See also* chastity
cellarer and assistants, 79
Cerisiers. *See* St.-Savin-sur-Gartempe, France
Cesarius of Arles, St., 201
chamberlain and assistants, 78–79
Chapel of Nine Altars (Fountains Abbey, England), 236–37
charity, monastic, 115–16, 248
Charlemagne, Emperor (d. 814), 58–59, 115, 200, 254. *See also* Carolingian renaissance
Chartreuse, La Grande, France, O.Cart., and Carthusian Order: Guigo I and, 91; hermitage at, 91–95; Hugh of Lincoln and, 92–93; life, liturgy, work at, 91–94; nature and natural beauty and, 146; in present times, 278; site of, 91
chastity, 196
Chaucer, Geoffrey: Augustine, St., and, 165; Augustinian canons and, 164–65; *Canterbury Tales* of, 165; friar of, 231; on monks and canons, 164–65; prioress of, 214, 216; satire and, 231
Chiusa, Italy. *See* Sagra di San Michele
chivalry, 209
Christ. *See* Jesus
Christian Brothers, 287
Christian Platonists of Alexandria, Egypt, 29, 31
Christina (princess, nun, perhaps abbess of Romsey), 203
Christina of Markyate, St., 17–19, 212–13
Chrodegang (bishop of Metz), 155
Church of the Holy Sepulchre, Jerusalem, 199–200

Cistercian Order: Ailred and, St., 186–91; art and architecture of, 139, 179–80, 181–86; Bernard and, St., 163–69, 179; Cassian and, 170; chapter houses of, 184–86, 189, 193; choir monks and, 8, 140, 169–72; class distinctions and, 13–14, 172; constitution of, 181–86; daughter houses of, 167–68, 180, 274; efficiency and, 178–81; expansion of, 10, 17; Fountains Abbey and, 242–43; Grandmont Order and, 13–14; historical perspective, 9–12; in Ireland, 271; lay brothers and, 169–72; manuscripts of, 11–12; map of, 167; nuns and, 211–14; Orden de Cristo and, 266; planning, 8–10; in Poland, 268; Puritanism and, 178–81; recruitment of, 172; Rievaulx and, 186–91; Rule of St. Benedict and, 169–70, 173; seclusion and, 173–78; self-sufficiency and, 173–78; spiritual adventure of, 191–95; in thirteenth century, 163; uniformity and, 8, 139, 181–86; women and, 18; work and manual labor and, 139, 173–78. See also Cîteaux, France

Cîteaux, France: abbey, 183–84; abbot and visitation, 10–11, 182; altar, 171, 181; architecture, 8–9, 179–80; art school in, 132; Bernard, St., at, 10–11, 163–69; chapter houses, 184–86, 189, 193; choir monks and, 179–80; daughter houses, 167–68, 180; documents and catalogue from, 11–12; expansion of order and, 10; foundation and early history, 8–17, 166; lay brothers and, 12–14, 169–72; map, 167; masons, 180; planning, 8–10; reformation, 15–16; water supply and, 184, 186; work and manual labor at, 173–78. See also Cistercian Order

cities, urban renaissance in (eleventh and twelfth centuries), 109–10, 121

Clairvaux, France, O.Cist.: daughter houses, 167, 180; foundation, 12. See also Fountains Abbey, England

Clare, St. (founder of Poor Clares or Minoresses, O.F.M. nuns), 20, 213, 228

claustra, 7, 78, 259–60

Clown, William (abbot of Leicester), 165

Cluny, France: abbots of, 103; Abelard and, 84; art and architecture of, 131, 133, 136; Bernard and, St., 82–83; books written at, 75–76, 139–40; customs of, 73–75, 172; daily routine at, 70–77, 86; daughter houses, 67, 274; deans at, 78; economic life at, 77–82; economy and, 117, 120; Gorze and, 67–69; Henry of Blois and, 118; hermits and, 14, 85; Hugh and, St., 83; influence of, 64–66, 263; Italy and, 65–66; monastic buildings in, 7; monastic movements in, 63; monastic officials at, 80; monastic tradition in, formation of, 64–69; nuns at, 203–4; Peter the Venerable and, 82–83; plan of, 74; as property of kings and princes, 103–4, 117; religious revival (tenth and eleventh centuries), 64–69; rituals and liturgy of, 74–75; Rule of St. Benedict and, 83; St. Andrew priory and, 160; Spain and, 65; in tenth and eleventh centuries, 64–69, 75–76; in twelfth-century renaissance, 74, 82–85; work and manual labor at, 72–73, 81–82, 120, 139–40. See also Urban II, Pope

Cnut, King of England (1016–35), 106

coenobites, 28, 32, 34, 45–46, 49

Colan Forest, France, 91, 166
Colchester, England, St. Botolph, Aug., 159
Cologne, Germany, Beguines in, 214
Columban, St., 55–56
Columcille (Columba), St., 55–56
commanderies, 196
community, 14, 95–99. *See also* cities
Conques, France, Ste. Foy or St. Faith, O.S.B., 199
Constable, G., 15–16, 18
Constance (Konstanz), Lake of, Germany, 62
conversi, 107
Corinthians, first book of, 26
Coulton, G. G., 134, 281
Counter Reformation, 281
courtly love, 21, 208
Coutances Cathedral, France, 250
craftsmen, 123, 133, 136, 138–39, 203. *See also specific types*
Craon Forest, France, 14, 206
crise du monachisme, la ("monastic crisis"), 153, 288
Crispin, Eve, 204
Cristo, Orden de, 266
Cromwell, Thomas, 283
Crusades, 143, 197–98; First, 195, 207, 266; Fourth, 262; Second, 168, 191, 264–65; Third, 198. *See also* Albigensian Crusade
Cuxa, Saint-Michel-de-, France, O.S.B., 66, 263
Cyprus, monasteries in, 262
Czechoslovakia, monasteries in, 110–11, 262, 267–68

Damian, St. Peter. *See* Peter Damian, St.
Daniel, Walter (monk of Rievaulx, biographer of St. Ailred), 188
Dante, Alighieri, 276–77, 281
David, King of Israel, 94
David, King of Scotland (1124–53), 159–60, 186, 271–72
deans, monastic, 78

Denmark, monasteries in, 269–70
desert monks and hermits, 28, 30, 32, 86, 238
Diana, Temple of (at Nîmes), 127
Dietrich von Bern (Dietrich of Verona), 123
Dijon, France, 65, 133, 274
Diocletian (Roman Emperor), persecution under, 27
Dominic of Caleruega, St. (c. 1171–1221): Augustine, St., and, 158; Augustine's Rule and, 225–26; Francis and, St., 225; monument of, 227; Order of, 156–57, 224, 225–32
Dominic, St., Santo Domingo of Silos (1000–1073), 119–20, 130, 133
Dominican Order and Order of Preachers, 156–57, 224, 225–32
dormitories, 95–96, 185
Dorpat, Russia (formerly Esthonia), 268
Drang nach Osten ("Drive to the East"), 220
Dryburgh, Scotland, O.Praem., 220–21, 272
Dünamunde, Russia (formerly Latvia), O.Cist., 268
Dunstan, St., 67, 135
Durham, England, 129–30, 251; Cathedral priory, 189
Durrow, Ireland, early monastery, 55–56

Eadmer (monk of Canterbury, biographer of St. Anselm), 142–45, 147
Eberbach, Germany, O.Cist., 95–96, 183
Ecclesiasticus, 210–11
Eden, garden of, 131
Edgar the Atheling, 203
Edgar, King of England (959–75), 102, 105
Edith (wife of Otto I), 203

Edward the Confessor, King of England, 112
Edwin, King of Northumbria, 202
efficiency, 178–81
Eglentyne, Madam (Chaucer's prioress), 216
Egypt: Cassian in, 38; Egyptian desert monks and hermits in, 28, 30, 32, 86, 238
Einsiedlen, Switzerland, O.S.B., 278–79
Ela (countess of Salisbury, abbess of Lacock), 214–15
Elbe (river in Germany), 220, 268, 275
Eleanor of Aquitaine, Queen of England, 208–9
Eleanor, Queen of Castille, 212
Elizabeth I, Queen of England, 105
Elizabeth of Schönau, St., 214
endowments, 204–5
England: abbesses and prioresses in, 57; art and architecture in, 128–29, 132; Augustinian canons in, 158–62; Benedictine Order in, 60–61; Bernard and, St., 11; centers of monastic life in, 33; Germany versus, 18–19; monasteries in, 18–19, 33, 55, 104; Norman Conquest and, 102–3, 110, 129; nuns in, 18–19; in tenth and eleventh centuries, 110
Ephesians, Epistle to, 26
Espec, Walter, 186
Esrom, Denmark, O.Cist., 270
Essen, Germany, O.S.B., 257; abbesses and prioresses in, 203; Cathedral, 203; nuns in, 203
Esser, K. H., 180
Estouteville, Cardinal de, 252
Ethelwold, St., 67, 135
Eugenius III, Pope (1145–53), 10, 168
Evagrius of Pontus (c. 346–99), 31, 39
Eve, 19–20, 37. See also Adam and Eve
Ezekiel (prophet), 131

Falkenau, Russia (formerly Esthonia), O.S.B., 268
Farfa, Italy, O.S.B., 65
Fécamp, France, O.S.B., 65–66
Felix, St., 253–54
Ferdinand I, King of León-Castile, 119–20
fish and fishpond keepers, 81
Flanders, Beguines in, 214
Fleury, Saint-Benoît-sur-Loire, France, O.S.B., 54–55
Florence, Italy, 109, 122
Foliot, Gilbert (bishop of Hereford and London), 243
Fontaine-lés-Dijon, France, 167
Fonte Avellana, Italy, 89
Fontevrault, France, and Order of Fontevrault, 208–9, 216
Fossanova, Italy, O.S.B. then O.Cist., 163, 273–74
Fountains Abbey, England, O.Cist.: Bernard and, St., 238–39; Chapel of Nine Altars, 236–37; chapter houses, 184–85, 242; church, 242; Cistercian Order and, 242–43; colonies of, 270; domestic buildings, 239–43; Fountains Hall, 239; lawns and landscape, 237–39; plan, 236; Salle des Chevaliers and, 249; site, 236–37
Fountains Hall (Fountains Abbey, England), 239
Fourth Latern Council (1215), 60, 225
France: art and architecture in, 127–28, 132; Augustinian canons and, 157–58; centers of monastic life in, 33; Francia, West, 57; Gaul, 33, 55, 57; hermits in, 153; Île de France, 249–50; monasteries in, 103; under Napoleon, 123, 278, 285, 291; in twelfth-century renaissance, 127
Francis of Assisi, St. (founder of O.F.M. [c. 1181–1226]): background of, 223; career of, 225–32; Clare and, 20, 228;

death of, 229; Dominic and, St.,
225; influence of, 87; nature and
natural beauty and, 146; nuns
and, 213; Rule of, 223; St.
Stephen and, 13; shrine of, 229.
See also Franciscan Order
Franciscan Order: nuns, 213–14;
poverty, 231; recruitment of lay
brothers and, 14; in thirteenth
century, 224
French Revolution, 285
friars: Chaucer's portrait of, 231; in
twelfth and thirteenth centuries,
219–22. See also specific orders
frontals. See altars and frontals
Fruttuaria, Italy, O.S.B., 65, 273–74
Fulda, Germany, O.S.B., 57

gardening and gardeners, 79–81
Gaul. See France
Gelasius II, Pope (1118–19), 217–18
Genesis, book of, 139
Geneva, Lake of, 178
Geoffrey de Gorron (1119–46), 19
Geoffrey of Clairvaux, 241–42
Geoffrey of Monmouth, 143
Gerard (Cistercian monk, brother of
St. Bernard), 193–94
Gerhoh, 159
German Romanesque art and archi-
tecture, 128–29
Germany: art and architecture in,
128–29, 132; Augustinian canons
in, 158–62; East, 110–11; England
versus, 18–19; monasteries in,
18–19, 104, 205, 274–75; nuns in,
18–22, 202–3; political power of,
102–3; in tenth and eleventh
centuries, 110–12
Gernrode, Germany, 128
Gervasius, St., 254
Gilbert (brother, Cluniac hermit), 84
Gilbert, St. of Sempringham, 14, 19,
211, 222
Gilbertine Order, 14, 19
Glastonbury, England, O.S.B., 7, 68

Gloucester, England, Abbey, O.S.B.,
160, 186; sister house in, 160
gnosis, 31
Godehard, St. (bishop of Hilden-
sheim), 68–69
Golden Altar (San'Ambrogio, Milan,
Italy), 253–55
Gorze, France (formerly Germany),
O.S.B., 7, 67–69, 114, 139
Gothic art and architecture, 127,
130, 133, 249–50
Gotland (island), 269
Gottfried von Strassburg, 21
granarer, 79
Grandmont Order, 13–14
Grandmont, France, 12–14
Greece, monasteries in, 262. See also
Byzantine Empire, Byzantium
Gregory the Great, St., Pope Gregory
I (590–604), 53–55; Benedict
and, St., 54; Dialogues of, 54
Gregory VII, Pope Hildebrand
(1073–85), 89, 114, 157, 159, 256,
266
Grenoble, France, bishop of, 91
Gualbert, St. John, 88
Guigo I (prior of the Chartreuse), 91
Guy de Thouars (King Philip II's
vassal), 248

habits, monastic, 78, 80
Haito (bishop-abbot of Reichenau),
7
Heidenheim, Germany, double
monastery, 57
Heloise, 17–18, 144, 147, 209–11
Henry I, King of England (1100–35),
112, 117–18, 160–61, 186
Henry II, King of England
(1154–89), 110, 160, 198, 208–9,
248
Henry II, St., King of Germany,
Western Emperor (1002–24), 69,
102, 105
Henry IV, King of Germany, Western
Emperor (1056–1106), 159, 256

Henry V, King of Germany, Western Emperor (1106–25), 217
Henry VIII, King of England (1509–47), 199, 283, 285
Henry of Blois (abbot of Glastonbury, bishop of Winchester), 112, 118
Hereford, bishop of. *See* Foliot, Gilbert
heresy, 42–43, 222, 265
hermitage, 95–99
hermits: Carthusian Order, 90–95; Cluny and, 14, 85; community and, 14; in Egyptian desert, 28, 30, 32, 86, 238; in France, 153; Franciscans and; in Italy, 86–87, 153; Peter Damian, St., 87–90; Romuald, St., 87–90. *See also specific names*
Herrad (abbess), 211
Hilda of Whitby, St., 57, 202
Hildebrand, Pope. *See* Gregory VII, Pope
Hildegard, St. (abbess of Bingen [1098–1179]), 17–18, 211
Hildesheim, Germany, 123; bishop of, 69
Hirasau, Germany, O.S.B. abbey in, 73; architectural style and, 136; monastic movements in, 63, 69
history, writing of, 142–43
Holborn. *See* London, England
Holy Land. *See* Palestine
Holy Trinity (cathedral), 159
honey, 80–81
Honorius Augustodunensis, 142
Honorius III, Pope (1216–27), 223
Hospital of St. John of Jerusalem, 195–96
Hospitallers, Order of Knights, 196–97, 266. *See also* Knights Templars
hospitals, 80, 195–96
Hovedö, Norway, O.Cist., 270
Hradcany. *See* Prague, Czechoslavakia
Huby (abbot), 240

Huelgas, Las (near Burgos, Spain), O.Cist., nuns, 212, 214
Hugh of Avalon. *See* Hugh of Lincoln, St.
Hugh of Lincoln, St. (monk of the Chartreuse, prior of Witham, bishop of Lincoln [1186–1200]), 92–94, 97–98
Hugh, St. (abbot of Cluny [1049–1109]), 64, 68–69, 75, 82–83, 114, 117, 120, 204
Huguenot attacks on monasteries, 284
humanism, 143–49, 192
Hungary, monasteries in, 262, 268
Hyde. *See* Winchester, England

Iberian peninsula, 266
Ignatius Loyola, St., 284
Île de France, 249–50
infirmarer, 79–80
infirmaries. *See* Hospitals
Innocent III, Pope (1198–1216), 223–25
Institutio Canonicorum (816–17), 155
Iona, Scotland, early monastery, 56
Ireland: Augustinian canons in, 158–62; Cistercian Order in, 271; monasteries in, 55–56, 262–63, 269–71
Isaac, Abba, 42
Isabel of Angouléme, Queen of England, 209
Isaiah, book of, 75–76
Islam: architecture and, 130; Peter the Venerable and, 84; in Spain, 197, 262–63
Islamic architecture, 130
Italy: art and architecture in, 127; Augustinian canons in, 157–58; Cluny's influence in, 65–66; hermits in, 86–87, 153; monasteries in, 103–4, 263; monastic tradition and, 87; social change in, 109; in twelfth-century renaissance, 127
iuvenes, 107

Jacoba of Settesoli, 213
Jacob's ladder, 281
Janauschek, Father, 11
Jarrow, England, early monastery, 6, 54
Jedburgh, Scotland, Aug., 272
Jerome, St., 37–38, 89, 201
Jerusalem, 195, 198–99; Church of the Holy Sepulchre in, 199–200
Jesus: cult of human, 143–44; nature and natural beauty and, 139; teaching of, 26
John Gualbert, St., 88
John of the Cross, 284
John, King of England (1199–1216), 209, 248
John, St. (apostle and evangelist), 207
Jordan of Saxony, O.P., 230
Joseph II, Emperor, 285
Joseph in Egypt, 148
Jumièges, France, O.S.B., 65–66, 129, 251

Kelso, Scotland, O.S.B. Tironian, 272
Kingswood, England, O.Cist., 186
Kirkstead, England, O.S.B., 270
Knights Templars, 195–200, 266
Knowles, David, 8–9, 45, 281
Knox, Ronald, 157

labor. See work and manual labor
Lacock, England, Aug., nuns, 214–16, 279
La Ferté, France, O.Cist., 167
Lanfranc, Archbishop, 7
Laon, France, bishop of. See Bartholomew
Latin language, 192
Lawrence, St., 92
lay brothers, 12–14, 169–72, 196–97. See also specific names
lay offerings, 117–20
Lazarus, St., church of, 133
Leicester, England, Aug., 161
Leo IX, Pope, St. (1048/9–54), 89, 114
Leo XIII, Pope (1878–1903), 60–61

Leoba (Anglo-Saxon abbess in Germany), 57
Leofric (d. 1066), 112
León-Castile, kingdom of, 117, 119
Le Perche, France, 207
Le Puy, France, 199
Lézat, France, O.S.B., 66
Libellus de diversis ordinibus ("On the Different Orders"), 162–63
liberalism, 286
libraries, monastic, 53
Liège, Belgium, 22, 214
Lincoln, England. See Hugh of Lincoln, St.
Lisbon, Portugal, 264
liturgical movement, 58
Lives of the fathers (of the desert), 28–32
Livy, 76
Llanthony Prima, Scotland, 160
Llanthony Secunda, Scotland, 160
Lombards and destruction of Monte Cassino, 54
Lombardy, 65, 122, 128, 273
London Charterhouse, 99
London, England, 159, 198
Lorsch, Germany, Roman villa rustica, 6–7
Louis the Pious, Emperor (814–40), 59
Louis VII, King of France (1137–80), 94–95
Louis XIV, King of France (1643–1715), 77
Lucca, Italy, 109, 122, 157
Lucchesi, 158
Luke, book of, 27
Luxeuil, France, early monastery, 55
Lyse, Norway, O.Cist., 270

Mabillon, Dom J., 284–85
Mâconnais, France, 80, 103
Madonna. See Mary, Blessed Virgin
Magdeburg, Germany, 22
Mainz, Germany, Cathedral, 129, 133

Malachy, St. (archbishop of Armagh), 270–72
Mâle, Emile, 133
Malta, 262
Mammon, 114, 121
Map, Walter, 238
Marcigny, France, Cluniac nuns, 203–4
Margaret, St., Queen of Scotland, 203, 271
Maria Laach, Germany, O.S.B., 69, 134
Marist Brothers, 287
Markyate, England, O.S.B. nuns, 19, 212–13
marriage, 26–27, 108, 290–91
Marseille, France, 38–39
Marshal. See William Marshal
Martha and Mary, 41, 154, 218, 228
Martin, St. (monk, later bishop of Tours), 38, 199
Mary Magdalene, St., shrine of, 199
Mary, Blessed Virgin, 143–44, 204, 219
masons, 81, 123, 136, 179–80
Matilda (abbess of Essen, abbess of Quedilinburg), 202–3
Matilda, Queen of England, 159–60, 203, 205, 271
Matthew, book of, 25–26
Maulbronn, Germany, O.Cist., 177–78, 183, 268
Maurus, St. (Maure), Rule of, 164
Mazan, France, O.Cist., 184
Mechtild of Magdeburg, 22
Mellifont, Ireland, O.Cist., 270
Melrose, Scotland, O.Cist., 272
Mendicant Orders. See Augustinian and Austin friars; Carmelite friars; Dominican Order and Order of Preachers; Franciscan Order
Mercia (English kingdom), 202
Merveille, 248–51
metalwork, 131–32
Metz, France, 155
Michael, St., and his cult, 245, 249
Milan, Italy, 65, 89, 154, 256–57

Milburga, St., 280–81
Milton, John, 97
missionary work, 219
Mlada-Maris, Princess (abbess of Hradcany), 267
Modena, Italy, 122
Moissac, France, O.S.B., 67, 130–31, 133, 136
Molesme, France, O.S.B., 166
monasteries, as property of kings and princes, 100–106
monastic buildings: Cluniac, 7; dormitories, 95–96, 185; endowments and, 204–5; in Gorze, 7; knowledge about, 5–8; in present times, 278–79; resources directed toward, 116–17, 124; sculpture, 131. See also specific names
monastic church: altars and frontals, 75, 128, 180–81; apses, 180–81; furnishings and ornaments, 75, 131; square east end and, 180; in twelfth-century renaissance, 127–32. See also specific names
monastic crisis (la crise du monachisme), 153, 288
monastic daily routine, 70–77, 86
monastic geography of Europe (1300), 261–77
monastic officials: almoner, 79–80; cellarer and assistants, 79; chamberlain and assistants, 78–79; at Cluny, 80; deans, 78; economy and, 77–82; fishpond keeper, 79; gardener, 79; granarer, 79; infirmarer, 79–80; refectorer, 79; Rule of St. Benedict and, 78, 80; sacrist, 80–81; winekeeper, 79; work of, 73
monastic schools, 147–48
monastic tradition: Augustine and, St., 35–38; Basil and, St., 34–35; Bede and, 57–58; from Benedict of Nursia to Benedict of Aniane, 52–62; Carolingian, 62; Cassian and, 32, 38–43; centers of, 33; Cluny and Gorze and, 64–69; in

eleventh century, 64–69, 75–76, 134, 153; expansion of, 101–2, 110; in 1500, 282–92; Italy and, 87; lay offerings and, 117–20; learning and, 52–55; origins of, 25–33; patronage and, 113; recruitment in eleventh and twelfth centuries, 106–7, 111, 124–25; Reformation and, 113–15; Rule of St. Benedict and, 61–62, 153; social change (1050–1150), 107–17; in tenth century, 62–64; in 1300, 261–77; from 1300–1500, 278–82; in twelfth-century renaissance, 134–37; women's movement, 17–22, 57; work and manual labor in, 36–37, 72–73, 81–82

Mongols, 262

monks: Augustinian canons and, 162–63; Benedict and, St., 259; boys, 107, 111; Chaucer on, 164–65; choir, 122, 169–72; at Molesme, 166; of Mont Saint-Michel, 8; nature and natural beauty and, 97, 145–46; parochial life, 50; privacy and, lack of, 76–77, 122; Romanesque art and, 132–34; in Syria, 238. *See also specific names*

Monkwearmouth, England, early monastery, later O.S.B., 6, 54

Monreale Cathedral, Sicily, O.S.B., 267

Mont Saint-Michel, France: abbey, O.S.B., 246; almonry, 244, 248; architecture, 249–50; cult of St. Michael and, 245; Mabillon and, 284–85; monks of, 8; plan, 244; Salle des Chevaliers, 244; spire, 251–52; town, 246–47; William of Volpiano's influence on, 66, 246

Montalembert, 134

Monte Cassino, Italy, O.S.B., 44, 52–54, 57, 130, 267, 273

Monte Gargano, Italy, 245

Montpellier, France, 60

Montserrat, Spain, O.S.B., 67

Morimond, France, O.Cist., 12, 167, 268–69

Mount Grace, England, O.Cart., 99

Mount Horeb, 97

Mount Sinai, 97

Mozarabic influences, 131

Much Wenlock, England, 279–82

Muslims. *See* Islam

Napoleon, 123, 278, 285, 291

nature and natural beauty, monks and, 96–97, 139, 145–46

Nevers. *See* William

New College, England, 8

New Testament, 26–27, 42, 141. *See also specific books*

Nicholas Brakespeare. *See* Adrian IV

Niebelungenlied, 123

Niederaltaich, Germany, abbey, O.S.B., 68

Nilus, 87

Nîmes, France, 127

Norbert of Xanten: Bernard and, St., 211, 218, 220; canon regular of, 219; career of, 218–19; influence of, 220; nuns and, 213; and Premonstratensian Order and, 211, 217–19; St. Augustine's Rule and, 218

Norman school of art, 132

Normandy, France, 159. *See also* France

Northumbria (English kingdom), 56

Norway, monasteries in, 269–70

nuns: Augustine and, St., 37; Bridgettine, 214; Cistercian, 211–14; Cluniac, 203–4; endowments and, 204–5; in England, 18–19; Essen, Germany, 203; Francis and, St., 213; Franciscan, 212–13; in Germany, 18–22, 202–3; at Lacock, 214–16, 279; Las Huelgas, 212; Markyate, 19, 212–13; Norbert and, St., 213;

Paraclete, 210; in Prague, 267; Romsey, 203; St. Cesarius of Arles, 201; Shaftesbury, 209; Wilton, 203. *See also* abbessess and prioresses; *specific names*; women's movement
Nydala, Sweden, O.Cist., 270

obedience, 44, 48–49, 196
oblate monks, boys, *pueri,* 107
Odeler, 148
Odensee, Denmark, O.S.B., 269
Odilo, St. (abbot of Cluny [994–1049]), 64, 68, 117
offerings, lay, 117–20
Old Castile, 263
Old Testament in bronze and stone, 123
Oliba (abbot), 66–67
opus Dei (God's work), 52, 61, 172, 260
Orden de Cristo, 266
Orderic Vitalis (monk of St.-Évroult, chronicler), 135, 142, 146–48
Origen, 29, 113
ornaments. *See* monastic church
Osma, Spain, Cathedral of, 158
Ostia, Italy, cardinal bishop of, 89
Oswald, St., 67
Otto I the Great, King of Germany, Western Emperor (936–73), 102, 105, 202
Otto II, King of Germany, Western Emperor, 202
Oxford, England, 8

Pachomius, St., 28, 32, 238
Palestine, 34, 38, 197, 262
papal reform, 113–15, 153–54, 278–79
Paraclete, France, O.S.B. nuns, 209–10
Parma, Italy, 122
Paschal II, Pope (1099–1118), 217
Passau. *See* Altmann, St.
Patrick, St., 55
patronage, 113

Paul, St. (apostle), 26–27, 30, 148
Paula, 37
Pembroke. *See* William Marshal
Perugia, Italy, 229
Peter (archbishop of Milan), 254
Peter Damian, St., 87–90, 145, 148, 155, 157, 163, 207, 227
Peter the Venerable (abbot of Cluny [1122–56]), 82–85, 117–18
Petronilla of Chemillé (abbess of Fontevrault), 207, 216, 219
Philip II, Augustus, King of France (1108–1223), 248–50
Philip IV, the Fair, King of France (1285–1314), 199
pilgrims and pilgrim centers, 199
Pirmin, St., 57
Pisa, Italy, 109, 122; Camaldolensian house, 97
plague (1340s), 108, 174, 283
Plato, *Dialogues* of, 40
Poblet, Spain, O.Cist., 183, 264–65
Poitiers, France, 132
Poitou. *See* William IX
Poland: Cistercian Order in, 268; monasteries in, 262–63, 267–69
Pons (abbot of Cluny), 82
Pontefract, England, Cluniac priory, 243
Pontigny, France, O.Cist., 167
Pope, Alexander, 261
popular religious movement, 58
Portiuncula, Italy, chapel, 227
Portugal: Knights Templars in, 197; monasteries in, 263; religious history in, 263
poverty, 101, 115, 196, 231
Prague, Czechoslovakia, nuns and monks in, 267
prayer, meditation and spiritual readings, 42
preceptories, 196
Premonstratensian Order: Augustine and, St., 157; canon of Liège and, 162; expansion of, 163; Norbert and, St., 211, 217–19; in Poland, 268; in Scotland, 272

prioresses. *See* abbesses and prioresses

Protasius, St., 254

Protestantism, 281, 283–84

Provençal lyric, 208

Provence, France, 38, 127, 158, 178, 263, 278

pueri, 107

pueri dominate, 107

puritanism, 42, 61, 178–81

Pyx. *See* monastic church

Qur'an, 84

Rainald (monk of St.-Évroult), 148

Rancé, Armand (founder of Trappists), 285

Raymond du Puy, 196

recluse, life of, 85

recruitment of clergy, 106–7, 111, 124–25, 289–90

refectorer, 79

Reformation, 113–15, 153–54, 278–79

Regula magistri (Rule of the Master), 5, 44–45

Reichenau, Germany, 7, 57, 62, 128–29

Reichersberg, Germany, Aug., 159

Renaissance. *See* Carolingian renaissance; Twelfth-century renaissance; Urban renaissance

Rennes, France, 207

Revelation, book of, 131, 245

Rhine (river), 38, 274

Rhodes, 262

Rhône (river), 128, 274

Richard de Rodez (abbot of Saint-Victor, Marseille, and cardinal), 67

Richard I, King of England (1189–99), 198, 209, 246

Richelieu, Cardinal, 284

Rievaulx, England, O.Cist., 186–91

Ripoll, Spain, O.S.B., 66–67, 263

Robert of Arbrissel, St. (founder of Fontevrault), 18, 207–8, 219

Robert of Molesme, St. (founder of Cîteaux), 91, 141–42, 166

Robert of Torigny (abbot of Mont Saint-Michel), 248

Roger (monk of Helmarshausen, perhaps Theophilus), 139

Roman Catholic religious, in present times, 286–92

Roman Empire, 33, 113

Romanesque art and architecture, 122, 127–28, 130, 132–34

Rome (city), 157, 199

Romsey, England, O.S.B. nuns, 203

Romuald, St., 87–90, 267

Rouen Cathedral, France, 250

Rule of the Master. *See Regula magistri*

Rule of St. Benedict: Augustinian canons and, 164–65; Bede and, 56; for beginners, 46–48, 88; Camaldoli and, 87–88; Carthusian Order and, 156; Cassian and, 39, 46, 48–49, 141; Cistercian Order and, 169–70, 173; *claustra* of, 7, 78, 260; Cluny and, 83; counsel and, 49; dissemination of, 59–60; *Institutes* and, 39; knowledge about, 5–6; meat (prohibition of), 71, 81, 210; monastic officials and, 78, 80; monastic tradition and, 61–62, 153; monks and, virtues of, 259; obedience, chastity, poverty and, 44, 48–49; oldest surviving text of, 59, 75; oratory, worship, *opus Dei* and, 52, 61; prayer, meditations, spiritual reading and, 50–52; *Regula Magistri* and, 44–45; work and manual labor and, 50, 72–73

Russia, monasteries in, 262

sacrist, 80–81

Sagra di San Michele (or Chiusa), 144

Sahagún, Spain, O.S.B., 263

Saint-Bénigne, 274

Saint-Benoît-sur-Loire, 58, 116

Saint-Denis, France, abbey, O.S.B., 130–31, 134, 145
Saint-Étienne, Caen, 129
Saint-Évroult, France (home of Orderic Vitalis), 148
Saint-Guilhem-le-Desert, 60
Saint-Guilhem-le-Desert, France, O.S.B., 146
Saint-Gilles, France, 127, 133, 199
Saint-Martin-du-Canigou, France, 67
Saint-Maur, Congregation of, O.S.B., 284
Saint-Odile, Germany, 211
Saint-Riquier, France, O.S.B., 257
Saint-Ruf, near Avignon, France, Aug., 158, 160
Saint-Savin-sur-Gartempe, France, 132
Saint-Trophime, France, 133
Saint-Victor, Marseille, France, 263
Saint-Wandrille, England, 246
Sainte Foy (St. Faith) at Conques, 199
Salerno, Italy, 66
Salisbury Cathedral, England, 250
Salle des Chevaliers, 244, 249
salvation, 102
Salzburg, Austria, 159
San Frediano priory, 158
San Juan de la Peña, Spain, O.S.B., 67
San Lorenzo, Italy, 257
San Miniato, Italy, 122
San Paolo fuori le Mura (Rome), 66, 267
San Romerio (hermitage), 14
San Zeno Maggiore, Italy, abbey, 121–25, 154
Sankt Gallen, St. Gall, Switzerland: Codex Sangallensis in, 59; early monastery in, 55, 62
Santa Leocadia abbey, 158, 160
Sant'Ambrogio, Milan, Italy: Ambrose and, St., 253–54; atrium, 257; Basilica of, 252–54; city of Milan and, 256–57; Cluny and, 65; domestic buildings of, 259–60; Golden Altar of, 253–55; monks at, 255; plan, 253; tithes

and, 154; western chapels and courtyards and, 257–58
Santes (Santas) Creus, Spain, O.Cist., 264
Santi Quattro Cornati, Rome, Italy, 257
Santiago de Compostela, Spain, Cathedral and Order, 199, 263, 266
Santo Domingo. *See* Dominic, Silos
Sarabaites, 32
Saracens, slaughter of, 146
satire. *See* Chaucer; Map
Savigny, France, Savigniac, then O.Cist., 207
Scandinavia, 262. *See also* Denmark; Norway; Sweden
schism in papacy (1130), 168
Schönau. *See* Elizabeth of Schönau, St.
schools, monastic, 147–48
Schwyz (Swiss Canton), 279
Scotland: Augustinian canons in, 158–62; monasteries in, 55, 271–72; Premonstratensian Order in, 272
sculpture, 128, 130–33
seculsion, 173–78
Sée (river in France), 159
self-sufficiency, 173–78
Sénanque, France, O.Cist., 95, 183–84, 186
Severn (river in England), 148
Shaftesbury, England, O.S.B., abbey and nuns, 209
Shakespeare, William, 206
Sherborne, England, O.S.B., 169
Shrewsbury, England, 148
Shropshire, England, 175
Sicily, 262, 266–67
Siena, Italy, 109
Silesia, monasteries in, 262–63, 268
Silos, Santo Domingo de, Spain, 119–20, 263
Silvacane, France, O.Cist., 178, 184
social change (1050–1150), 101, 107–17

Socrates, 40
Solesmes, France, O.S.B., 286
Solomon, King of Israel, 94
Song of Songs or of Solomon, 193
Sopwell, England, nuns, 19
Spain: art and architecture in, 131–32; Augustinian canons in, 157–58; Cluny's influence in, 65; Iberian Peninsula and, 266; Islam in, 197, 262–63; Knights Templars in, 197; religious history in, 263
Speyer Cathedral, Germany, 129, 133
Spoleto, Italy, 159
square east end of monastic churches, 180
St. Albans, England, O.S.B., 19, 251
St. Albans Psalter (art), 212
St. Botolph, England, 159
Stephen, Harding, St. (abbot of Cîteaux), 9, 12, 132, 168–69
Stephen, King of England, 112
Stephen of Grandmont, St., 11–12
Stephen of Lexington (abbot of Stanley and Clairvaux), 271
St. Gall plan, 7
St. Gall (Sankt Gallen), Switzerland, 7, 55, 59, 62
St. Mary's Abbey, York, 241–42
St. Maximin, Trier, 69
St. Michael's Mount, England, priory, O.S.B., 246
Suger (abbot of Saint-Denis), 130–31, 133–34, 145, 179
Swaan, W., 1–3
Swartwout, R. E., 134
Sweden, monasteries in, 269–70
Switzerland, abbeys in, 286
Symeon Stylites, St., 15, 40
Syria, 33–34, 38, 238

Taizé, France, Protestant community, 288–89
Tegernsee, Germany, abbey, O.S.B., 68
Templars. See Knights Templars
Temple Church, 199–200

Temple, William, 157
Teresa of Avila, St., 214, 284
Thecla (Anglo-Saxon abbess in Germany), 57
Theodoric the Great, 123
Theophilus, 137–39, 145
Thomas, St. (of Canterbury). See Becket
Thoronet, Le, France, O.Cist., 175, 178, 184
Thuringia, Germany, 57
Thurstan of Bayeaux (archbishop of York), 241, 243
Timothy, First Epistle to, 27, 37, 201
Tiron, France, O.S.B. Tironian, 207, 272
tithes, 115–16, 154
Toledo, Spain, 160, 267; Cathedral, 158, 160
Toulouse, France, 131, 225–26
Touraine, France, 206
Tours, France, 199
Trappe, La, O.Cist., and Trappists, 285
Tre Fontane, Italy, O.Cist., 274
Turin. See Sagra di San Michele
Turkey, 130
Tuscany, Italy, 88, 274
Twelfth-century renaissance: Anselm and, St., 143–49; apostolic life in, 140–42; architecture and crafts in, 127–32; beginning of, 126; biography in, 142–43; books in, 139–40; Cistercian Order and, 139–40; Cluny in, 82–85; France in, 127; history in, 142–43; Italy in, 127; monastic church in, 127–32; monastic tradition and, 134–37; Romanesque art and, 127–28, 130, 132–34; spread of, 126; Theophilus and, 137–39; variety and, 145
Tyniec (near Kraków, Poland), 267–68

Ulrich (monk of Cluny), 73–75, 78–80, 84

uniformity, 8, 139, 181–86
Urban II, Pope (1088–99), 114, 207, 266
urban renaissance, 109–10, 121

Valeria, St., 253–54
Vallombrosa, Italy, and Vallombrosan Order, 87–90, 97, 274, 278
Verona, Italy, 121–25, 154
Versailles, France, 77
Vézelay, France, 83, 131, 133, 136, 199
Victor III, Pope (1086–87), 66
Victor, St., 253–54
Villers-la-Ville, Belgium, O.Cist., 213
vineyards, 80, 120
Virgin Mother, cult of, 143–44
Vitalis de Mortain (abbot of Savigny), 207
Vitalis, St., 253–54
Vitry, Bishop Jacques de, 22
Vivarium, Italy, early monastery, 52–53

Waddell, Chrysogonus, 9
Waldburg or Walpurgis, 57
Waldensian Church, 222
Waldo (merchant of Lyon), 222
Wales: Augustinian canons in, 158–62; Benedictine Order in, 272; monasteries in, 160, 272
Wearmouth, England, early monastery, 6, 54
Werburga, St., 202
West Francia. See France, Francia
Whitby, England, 202
Wilfred of Ripon, York and Hexham, St., 54–55
William (monk of La Grande Chartreuse, ex-count of Nevers), 94–95
William IX (count of Poitou, duke of Aquitaine), 208
William Marshal (earl of Pembroke), 199

William of Hirsau (abbot), 69
William of Malmesbury, 142–45
William of Sens (architect), 136–37
William of Volpiano, St. (abbot of Fruttuaria), 65–66, 87, 246
William of Wykeham, 8
William Rufus (1087–1100), 105
William, St. (count of Toulouse, Guillaume d'Orange, Willehalm), 60, 146, 274
Wilton, England, O.S.B. nuns, 203
Winchester, England, 8, 68, 106, 171, 209, 251
wine and winekeeper, 79. See also vineyards
Witham, England, O.Cart., 99
Wolfram von Eschenbach, 21, 60, 146; Willehalm, 60, 146
women's movement, 17–22, 57. See also abbesses and prioresses; nuns
Worcester, England, 68
work and manual labor: Augustine and, St., 36–37; Benedict and, St., 139; Cistercian Order and, 139, 173–78; at Cîteaux, France, 173–78; at Cluny, 72–73, 81–82, 120, 139–40; of monastic officials, 73; monastic tradition and, 36–37, 72–73, 81–82; Rule of St. Benedict and, 50, 72–73
Worms Cathedral, Germany, 129, 133
Wulfhere, King of Mercia (657–74), 202
Wynnebald, 57

Xanten, Germany, cathedral chapter, 217

Yorkshire, England, 99

Zürich, Switzerland, 279
Zwingli, 279